# Rich Countries
## and
# Poor Countries

# About the Book and Author

In these ten graceful and learned essays, Professor Rostow addresses the future of the world and its economy from the perspective of his more than forty years of study and reflection on the problems of economic development. Rostow focuses on how we are to create and sustain a civilized and industrious world society in an international trading system beset by historic trends with enormous potential for disruption.

These powerful forces—including an industrial revolution of microelectronics, genetic engineering, robots and lasers, and the diffusion of high technology to low-wage areas—are creating different sets of irrevocably intertwined problems for nations around the world.

The issues are illuminated here by Rostow's mastery of economic history as well as the history of political economy. In addition to general discussions placing the issues historically and intellectually, there are essays highlighting the particular concerns of Mexico, India, Japan, and the Pacific Basin. In his final remarks, Rostow speculates on how the large economic trends affecting the superpowers may lead gradually to a truly significant lessening of East-West tensions. This book will be valuable for any citizen or student concerned about the future of the global economy.

W. W. Rostow is professor of political economy at the University of Texas, Austin. He has taught at, among other universities, Oxford, Cambridge, and MIT, and is the author of twenty-six volumes, among them *The Process of Economic Growth*, *The Stages of Economic Growth*, and *The World Economy: History and Prospect.*

# Rich Countries
## and
# Poor Countries

*Reflections on the Past,*
*Lessons for the Future*

W. W. Rostow

**Westview Press**
*Boulder & London*

Copyright © 1987 by W. W. Rostow

Published in 1987 in the United States of America by Westview Press, Inc.; Frederick A. Praeger, Publisher; 5500 Central Avenue, Boulder, Colorado 80301

Library of Congress Cataloging-in-Publication Data
Rostow, W. W. (Walt Whitman), 1916–
  Rich countries and poor countries.
  Includes index.
  1. Economic history.  2. Economic development.
3. International economic relations.  I. Title.
HC51.R665 1987    337    87-8280
ISBN 0-8133-0497-0

Printed and bound in the United States of America

The paper used in this publication meets the requirements of the American National Standard for Permanence of Paper for Printed Library Materials Z39.48-1984.

10    9    8    7    6    5    4    3    2    1

*To Elspeth*

# Contents

# *Preface*

These essays, written or delivered in the period 1983 to 1986, reflect an idiosyncratic aspect of the way I work. When developing a new set of ideas I generally conduct in counterpoint a series of tests. I try to apply the emerging new concepts to a range of particular problems or circumstances.

These exercises fulfill several purposes.

First, I learn whether the new ideas are viable. If they don't usefully illuminate problems that should fall within their range, they are not worth pursuing. But even if the experiments in application appear reasonably positive, I, at least, always learn something from them, and they thereby enrich the final version of the larger work on which I am engaged.

Second, in using such experimental exercises to fulfill the inevitable extracurricular speaking demands of modern academic life, one reduces the risk of boring others as well as the certainty of boring oneself by reaching into the sermon barrel. Audiences sense accurately whether what you have to say is part of a fresh, current exploratory effort or old hat; and the questions, discussion, or head-on debate in the wake of such talks is generally informative.

The particular setting for this book is the following. In July 1979 I finished the last of four related books centered on the history of the world economy. After that effort, which I had set as a goal more than thirty years earlier, I turned to another theme reflecting the years that I, like many of my generation, had spent in public service—the relation between ideas and action. Six case studies, each a short book, followed. I had nearly completed the last of these books when a year's leave of absence—earned by my wife for both of us—became possible. Because the final case study was devoted to the past and future of regional organization in Asia, we headed west from Austin,

Texas, on July 6, 1983, having sent ahead a draft of the book. During this trip, I talked with officials in fourteen governments of Asia and the Pacific and the heads of two major international agencies. These interviews and other experiences along the way permitted me to strengthen the final draft. Chapter 8 reflects some conclusions of that book.

The year abroad—with visits to thirty-four countries and intense speaking schedules for both of us—started me on my next major enterprise, which had been on my mind since the early 1960s and arose from one aspect of the reception accorded *The Stages of Economic Growth* (1960). Although much debated, that work was, as books go, something of a success. Many men and women in the developing regions and in Communist countries derived a great deal from the work. It was also widely read in Japan and the West. And it goes on having a life of its own. For example, it was recently published and widely circulated in China.

However, *The Stages* also stirred up a good deal of controversy, which I regarded as inevitable and appropriate for a new set of ideas and which I rather enjoyed. Only one aspect of the debate troubled me. I evidently failed to direct my fellow economists to a basic fact: *The Stages*, as I had explained in Chapter 2, was rooted in a dynamic theory of production and prices already elaborated in my earlier book, *The Process of Economic Growth* (1953, 1960). This failure of communication may have resulted from imperfections in my exposition. But in part, at least, it may also have resulted from the fact that *The Stages* emerged at just the time that two other methods of growth analysis came on stage: the neoclassical growth models launched in 1955 and 1956 in articles by Robert Solow, T. W. Swan, and James Tobin; and Simon Kuznets's great effort in organizing the statistical morphology of growth, which began to emerge in 1956. (My *Economic Journal* article on the take-off of developing countries appeared in March 1956.) It is possible that my insistence on the critical importance of the absorption of specific technologies in particular sectors—which neither of the other two highly aggregated methods of analysis were designed to handle—lay at the bottom of the lively but somewhat evasive and inconclusive controversy that followed.

Be that as it may, I decided in the 1960s that I would one day try to set out a final version of my theory of growth (not merely the stages) in a form that would more effectively dramatize the need for a disaggregated sectoral treatment of the process of invention and innovation and for treatment of other neglected features of the process of growth. That decision was brought into sharp focus by the almost obsessive interest and concern with the new technologies we encountered in 1983 and 1984—from Honolulu to Beijing, Seoul to Djakarta, New Delhi to Rabat, Verona to Uppsala, Moscow to London, and at all intervening stops. On returning home on July 1, 1984, I set to work on the long-contemplated study. Later in the year the notion emerged of beginning with a history of theories of economic growth over the past two and a half centuries and, against that background, presenting my own version. I can only report, about a thousand draft pages out, that it has been thus far a most rewarding academic enterprise. Chapter 1 of the present book suggests—and the other chapters elaborate—some of the large themes I now envisage the study will ultimately address.

The chapters of this book are, essentially, variations on those themes. Inevitably, therefore, there is a certain amount of repetition, even after editing. After considering the alternatives, I decided the best course was to accept that outcome rather than to deform the line of argument used on each occasion.

Five of these chapters have been previously published. I have edited out some of the more parochial passages that focused on the specific settings to which these essays and talks were addressed, but I have added brief prefatory notes explaining the circumstances. On the other hand, I have not rewritten these essays in the form of conventional chapters of a book.

*W. W. Rostow*
Austin, Texas

# *Acronyms*

| | |
|---|---|
| ADB | Asian Development Bank |
| AFDB | African Development Bank |
| ASEAN | Association of Southeast Asian Nations |
| CIAP | Inter-American Committee on the Alliance for Progress |
| ECA | Economic Commission for Africa |
| GDP | Gross Domestic Product |
| GNP | Gross National Product |
| IADB | Inter-American Development Bank |
| NATO | North Atlantic Treaty Organization |
| NIEO | New International Economic Order |
| OAS | Organization of American States |
| OCS | Outer Continental Shelf |
| OECD | Organization for Economic Cooperation and Development |
| OPEC | Organization of Petroleum Exporting Countries |
| SALT I | Strategic Arms Limitation Talks I |
| SDI | Strategic Defense Initiative |
| SIC | Standard Industrial Classification |

# ONE

# Reflections on the Past and Future of Political Economy

The American Economist *is an excellent magazine addressed to undergraduates doing honors work in economics. I confess I had never heard of it when I received the invitation, referred to in the essay that follows, from its editor-in-chief, Michael Szenberg. My initial reaction was as stated. I showed the invitation to my wife, along with essays by four predecessors in the series. She concluded firmly that I should accept and proceed. Her grounds were these: I was evidently having so much fun writing about the major figures in growth theory since the eighteenth century that there was danger of my losing a sense of the forest among the trees; and it was time, in mid-passage, to reflect on the large issues to which my current growth study was ultimately addressed. I accepted her argument, as I usually do.*

*This piece about the forest, written lightheartedly over a weekend, suggests where I seemed to be heading in the late winter of 1985–1986. It was published in the Fall 1986 issue of* The American Economist.

## I. COMPLEXITY, HUMOR, AND CREATIVITY

I have rarely received an invitation to which my initial reaction was more negative than Mr. Szenberg's gracious suggestion that I set down my philosophy of life. He was good enough to send along essays by four distinguished predecessors in this series. I found all of them illuminating and good to have in print. But still, the notion of pronouncing solemnly on my life philosophy made me reach out for some properly deflating *bon mot* of Mark Twain, Mr. Dooley, Will

---

Reprinted with changes from *The American Economist* (Fall 1986), pp. 3–12.

Rogers, or Groucho Marx. It was only when I began to understand the dual sources of my instinctive resistance that I concluded the enterprise might be doable.

First, I regard human beings and their behavior as too complex to be governed by a philosophy of life. David Hume, one of the wisest of men, put it memorably:[1] "These principles of human nature, you'll say, are contradictory: But what is man but a heap of contradictions." And in the same vein James Gould Cozzens, in *By Love Possessed*:[2]

> A man's temperament might, perhaps, be defined as the mode or modes of a man's feeling, the struck balance of his ruling desires, the worked-out sum of his habitual predispositions. In themselves, these elements were inscrutable. There were usually too many of them; they were often of irreducible complexity; you could observe only results. . . . The to-be-observed result was a total way of life.

This line of reflection led me once, when writing about our own society, to set aside the concept of national character as beyond my reach, in favor of describing our national style—how we went about our business.[3] It turned out that reasonably distinctive, persistent patterns of behavior could be observed and documented, despite their complexity.

The great philosophers and theologians, in most cultures, have tended to begin with some version of this complexity. For example, those two great scientist-poets of the human condition—Plato and Freud—simplified their systems down to three similar, interacting forces: the spirited side of man, appetite, and reason; the id, ego, and super-ego. And both elevated the triad, which Plato called the state within us, into their analyses of politics—a continuity in moving from micro- to macro-analysis economists have never been able to achieve.

It is this kind of perception about people—the marvelous "diversity and paradox in their . . . natures," to use a phrase of Elting Morison[4]—that leads the best politicians to conduct their business, even their most solemn business, in a context of humor. It is a way of underlining to themselves and their colleagues the need to take account of many perspectives before acting. It reminds decision-makers that the adversary—across the aisle or across the seas—is also trying to cope with a constituency equally divided by conflicting perspectives and pressures. And it conveys without cant the inherent disparity between the scale of the problems they confront and the capacities of mortal men.

In the Kennedy Presidential Library you can buy a coffee mug with an inscription from Aubrey Mennen which President Kennedy had inscribed on a silver beer mug he gave to his friend David Powers on his birthday in April 1962:

> There are three things which are real;
> God, Human Folly and Laughter.
> The first two are beyond our comprehension
> So we must do what we can with the third.

I take that to be part, at least, of the truth about the human condition.

A second conclusion follows from this perspective. An individual is unlikely to be the best judge of his life philosophy. But to return to Cozzens' phrase, "the to-be-observed result" of an individual in action over a sustained period of time may provide an approximation of what his operating philosophy of life, in fact, is. And it may differ a bit from what he quite honestly believes it to be.

The problem here is not unlike the difficulty we sometimes get into in our profession when trying to explain where our ideas came from; for example, Alfred Marshall on how he came to marginal analysis.[5] We may believe we remember whom we talked to, what we read, and what we thought in an accurate time sequence; although memory is notably faulty and self-serving as well. But even if a persevering historian could construct from documents such sequences—as historians of economic thought often try to do—they would not provide a reliable answer. Time sequences tell us nothing definitive about causation. Besides, as Winston Churchill is reported once to have remarked:[6] "Men often stumble over the truth, but most manage to pick themselves up and hurry off as if nothing had happened." And when the truth firmly grips us, it may emerge from some quite unlikely process. Keynes, for example, explained how Isaac Newton made his discoveries: through intuition operating in periods of uniquely sustained concentration—the mathematical rationale for which he did not bother to write down until much later when pressed to do so.[7] Or the process may be as messy as Watson's description of finding DNA. With the rise of Artificial Intelligence we may learn to call creativity interaction among parallel super-computers with large idle capacity; but, in the end, creativity is the bringing together of strands never brought together before—like a good joke. And thus far impenetrable human capacities like intuition continue to play a large part.

Mennen is right. There is an ample supply of folly in the world. But there is also magic.

To return to my assigned theme, it turned out that the two sources of resistance to the invitation, once identified, were, after a fashion, the beginnings of a response.

This is the case because I do believe these reflections bear not only on how I've gone about my business as an economist but, more importantly, on the abiding schism in our profession, and the crisis which many perceive economists must try to resolve if we are to serve humanity well over the next century.

## II. NEO-NEWTONIANS AND BIOLOGISTS

At the risk of considerable over-simplification, it is fair to say that economists have for long been divided between what might be called the neo-Newtonians and the biologists. I belong with the biologists.

The distinction was never more vivid than in the moving effort of Ricardo and Malthus—polar representatives of the two schools—to establish why they disagreed so profoundly and could not resolve their differences. Here were men engaged for twelve years (1811–1823) in intense dialogue, focused on essentially the same issues, their friendship suffused with an authentic mutual affection and the kind of respect that comes when two human beings know each is striving with total integrity to find answers to large questions. But their endless exchanges, face-to-face and in a correspondence of 167 known letters, remained almost—not quite—a dialogue of the deaf.

Malthus explained their differences as follows:[8]

> The principal cause of error . . . among the scientific writers on political economy, appears to me to be a precipitate attempt to simplify and generalize. While their more practical opponents draw too hasty inferences from a frequent appeal to partial facts. . . .
>
> In political economy the desire to simplify has occasioned an unwillingness to acknowledge the operation of more causes than one in the production of particular effects. . . . The first business of philosophy is to account for things as they are. . . .

Ricardo found "one great cause of our difference in opinion" in Malthus' concern with "immediate and temporary effects" whereas he [Ricardo] puts them aside and fixes his "whole attention on the permanent state of things which will result from them. Perhaps you estimate these temporary effects too highly, whilst I am too much disposed to under-value them. To manage the subject quite right they should be carefully distinguished and mentioned, and the due effects ascribed to each."[9] But, of course, Ricardo didn't bring about this reconciliation. He continued, in Schumpeter's phrase, with the Ricardian Vice, piling up abstract assumptions until "the desired results emerged almost as tautologies."[10]

Marshall did seek a reconciliation. Despite his great neo-Newtonian gifts, mathematical appendices, and short-term equilibrium formulations, he was a convinced biologist. For example, probably in 1881 he formulated, in mathematical terms, a quite recognizable neo-classical growth model, vintage 1960's.[11] He then specified the determinants of the variables. For example, the rate of increase of the working force and its efficiency he viewed as dependent on six sub-variables, including "the evenness of income distribution," the strength of family affections, the willingness to sacrifice present for more distant enjoyment as it determines both age of marriage and willingness to invest in a good education. Faced with such complexities, the neo-Newtonian tends to bundle them up in a black box; shove the box into his equation; and to get on with often meaningless, elegant manipulations. Marshall put aside his model and wrote Book IV of the *Principles*.

Which way we go is determined, I suspect, like W. S. Gilbert's Liberals and Conservatives, by the time we were born into the world alive. In my case, although the outcome may well have been predetermined, the decision was made in my sophomore year at Yale where I majored in history. I wrote my freshman and sophomore term papers on aspects of the French Revolution and the English Revolution of the 17th century, and was much impressed by the gross inadequacy of Marxist or any other single cause explanations. As a sophomore, I was taught my first serious economics by Richard M. Bissell, just back from a year at the London School of Economics, at work on his doctorate, and a man with extraordinary gifts of exposition. He laid out both micro- and macro-theory in mathematical terms to four of us in a kind of black-market seminar on Thursday evenings. It was an extraordinarily exciting experience. I decided then, at the age of seventeen, that I would try to combine economic theory and economic history in just about the way I have done for the past fifty-two years.

By the spring of 1934 I had conducted my first experiment as an economist-historian: a paper of ninety-seven pages on the British inflation during the French Revolution and the Napoleonic Wars, the subsequent deflation, and the return to the gold standard. I began believing that the theoretical structures incorporated in D. H. Robertson's *Money* and Keynes' *Treatise on Money*, among other works, would provide a sufficient framework to explain what happened to prices. The beginning of my education as an independent economic theorist was the discovery that conventional monetary theory was incomplete and, on occasion, significantly misleading as a tool for explaining why prices moved as they did from 1793 to 1821. In the course of the exercise I came to understand the shrewdness of Wicksell's description of quantity theorists:[12] "They usually make the mistake of postulating their assumptions instead of clearly proving them"—a phenomenon that persists but surprises me less than it did.

I found that Thomas Tooke was a good deal wiser. He systematically introduced changes in costs, including those brought about by the new technologies. He also wove together the real and monetary factors, producing along the way a theory of effective demand (as opposed to the money supply) that clearly anticipated Wicksell and Keynes.[13]

The lesson of this first experiment was systematically reinforced with the passage of time. I found mainstream economics, including the so-called neo-classical synthesis, an incomplete framework for a serious economic historian or analyst of the current scene; and, as I learned more, I judged it increasingly necessary to introduce as systematically as I could political, social, cultural, and other non-economic forces as they bore on economic behavior.

We all know what kind of theory neo-Newtonians produce. But what about the biologists? What kind of theory can we produce if we feel impelled, in Malthus' phrases, "to account for things as they are"—and were—and to look for "more causes than one"? Marshall knew all too well what happens to the use of differential calculus when you introduce increasing returns: there is no unambiguous equilibrium position and no reversibility. One is confronted with "organic growth" in all its complexity, much as contemporary physical scientists are being forced to face up, in Ilya Prigogine's phrases, to "instability, mutation, and diversification where irreversible processes are constantly at work, and non-equilibrium is itself a source of dynamic order."[14] The economist-biologist answer, I believe, is to discern and try to inter-relate recurrent dynamic patterns operating in the past and at present.

I suggest five examples: the demographic transition; the occurrence over the past two centuries of four identifiable periods when major innovations clustered; the recurrence of major cycles of about nine years length from a peak in 1782 to one in 1937; the existence from 1790 to the present of four and a half cycles in the prices of basic commodities relative to manufactures; and the existence of a definable period of discontinuity in economic growth which I call the take-off and Kuznets, with virtually the same dates, called the beginning of modern growth.[15] And I would argue that beyond take-off (or the beginnings of modern growth) there are distinguishable stages which can be defined in terms of (i) the degree to which the pool of (then) modern technology has been absorbed and (ii) the operation of the income elasticity of demand.

These patterns are all authentically dynamic in the sense that both conceptually and in fact they can be dated. They all involve the movement over short time periods of Marshallian long period factors; and they can all be regarded analytically as aspects of the process of economic growth.

Three of the patterns are the result of lags of different lengths and other imperfections in the investment process leading to systematic over-shooting and under-shooting of dynamic optimum sectoral paths with wide-ranging macro consequences. The length of the cycles (and the related extent of over-shoot and under-shoot) is primarily determined by the length of the periods of gestation of the relevant types of investment.

All the patterns have, in fact, been altered or, in concept, could be altered by changes in institutions, policies, or technologies as, for example, the demographic transition has been altered by developments in medical technology. All the patterns are subject to deviations from calculated average behavior. At least three can not be understood without introducing directly into economic analysis non-economic variables which are often the source of deviations from average behavior.

Nevertheless, I believe they are authentic features of economic growth since, say, the 1780's. There is a hard scientific core to these related patterns. Something like this system with all its components brought together, rendered endogenous, and linked to more or less conventional macro-economics is what is required to fulfill Allyn Young's vision of "a moving equilibrium" and Schumpeter's unfulfilled dream of dynamizing the Walrasian model. It is also the clue to rendering the Leontief matrix authentically dynamic. I've used this system for just about thirty-five years—since I wrote *The Process of Economic Growth* (1953). I am now engaged in elaborating this structure in both prose and, to the extent possible, in mathematical form, assimilating along the way what I believe I have learned about growth over the three subsequent decades. In Warren Weaver's phrase, it is an exercise in "organized complexity."[16]

## III. THE ILLUSORY TRIUMPH OF THE NEO-NEWTONIANS

I evoke this enterprise here not to argue its merits but to underline how profoundly a minority position it reflects at this stage of the history of economic thought. In his essay [in *The American Economist*

(Fall, 1986)], Paul Samuelson says, I believe correctly, that it is not a virtue for economists to nurture their originality in isolation and not read their colleagues' work. I wouldn't quite rate it part of my life philosophy, but I have been a lifelong registered Democrat. I was brought up, however, by parents committed to the pre-1914 democratic socialist tradition, for which I retain an affectionate respect. There was authentic rejoicing in the household when Eugene Debs got a million votes in a presidential election. We were encouraged to feel comfortable in a minority position if we were so minded, but without a chip on our shoulder. And so I read the papers and books of my mainstream friends as Samuelson counsels. I'm simply as unimpressed in 1986 as I was with the quantity theorists of the period 1793–1821 when I read them in 1934.

Let me cite an example. The great boom in the world economy of 1951–1972 is conventionally presented as a triumph of modern macro-economics, a unique combination of low unemployment, rapid growth, and low rates of inflation, brought about because effective demand was held at an appropriate level (at least down to the mid-1960's) by a skillful combination of fiscal and monetary policy. Three critical forces have no place in this demand-side story on which we are now bringing up the young. First, a sharp movement in relative prices which granted the advanced industrial countries a favorable shift in their net barter terms of trade of about 20% between 1951 and 1964, when the absolute decline in basic commodity prices bottomed out. Second, the existence of a large backlog of automobile and durable goods technologies for Western Europe (an enormous backlog for Japan) which proved easy to absorb and diffuse because of the rise in real wages after 1951, which, in turn, partially reflected the favorable shift in the terms of trade. Third, in a perfectly natural process the leading sectors of the boom began to decelerate in the mid-1960's, yielding a slowdown in the rate of productivity increase and a tendency of the capital-output ratio to rise.

I would argue that what happened in 1972–1974 and subsequently in the world economy can not be understood without introducing these factors plus the gathering tension in commodity markets as grain stocks fell in relation to world consumption levels and U.S. dependence on oil imports rose with oil and gas production topping out in 1970–1971. These proved to be macro- not simply micro-phenomena when the explosion of grain and oil prices came in 1972–1974.

I submit that this image of the great post-1951 boom coming under progressive strain from the side of basic commodity supplies and relative prices as well as from a reduced technological backlog requires considerable modification in the theoretical structure we now teach our students.

But if all this came to rest simply in a debate on the causes of the great boom of the third quarter of the twentieth century, its attenuation and demise, Mr. Szenberg could legitimately take the view that I hired the wrong hall. But if, against this background, we look ahead to the problems of political economy over, say, the next 50–100 years, I believe issues of how we view the world and our fellowmen emerge as well as the need for quite fundamental changes in our methods of analysis.

## IV. THE CENTURY AHEAD

The first century of political economy—from, say, Hume and Smith to J. S. Mill and Marx—centered on economic growth, its potentialities and limits and their implications for relative prices and distribution. But Mill and Marx, while rooted in the older tradition, also opened the second century of political economy. They assumed an ongoing system existed based on more or less regularly expanding technological possibilities. They identified its inequities and elements of harshness. Although Marx might not be happy with my formulation, they both asked, in effect, how the system could be rendered humane and civilized in terms of the abiding values of Western culture and its religions. Mill, a passionate environmentalist and designer of the democratic welfare state, provided, of course, quite different answers than the bloody revolutions counseled by Marx; but they and their contemporaries launched a century and more in which the central question of political economy became a kind of zero-sum struggle for the allocation of resources from a pie which, except for the interwar traumas, could be assumed to be expanding. Should resources be allocated to welfare or to nurture private consumption and investment? The revolutionary rise of welfare outlays from an average of about 14% to 24% of GNP in the major OECD [Organization for Economic Cooperation and Development] countries between 1960 and the mid-1970's brought that phase to a rather dramatic close. The fate of the social and physical infrastructure of the advanced industrial countries depends, I believe, not on the power of conservative versus liberal politicians but on how the political process responds to the new question which is upon us but not yet faced and dealt with in the United States and Western Europe. That response or failure to respond will determine whether or not the pie can continue to expand and sustain and refine the amenities we have thus far achieved.

The central question for political economy in the presently advanced industrial countries during the third century of modern growth already is—and will increasingly be—the question David Hume posed in 1758, a quarter century before the first wave of modern industrial innovations began to assert itself. He asked what would happen to front-runners who first develop the skills of large scale trade, the specializations that go with the exploitation of comparative advantage, including improvement in "the mechanic arts," when their success stirs a "fermentation" in less advanced societies which proceed to imitate the more advanced but with the advantage of lower wage rates.[17]

Hume's answer, in response to the mercantilist instinct to throttle the late-comers in the cradle, was that the front-runner could enjoy the advantages of expanded two-way trade with the aspiring country if it maintained an open trading system; but to sustain the inevitably intensified competition it would have to remain "industrious and civilized." Here is Hume's summation:[18]

Nor needs any state entertain apprehensions, that their neighbours will improve to such a degree in every art and manufacture, as to have no demand from them. Nature, by giving a diversity of geniuses, climates, and soils to different nations, has secured their mutual intercourse and commerce, as long as they all remain industrious and civilized. Nay, the more the arts increase in any state, the more will be its demands from its industrious neighbours.

His quite detailed technical description of the adjustments required by the front-runner economists would subsume as a demonstration of a high elasticity of substitution.

In our day, of course, a high elasticity of substitution involves the generation and diffusion of the fourth great wave of innovations which emerged commercially round about the mid-1970's: microelectronics, genetic engineering, a batch of new industrial materials, the laser, robots, a communications revolution combining several of the other new technologies. The implications of these and no doubt other major technological innovations will unfold over the decades ahead and offer to the more advanced industrial societies an opportunity to maintain themselves near the front of the queue if they bestir themselves.

But there is no cause for complacency if we are to fulfill Hume's conditions. At the moment, we tend to focus on Japan as the great challenger; but behind Japan, South Korea, Taiwan, and other vital states of Southeast Asia are gearing up to go high-tech; India and China, despite their enormous problems, will not be far behind; nor, I predict, will Brazil and other Latin American countries.

I hold this view because of a virtually unnoticed revolution in the technologically more advanced developing countries. Overall, the proportion of the population aged 20–24 enrolled in higher education in what the World Bank calls "lower middle income" countries rose from 3 to 10% between 1960 and 1982; for "upper middle income" countries the increase was from 4 to 14%.[19] The increase in India, with low income per capita but a vital educational system was from 3 to 9%. To understand the quantitative meaning of these figures it should be recalled that in 1960 the proportion for the U.K. was 9%, for Japan 10%.

There has been, moreover, a radical shift towards science and engineering. In India, for example, the pool of scientists and engineers has increased from about 190,000 in 1960 to 2.4 million in 1984— a critical mass only exceeded in the United States and the Soviet Union. In Mexico, for example, the annual average increase in Mexican graduates in natural science was about 3%, in engineering 5%, in the period 1957 to 1973. From 1973 to 1981 the comparable figures were 14% to 24%, respectively—an astonishing almost five-fold acceleration.

Even discounting for problems of educational quality, the potential absorptive capacity for the new technologies in the more advanced developing countries is high. Their central problem—like that of most advanced industrial countries—is how to make effective the increasingly abundant scientific and engineering skills they already command. This requires, in turn, an ability to generate and maintain effective, flexible, interactive partnerships among scientists, engineers, entrepreneurs, and the working force. For the United States, I would predict, the outcome will depend not only on the pace at which we generate the new technologies but on the pace at which we diffuse them to old basic industries, agriculture, and the services.

## V. WHAT IS TO BE DONE: POLITICS

If my view of the challenge posed by the new technologies in the world economy is roughly correct, a radical change in the contours of politics is required in the United States and Western Europe. The change, put simply, is from primary emphasis on a zero-sum conflict over the allocation of what has been assumed to be an automatically expanding pie to sustained communal cooperation to assure that the pie will, in fact, continue to expand.

A quick glance at national politics in the United States would not appear to justify a high degree of optimism. The 1984 presidential campaign was conducted in terms which roughly characterized every election since 1896, at least; i.e., protection of the private sector from government intrusion versus equity for the disadvantaged. We are maintaining our standard of life by borrowing abroad—much like New York City under Mayor Lindsay. At home we have inflicted on ourselves belatedly an awkward chastity belt called Gramm-Rudman to control apparently irrepressible passion for expenditure or unconquerable resistance to the austere discipline of taxes. At first sight, we give every sign of preferring to go down in the style to which we have become accustomed rather than facing reality.

But that's not quite the way it is. Beneath the surface some fifty high-tech highways, all of which will not flourish, have nevertheless, been built by intimate cooperation among the private sector, state and local governments, the universities, and, quite often, representatives of labor. Large segments of labor and management are aware that they have come to a new phase in their history, and new kinds of cooperation will be required if the American industrial structure is to continue to flourish and sustain both constituencies. Thus, for example, the Saturn experiment and a good many other examples of a partnership spirit achieved by a simple shared desire to survive. A heightened sense of community will no doubt be generated by such ventures but they are the immediate product of Dr. Johnson's dictum: "Depend upon it, sir, when a man knows he is to be hanged in a fortnight it concentrates his mind wonderfully."

Similarly, successful governors in the states, Republican and Democratic, as well as successful mayors in hard-pressed cities, reach out to damp confrontation and unite their communities, as New York City was united to avoid bankruptcy some years ago.

Often in American history national political trends and styles are foreshadowed in the states; and I believe this is happening, although no national political figure or party has yet found the terms and defined the agenda that would rally the nation for the long test of our viability as a society that has already begun. Right now we are buying time at high cost down the road; but we are clearly not meeting that test.

## VI. WHAT IS TO BE DONE:
## POLITICAL ECONOMY

If we take our objective from Hume it comes to this. We must sustain a civilized and industrious society capable of remaining viable in an open trading system in a world undergoing a powerful multidimensional technological revolution which will diffuse rapidly to lower wage rate developing regions as well as to the advanced industrial countries, affecting, in the end, virtually every sector of each of the world's economies. Clearly, this objective has a good many implications for the future shape of political economy, of which I shall cite only a few examples.

First, mainstream economics should, at last, concern itself in a serious, sustained way with the generation and diffusion of technologies. An inability to deal with this process as part of the central body of economic theory has been a characteristic of our trade for two centuries.[20] Incrementally increased productivity flowing from the enlargement of the market was quite legitimate in the time of Hume and Smith, before the industrial revolution; but once major technological change began, including large discontinuous change, specialization of function covered only a small part of the process, as did economies of scale even with their Marshallian refinements. The Schumpeterian insights on innovation were basically correct, but never absorbed into mainstream economics. Models were designed so as to split investment between the endogenous operation of the accelerator and something called exogenous investment coming along from time to time at random or at the stochastic will of drunken gods. The highly aggregated models generated in modern macro-economics had no place for an R&D investment sector out of which inventions were generated in response to more or less conventional market calculations, or for a dynamized Leontief matrix which would track out their impact on other sectors and the aggregates. Nor do economists clearly distinguish the tasks of entrepreneurship in maximizing profits under Marshallian short-period assumptions and under conditions of rapid discontinuous change in production functions—a major flaw in mainstream economic theory, an almost fatal flaw in the curricula of our business schools.

There are, of course, differences between the investment process in the R&D sector and that in more conventional sectors. Serendipitous results are perhaps more frequent and Murphy's Law somewhat more active. As in the wildcat search for new oil and gas reserves, a few rich payoffs must cover losses on many dry holes. But, at least since the mid-eighteenth century in Britain, R&D should be accounted an investment sector; and the flow of inventions into the economy viewed as an endogenous aspect of the growth process. Clearly, there is a long and quite revolutionary theoretical and empirical agenda before us if our craft is to be rendered relevant to a world economy where the generation and diffusion of new technologies is, and will remain, a central phenomenon. And that agenda will have to combine new theoretical concepts, the mobilization of statistical data in new forms, and the introduction of a good deal of non-economic analysis, including the institutional linkages of science, engineering, entrepreneurship, and the working force.

Second, building not only on Hume's suggestive observations but also on Folke Hilgerdt's classic League of Nations study, *Industrialization and Foreign Trade*, economists should extend our understanding of the positive and negative impact on front-runner A as late-comer B learns to exploit the hitherto unexploited backlog of technologies and narrows the gap in real income per capita. This kind of analysis should include all the factors—including non-economic factors—that economists group under the elasticity of substitution. The post-1945 experience of the world economy offers rich empirical materials for dynamic studies of this kind.

Third, as already suggested, a new definition is required of the appropriate role of labor in the transformation ahead and of the widened area of authentic mutual interest in labor-management cooperation. Labor has, for a century, by and large concentrated on maximizing its short-run gains in each sector, in a zero-sum struggle over the expected spoils in that sector. Now, new issues have asserted themselves; for example, the long-run level of employment in particular sectors, the sectoral and over-all rates of productivity increase, the intensity of international competition in particular sectors, the international value of the dollar, and the appropriate role of an incomes policy. And one can detect a parallel changing agenda under discussion among thoughtful business leaders. In redefining their objectives in the new international setting and the appropriate relations between them, business and labor could be helped by fresh thought from first-rate economists.

This, of course, is not all. There are other difficult problems which evidently deserve sophisticated attention. How do we avoid yo-yo oscillations in the world energy markets? How do both advanced industrial and developing countries work their way out of their different but equally pathological agricultural policies in ways that are politically acceptable? How do we deal internationally with gross environmental degradation; for example, forests, rivers, and acid rain? How do we deal with the developing nations which have not yet moved into take-off or beyond in, for example, Africa south of the Sahara, and the small Pacific islands? What is the appropriate relation between the industrial countries and the more advanced developing countries in, for example, the Pacific Basin and the Western Hemisphere? And, of course, what lessons are to be learned about the possibilities and limits of fiscal and monetary policy since the end of 1972 and the optimum form for incomes policies at a time when the vitality and flexibility of the private sector are also of critical importance?

Without laboring the point, it is clear that contemporary mainstream economics is not now coming to grips with some such array of palpably urgent and relevant problems. Our graduate students are, by and large, taught to respect the primacy of method and technique; and problems are cut down to the size the chosen techniques can handle. With admirable candor, Robert Solow put it this way:[21]

> I suspect there is an inner logic that pushes people like me to over-develop the technical apparatus, First of all, if you are good at it, you have a competitive advantage that you will want to use. Besides, it is easier to invent technical variations than to have new ideas. So that is what they will publish in the academic journals.
>
> "Does it matter? It may. People who spend their lives making elaborate distinctions will come to believe that the distinctions are important. They may get so wound up in the performance that they forget to ask if it is making sense. They may choose their assumptions for convenience instead of plausibility and then forget where the assumptions came from.
>
> "If you are nodding your head, I come to the strangest news of all. No one has found a better way of doing economics.

As for the last sentence, I would respectfully respond, to paraphrase John Kennedy, "I think we can do better."

I suggest it might be wholesome for all of us to look back and recall what our discipline was like in its classic origins and, indeed, down to a half century ago: from, say, Hume and Adam Smith through J. S. Mill, Alfred Marshall, and Knut Wicksell to Keynes, Hansen, Myrdal and the others who fought to use political economy to save democratic societies from destruction in the Great Depression. They took the problem, as they perceived it in all its complexity, made it their discipline, bringing to bear insights from every direction. Their efforts included, but were not limited to, the refinement of the concepts of economic theory as they inherited them cumulatively from the past. They acknowledged that they were driven by moral objectives, abhorred the human degradation imposed by poverty, looked to economics and economists, in the phrase of Keynes' famous toast, as the "trustees not of civilization but of the possibility of civilization." And they would have all, I believe, signed on to the dictum that appears on the first page of the Preface to all the editions of Mill's *Principles*: "Except on matters of mere detail, there are perhaps no practical questions, even among those which approach nearest to the character of purely economical questions, which admit of being decided on economical premises alone."

Our generation has deviated radically from the best in the tradition of our profession—at great cost.

Evidently we can't and shouldn't go back. Evidently we should not lose what we have gained in command over increasingly sophisticated techniques of mathematical and econometric analysis. But it is time for us to discipline those techniques to the large problems we confront and accept Alfred Marshall's well grounded judgment that such methods can, at most, constitute "a necessary introduction to a more philosophic treatment of society as an organism."[22]

## VII. A BIT OF "LIFE PHILOSOPHY"

There is a reason for urging this course which transcends any I have thus far evoked. Modern political economy arose in Western Europe, in both its French and British branches, in opposition to the mercantilists. The physiocrats argued powerfully for the critical importance of agriculture—even overdoing it a bit—in opposition to mercantilist neglect. Hume argued boldly for the British interest in the prosperity of France. Smith argued against a regime of colonies. In Britain their arguments gained ground; but the fact is that Britain was at war for just about forty years during the eighteenth century. In such an age there was a considerable logic to mercantilist doctrine.

If my view of what lies ahead is broadly correct, the world economy and polity face an unprecedented adjustment over the next century. The advanced industrial countries (including the U.S.S.R. and Eastern Europe) now constitute about 1.1 billion people or, say 24% of the world's population. At least 2.6 billion people, or about 56%, live in countries which will, I would guess, acquire technological virtuosity within the next century; and this will happen sooner rather than later. Moreover, population, in the decades ahead, will increase more rapidly in the latter than the former group. We are talking about a great historical transformation.

There can be important economic advantages to the early-comers as the late-comers move towards technological equivalence. But, evidently, the process could generate all manner of mercantilist frictions and dangers—even mortal dangers in a nuclear age. It will take strength, unity, poise, and inner confidence for the presently advanced industrial nations to maintain their vitality and play a constructive part in helping the world community, as a whole, through this complex and potentially explosive adjustment.

For thirty-five years I have committed a good deal of time and thought to economic development in Latin America, Africa, the Middle East, and Asia. I have come to know as colleagues and brothers-in-arms a great many of the development economists, planners, and administrators in these regions. And I have gone out from the capital cities to many villages in a good many countries from the Peruvian Andes to Iran and Korea, and seen in the faces of men, women, and children the terrible dehumanizing burden of poverty not quite overcoming the magical determination to live, love, and laugh.

The associations that arose from this commitment were among the most rewarding of my professional life. They reinforced a lesson which is the one we shall most need in the generations ahead if we are to come through the dynamic transition we confront in reasonably good order, a lesson to which I have often been driven back, incorporated in the lines of the poet after whom I happen to be named:

One though ever at the fore—
That in the Divine Ship, the World,
 breasting Time and Space,
All peoples of the globe together sail,
 sail the same voyage,
Are bound to the same destination.

## NOTES

1. David Hume, *Philosophical Works*, T. H. Green and T. H. Grose (eds.), London: Longmans Green, 1912 edition, Vol. III, p. 238.

2. James Gould Cozzens, *By Love Possessed*, New York: Harcourt Brace Jovanovich, 1957, p. 353.

3. "The National Style" in Elting E. Morison (ed.), *The American Style, Essays in Value and Performance*, New York: Harper, 1958, pp. 246–313.

4. *Ibid.*, p. 321.

5. See, for example, Joseph A. Schumpeter, *History of Economic Analysis*, New York: Oxford University Press, pp. 837–840.

6. Quoted, Alexander B. Trowbridge, *Private Leadership and Public Service*, Washington, D.C.: National Academy of Public Administration, 1985, pp. 14–15.

7. J. M. Keynes, "Newton the Man," in *Essays in Biography*, London: Rupert Hart-Davis, 1951, pp. 310–323.

8. T. R. Malthus, *Principles of Political Economy*, second edition, New York: Augustus Kelley, 1951 (reprint), pp. 4–12.

9. Piero Sraffa (ed.), with the collaboration of Maurice Dobb, *The Works and Correspondence of David Ricardo*, Vol. VII, Cambridge: at the University Press, 1952, p. 120.

10. J. A. Schumpeter, *op. cit.*, pp. 472–473.

11. J. K. Whitaker (ed.), *The Early Economic Writings of Alfred Marshall, 1867–1890*, Vol. 2, London: Macmillan, 1975, pp. 305–316.

12. Knut Wicksell, *Lectures on Political Economy*, Vol. 2, *Money*, E. Classen, Trans.; Lionel Robbins (ed.), New York: Macmillan, 1934, pp. 159–160.

13. On Tooke as a forerunner of Wicksell and Keynes, see, for example, Alvin H. Hansen, *Monetary Theory and Fiscal Policy*, New York: McGraw-Hill, 1949, pp. 87–89.

14. The phrases are drawn from Professor Prigogine's lecture "Order Out of Chaos," a public lecture delivered at The University of Texas at Austin, November 18, 1977, on the occasion of the announcement of his Nobel Prize award.

15. For reference to Kuznets' dating and analysis of discontinuity in relation to mine, see W. W. Rostow, *The World Economy: History and Prospect*, Austin: University of Texas Press, 1978, pp. 778–779.

16. Warren Weaver, "Science and Complexity," *American Scientist*, Vol. 36, 1948.

17. See, notably, Istvan Hont, "The 'rich country–poor country' debate in Scottish classical political economy," Chapter 11 in Istvan Hont and Michael Ignatieff (eds.), *Wealth and Virtue: The Shaping of Political Economy in the Scottish Enlightenment*, Cambridge: at the University Press, 1983.

18. *David Hume: Writings on Economics*, edited and introduction by Eugene Rotwein, Madison: University of Wisconsin Press, 1955, p. 80.

19. *World Development Report 1984* and *1985*, New York: Oxford University Press, 1984 and 1985, Table 25, pp. 266–267 and 222–223, respectively.

20. See, for example, my "Technology and the Price System," Chapter 4 in *Why the Poor Get Richer and the Rich Slow Down*, Austin: University of Texas Press, 1980.

21. Robert M. Solow, "Why People Make Fun of Economists," *The New York Times*, December 29, 1985, Business Section, p. 2.

22. Alfred Marshall, *Principles of Economics*, eighth edition, London: Macmillan, 1930, p. 461.

# The World Economy Since 1945:
# A Stylized Historical Analysis

As the second paragraph of the essay that follows suggests, I accepted that somewhat extraordinary—even megalomaniac—subject assigned me by Michael Thompson (of the University of London) while in Italy, about midway through a year's leave of absence. Perhaps the charm of the Villa Serbelloni on Lake Como tipped the balance. But I was lucky to have three solid months at Oxford with almost no responsibility other than to write this piece—a rare dispensation in modern academic life. It was delivered at the annual gathering of British economic historians, which took place in Glasgow in April 1984. The essay was published in the May 1985 issue of The Economic History Review—forty-seven years after my first professional article appeared in that journal.

For those who may be interested, I consulted a senior member of the music faculty at Oxford to establish the maximum number of themes Bach managed to weave together in counterpoint (end of second paragraph).

The need to nurture the sense of community to transit successfully the problems confronted in the 1980s within and among the nations of the Atlantic world—a need defined at the close of this chapter—has appeared increasingly urgent with the passage of time since April 1984.

From the perspective of economic theory, the concepts chosen to give shape to the story told here constitute three of the major differences between the analytic structure I have developed and mainstream economic theory. The principal additional difference is my insistence that noneconomic factors must be introduced systematically into the analysis of any major historical or contemporary economic problem.

Reprinted with permission from *The Economic History Review, Second Series*, vol. 38, no. 2 (May 1985), pp. 252–275.

Preparing this year's Tawney Memorial Lecture has been a gratifying adventure. In the first place it led me to recall a meeting with Tawney in 1950 at the home of Michael and Cynthia Postan. Wrapped about in his heavy brown tweeds, pipe ashes descending into their ample folds, Tawney seemed a John Bullish sort of man, all-of-a-piece, but with eyes alert and sensitive suggesting the complexity which, in fact, distinguished his mind and character—a complexity which soon emerged in conversation. The task also led me to re-read a good deal of Tawney's more familiar writing and to read for the first time his *Commonplace Book* and *The Attack and Other Essays* which Cynthia Postan and Peter Mathias, respectively, urged on me. As you will see, it was in these latter pieces that I found strands of thought, commitment, and passion which linked naturally to the broad conclusions of my paper. Tawney was, evidently, too grand and serious a figure to be introduced cosmetically into our proceedings this morning. When I began, I had not, in fact, expected my subject would relate to his work. I was rather surprised and pleased when it did.

I assume, of course, full responsibility for the somewhat spacious subject of my talk; although I should perhaps note that it was suggested by Michael Thompson last December when he had to extract a quick decision from me—in Italy—to satisfy the schedule of the printer of our programme. This is how he defined a possible theme: ". . . reflections on general trends in the performance of the advanced economies since the Second World War and how far these may have modified your own earlier ideas on a general model for the path of economic development". In conducting this stylized mapping of a large terrain, I recalled a paper I recently wrote entitled "Cycles and the Irreducible Complexity of History".[1] It identified some half-dozen types of cycles and explored the problem posed by their concurrence. In delivering the paper I observed that the flow of history was like a piece of music with a good many contrapuntal themes unfolding at the same time; but—unlike the work of Bach and other masters— they rarely yielded a harmonious result. I am reliably told that Bach managed up to five themes in the final Goldberg variation. With appropriate modesty I shall confine myself to three.

I

I shall begin by stating the three themes which are concepts derived from the study of modern economic history. I shall then examine broadly how variables reflecting these concepts moved over the past four decades, affecting both the advanced industrial North and the developing South, recognizing, of course, that these convenient designations are rather drastic abstractions and, indeed, not even geographically accurate. Next comes an exercise in applying the concepts to four time-phases: 1945–51; 1951–72; 1972–9; 1979–84. Finally, I shall pose a few large questions of policy that are likely to shape the future, relating some of them to Tawney.

The analytic concepts I shall use throughout are these:

First, *the stages of economic growth*.[2] It is here elaborated to take account of the relationship between the stage of growth and rate of growth.[3]

Second, *trend periods with respect to the prices of basic commodities relative to those of manufactures;* that is, the global inter-sectoral terms of trade. This relationship is, of course, reflected in national and inter-regional net barter terms of trade depending on the composition of exports and imports and the amplitude of fluctuations in their components. Irregular long cycles in this variable are the primary basis for my interpretation of the long cycles in prices, money wages and interest rates—starting round about 1790—which Kondratieff identified and which, in my view, continue down to the present.[4]

Third, *the ebb and flow of major innovations in the world economy*, including the timing of their diffusion. Here the concept appears rather dramatically as the waning in the second half of the 1960s of the Third Industrial Revolution and the emergence since, say, the mid-1970s, of the Fourth. The Fourth Industrial Revolution is taken to embrace micro-electronics, genetics, robots, lasers, new industrial materials, and new methods of communication.[5] (The four industrial revolutions are illustrated in Figure 2.1.)

I shall now say a few words about how these three concepts make their appearance in the broad sweep of economic affairs since 1945.

II

The post–World War II story of the North is marked by the following major features which relate to stages of economic growth: the substantial catching up of western Europe with the United States in terms of High Mass Consumption; and the extraordinary swift movement of Japan from Technological Maturity to High Mass Consumption at the western European level (Table 2.1 and Figure 2.2); the movement of all the advanced industrial countries into a phase of extremely rapid increase in outlays on education and other social services, including a large expansion of GNP allocated to transfer payments. Between 1960 and 1980 social outlays rose in the seven major OECD countries from 14 per cent to 24 per cent of GNP. I

Figure 2.1. *Four Industrial Revolutions Illustrated: United States, 1790–1983*

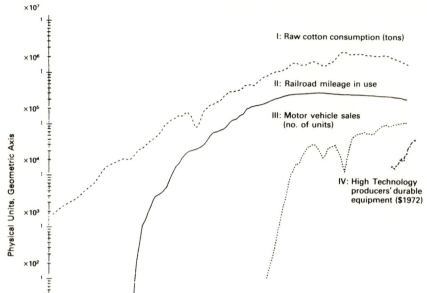

Note: As the text indicates, each of the industrial revolutions identified here is wider than the four series used in Figure 2.1 to illustrate its timing and broad contour.

*Sources:* For raw cotton consumption, railroad mileage, and motor vehicle sales see sources cited in *The World Economy: History and Prospect*, pp. 679-80, which have been used for up-dating. "High Technology producers' durable equipment" consists of office and store equipment including computers, communications equipment, photographic instruments, and scientific and engineering instruments. Measurement is in billions of 1972 US dollars. The index was constructed from data organized by the Bureau of Industry Economics, US Department of Commerce. Components of the series are to be found in: *1983 U.S. Industrial Outlook* (Washington, DC: US Department of Commerce, January 1983), pp. 27-5 and 6, 29-4, 34-5 and 36-4. See also Appendix A, under appropriate SIC numbers. Like cotton textiles but unlike railroads and motor vehicles, the high technology index starts from a relatively high level. This occurs because in both cases revolutionary new technology was introduced into an already existing industry.

Table 2.1. *Relative Growth Rates, 1950–1979 (GDP per capita) %*

|  | Western Europe† | Japan | United States |
|---|---|---|---|
| 1950-1973 | 3·7 | 8·4 | 2·2 |
| 1973-1979 | 2·0 | 3·0 | 1·9 |

† Arithmetic average

*Source:* Adapted from Angus Maddison, *Phases of Capitalist Development* (Oxford, 1982), p. 44.

Figure 2.2. *Automobile Registration per Million Population: Six Countries, 1900–1972* (*smoothed*)

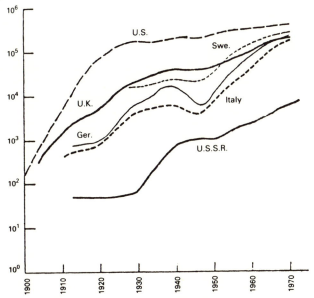

*Sources*: for all countries excepting Sweden, 1900-58, W. W. Rostow, *The Stages of Economic Growth*, pp. 168-71, where detailed sources are indicated. Sweden from 1930 and all other countries, 1958-75 (except the USSR), *Automobile Facts and Figures* published annually by the Automobile Manufacturers Association, Detroit (name changed to Motor Vehicle Manufacturers' Association in 1972). USSR, after 1957, from *World Motor Vehicle Data* (Detroit Motor Vehicle Manufacturers' Association, 1974), p. 113 (US Department of Commerce figures), and earlier editions.

have associated these movements with a possible post-High Mass Consumption Stage, the Search for Quality.[6]

The most important movements in the South during this period were the transitions of the world's two most populous nations—India and China—into Take-off in the early 1950s, and the later transition of a good many major developing countries (including India and China) from Take-off to the Drive to Technological Maturity.

It is the combination of the catching up of western Europe and Japan in High Mass Consumption and the transition of many developing countries into the Drive to Technological Maturity which accounts for the uniquely high real growth rates of the period 1951–72; for, as Figure 2.3 and Table 2.2 demonstrate, growth rates tend to be at their maximum at per capita real income levels associated with the Drive to Technological maturity.[7] They decelerate progressively in High Mass Consumption, mainly because the income elasticity of demand decrees disproportionate increases in demand for services as

Figure 2.3. *Income Levels, Annual Growth Rates, and Approximate Stage of Growth, 1960–1970*

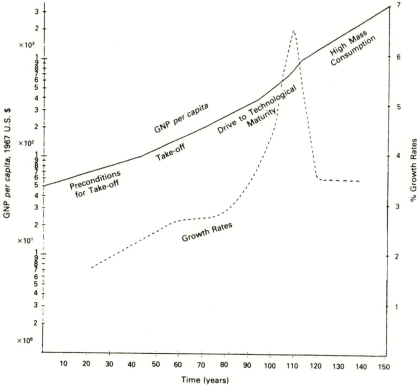

real income rises. Historically, services have been associated with lower rates of productivity increase than manufactures, although the new technologies may alter that relationship for certain service sectors in the future. As noted earlier, the lag in High Mass Consumption of western Europe and Japan behind the United States—and the pool of unapplied technologies therefore available to them after 1945—provided a phase of higher than normal growth for that stage.

During the first postwar quarter century, then, the position of the world economy in terms of stages was particularly favourable for growth rates, so long as the growth process itself proceeded strongly; and, as we all know, the growth process moved forward quite handsomely in the North until the deceleration of the late 1960s. In the South, deceleration came about a decade later. An explanation of

Table 2.2. *Income Levels and Growth Rates, 1960–1970*

| | Population 1967 (millions) | GNP per Capita 1967 US$ | Average Annual Growth Rate 1960-1970 | Approximate Stage of Growth |
|---|---|---|---|---|
| | | $ | % | |
| United States | 199 | 3,670 | 3·2 ⎤ | High Mass |
| Group 1 ($1,750-$3,670) | 307 | 3,120 | 3·4 ⎬ | Consumption |
| Group 2 ($1,000-$1,750 | 238 | 1,490 | 3·5 ⎦ | |
| Group 3 ($700-$1,000) | 444 | 930 | 6·5 ⎤ | Drive to |
| Group 4 ($400-$700) | 161 | 550 | 4·4 ⎬ | Technological |
| Group 5 ($200-$400) | 299 | 270 | 2·9 ⎦ | Maturity |
| Group 6 ($100-$200) | 376 | 130 | 2·6 | Take-off |
| Group 7 ($50-$100) | 1,580 | 90 | 1·7 | Pre-conditions |
| World | 3,391 | 610 | 3·2 | |

*Source:* Thorkil Kristensen, *Development in Rich and Poor Countries: A General Theory with Statistical Analyses* (Praeger Publishers, New York, 1974), pp. 156-9. Stages added by W. W. R.

these phases of extraordinarily high growth rates and of subsequent deceleration lies substantially in the behaviour of the second and third variables (the prices of basic commodities relative to manufactures) and the ebb and flow of technological change. And to these we now turn.

### III

There is, of course, no agreed explanation among economists for the long cycles Kondratieff identified. Indeed, some question the existence of such cycles. The three main contesting theories, among those who regard the long cycles as dated by Kondratieff as a serious phenomenon, are: cycles in technological innovation; cycles in growth rates and average levels of unemployment; cycles in the prices of basic commodities relative to manufactured goods. W. Arthur Lewis has also focused primarily on the latter as the major cause of the fluctuations Kondratieff identified.[8]

Relative prices and terms of trade movements emerge clearly in Figures 2.4 and 2.5. The relatively high postwar commodity prices down to 1951 complete, in my view, the fourth Kondratieff upswing; the fourth Kondratieff downswing follows down to 1972, but it progressively decelerates in the 1960s. The fifth Kondratieff upswing begins with an explosive upward shift in basic commodity prices starting at the close of 1972, a shift foreshadowed by an attenuation of the global inventory and reserve positions in grain and oil during the 1960s. The sharp relative price reversal of 1972–4 was followed by oscillation in a high range and a cycle in which the upward pressure on basic commodity prices appears to have weakened. In these irregular features both the fourth Kondratieff downswing and fifth Kondratieff

Figure 2.4. *Relative Price Movements, 1876–1982*

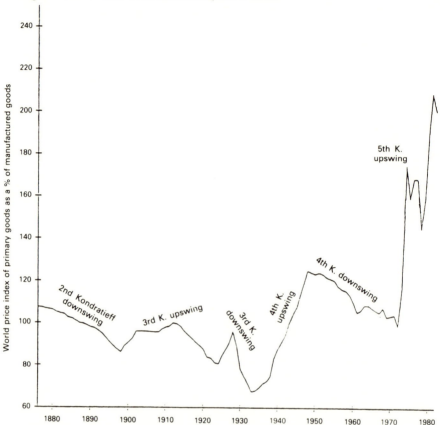

*Source*: Folke Hilgerdt, *Industrialization and Foreign Trade* (New York: League of Nations, 1945), p. 18, updated from *United Nations Statistical Yearbooks*.

upswing conformed rather well to historical precedent; for these cycles did not unfold as the smooth sine curves Schumpeter depicted by way of illustration.[9]

Specifically, before 1914 upswings began with a sharp initial rise lasting a few years, after which the relative price of basic commodities oscillated in a high range. Of the trend rise in British prices in the first Kondratieff upswing, 66 per cent occurred between 1798 and 1801; in the second, 71 per cent between 1852 and 1854; in the third 57 per cent between 1898 and 1900. The world economy experienced such a convulsive rise in 1973–5, with subsequent oscillation in a high range.

Figure 2.5. *Relative Prices, 1951–1982, USA*

A. Crude Materials and Finished Goods Prices

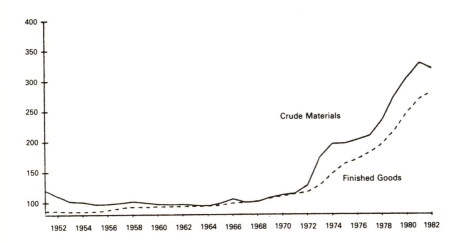

B. Ratio of Crude Materials to Finished Goods

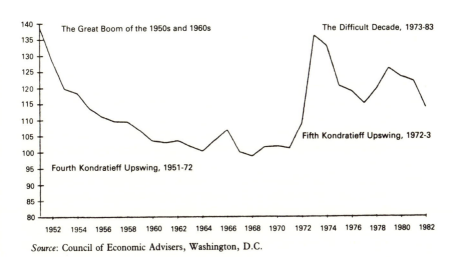

*Source*: Council of Economic Advisers, Washington, D.C.

Similarly, all four of the Kondratieff downswings began with an extremely sharp downward shift in the relative prices of basic commodities which subsequently decelerated, levelled off, or oscillated in a low range. This happened after the relative price peaks in 1812–13, 1873, 1920 and 1951.

There was a third, fairly consistent, irregularity. The upswings and downswings usually exhibited an interval or cycle in which the trend movement abated or reversed, and then asserted itself again. In the British case, for example, the cycles of 1803–8, 1832–7, 1862–8, 1886–94, 1904–8, all, to a significant degree, ran against the trend, after which the trend pattern reasserted itself before a definitive reversal occurred. I shall raise the question later as to whether we are now experiencing such an interval.

It should also be noted that relative price movements could have contrary effects within a particular economy. In 1945–51, for example, unfavourable relative price movements for most of the advanced industrial countries had a compensatory consequence. High basic commodity prices strengthened markets for manufactured exports in the countries producing basic commodities for the world markets. This situation was quite the reverse of that encountered after 1920.[10] The powerful decline in the relative prices of basic commodities in the 1950s undoubtedly provided a lift to real incomes in Japan and western Europe, accelerating their movement into and through High Mass Consumption; but the relative price decline also presented real difficulties for some developing countries whose terms of trade were depressed. Internally, however, relatively cheap energy, food and raw materials assisted the rapidly growing urban and industrial areas in the more advanced developing countries, encouraging their transition from Take-off into, or through, the Drive to Technological Maturity. The differential effects of energy price movements since 1973 on new energy exporting and importing regions within energy producing countries present a similar analytic complexity.

For the moment, I would simply note that, in one way or another, relative price movements have played an exceedingly important role in shaping the various phases of the world economy since 1945. Among other variables, they affected real incomes, the sectoral and regional distribution of investment, population movements, and the scale, composition and direction of trade. In addition, movements of basic commodity prices, which dominate the import price indexes of advanced industrial countries, helped determine the strength or weakness of the inflationary thrust within their economies both directly through their impact on price indexes and indirectly by damping or enhancing the impulse of labour to seek higher money wage increases.

IV

There are four major features of the post-1945 world economy, so far as innovation and the diffusion of technologies are concerned:

First, as noted earlier, the existence for western Europe and Japan of a large backlog of familiar, but hitherto not fully applied, technologies related, in particular, to the automobile and durable consumer goods sectors.

Second, the availability to all the advanced industrial countries (and, before long, to some of the more advanced developing countries) of certain technologies invented before 1939 but not fully elaborated and diffused, notably, synthetic fibres, plastics, and television. These became substantial sectors after the immediate postwar phase of reconstruction; but, along with some other important sectors of what I call the Third Industrial Revolution, they exhibited marked deceleration in the late 1960s.[11]

Third, a large backlog of unapplied technologies was available to the developing countries throughout the past four decades. They were absorbed at a rate determined by their initial stage of growth and the rate of build-up of their absorptive capacity.

In passing, I might note three distinctive characteristics of the Fourth Industrial Revolution as I perceive it. They are not central to this essentially historical argument, but they do bear on my final references to policy and to Tawney.

First, rather more than most of the industrial revolutions of the past, this one is closely linked to areas of basic science which are rapidly evolving. The fate of particular sectors and even whole national economies is likely to depend on success or failure in bringing into firm and steady partnership the domains of basic science, creative engineering, entrepreneurship, and the work-force.[12]

A second characteristic of the Fourth Industrial Revolution is that it seems fated to be ubiquitous. It is likely to transform—indeed, it is already beginning to transform—the older basic industries. I would guess that in the advanced industrial countries motor vehicles, machine tools, steel, and even textiles will be high-technology industries in a thorough-going way in a decade or so. But the new technologies will equally affect agriculture, forestry and animal husbandry; and, as is already observable, they will have revolutionary effects on a wide range of services: communications and medical care, education and banking.

A third characteristic of the new technologies is that, in different degree, they are, and will increasingly be, relevant to the South as well as the North, depending on each developing country's stage of growth and rate of build-up of its absorptive capacity.


## V

Having introduced the three working concepts, I shall now look a bit more closely at each of the four periods into which I have divided the saga of the postwar economy. The analytic perspective will remain the three-sided prism I have now defined and illustrated.

For the North, as we all know, the first six postwar years were a great surprise. In 1945, the leading macro-economists of the western world could perceive no forces likely to prevent, perhaps after a brief restocking boom, a return to depression. Their minds turned, therefore, to public policies that would mitigate unemployment more effectively than in the 1930s. In Europe, quite particularly, there was still in the back of many minds memories of the 1919–21 sequence of boom and bust, followed by a succession of difficult problems only half-solved in the 1920s and which gave way to the tragedies of the 1930s. The one outcome not generally envisaged was an almost unbroken quarter-century surge of recovery and growth.

Initially, agriculture lagged but global industrial production, excluding the United States, reached its prewar peak by 1948, despite the low level of the German economy. It was 37 per cent higher in 1951, by which date agriculture had pretty well recovered, except in eastern Europe.

Table 2.3 exhibits the rather remarkable British figures for the initial postwar interval. It clearly reflects the extraordinary export effort required down to 1950 to earn a lower volume of imports than in 1938, in the face of a decline in earnings from capital abroad and the adverse terms of trade which marked the final phase of the fourth Kondratieff upswing. The British terms of trade were 15 per cent less favourable in 1947 than in 1939, 33 per cent less favourable in 1951 than in 1938.

As for stage of growth, the recovery of living standards in the North was, essentially, along prewar lines, although the continuation of British food rationing down to the early 1950s consolidated important and benign changes in the British diet begun during the war. Western Europe as a whole had been moving towards the patterns of High Mass Consumption during the interwar years: much more slowly than in the United States in the 1920s, more quickly in the 1930s. But prewar automobile density in Britain and France was less than a quarter that in the United States. Interwar Japan was completing the Drive to Technological Maturity, converting its growing virtuosity

Table 2.3. *Index Numbers of Expenditure and Gross National Product at Constant Factor Cost: United Kingdom, 1938–1950 (1938 = 100 at Constant Market Prices)*

| | Consumers' Expenditure | Public Authorities' Expenditure | Gross Domestic Fixed Capital Formation | Exports, Goods and Services | Imports, Goods and Services | Net Property from Abroad | Gross National Product |
|---|---|---|---|---|---|---|---|
| 1938 | 100 | 100 | 100 | 100 | 100 | 100 | 100 |
| 1944 | 85 | 438 | 28 | 68 | 90 | 22 | 119 |
| 1945 | 90 | 356 | 32 | 55 | 86 | 21 | 111 |
| 1946 | 100 | 195 | 81 | 93 | 86 | 21 | 110 |
| 1947 | 103 | 138 | 94 | 93 | 87 | 30 | 107 |
| 1948 | 104 | 132 | 101 | 114 | 85 | 43 | 111 |
| 1949 | 106 | 140 | 111 | 126 | 91 | 39 | 114 |
| 1950 | 109 | 140 | 117 | 144 | 92 | 62 | 119 |

*Source:* C. H. Feinstein, *Statistical Tables of National Income of the UK, 1855-1965* (Cambridge, 1976), from Table 7, T21.

Table 2.4. *Private Automobiles in Use per Million Population, Selected Countries: Prewar Peak, 1951, 1955*

| | United States | United Kingdom | France | Germany | Italy | Japan |
|---|---|---|---|---|---|---|
| **Prewar peak** | 222,000 (1941) | 43,600 (1939) | 49,000 (1939) | 19,000 (1938) | 6,710 (1939) | 1,200 (1935) |
| 1951 | 277,000 | 48,600 | 37,900 | 14,100 | 9,010 | 680 |
| 1955 | 316,000 | 71,100 | 69,300 | 33,100 | 18,200 | 1,710 |

*Source:* See statistical source references, *Stages of Economic Growth* (Cambridge, 1960, 1971), Appendix A, pp. 168-9.

to military purposes after 1931, and persisting with essentially traditional patterns of consumption.

By 1951 there was some slight suggestion in the data of the coming
diffusion on a mass basis of the automobile; but the dramatic changes
began thereafter, as the surge between 1951 and 1955 suggests (Table
2.4).

As for the developing South, the setting for economic progress, in
narrow terms, was quite propitious. Rapid recovery and growth in
the North (after 1945) provided strong export markets at good terms
of trade compared to prewar levels. In 1948 the terms of trade for
developing market economies, in United Nations' parlance, were 20
per cent above the 1938 level, and in 1951 49 per cent. But, excepting
Latin America, politics and struggles for power dominated. There
were drives for independence against a colonial structure fatally
weakened by wartime developments. There were military or insur-
rectionary campaigns which often merged clashes of ideology and
personal ambition to exploit the transient plasticity of the postwar
world. These absorbed the bulk of the talent and energy of leaders
in Asia, the Middle East and Africa. The ending of the Korean War
and the launching of the First Five-Year Plans in China and India in
the early 1950s mark the beginnings of a phase of higher, but not
over-riding, priority for economic and social objectives in the South.

As Europe moved more persuasively into recovery and growth in
1948–9, with the Marshall Plan in place, the South began to claim
attention and resources from the North in support of increasingly
articulated aspirations for modernization and economic growth. Under
such pressures the United Nations launched a technical assistance
programme in 1949 as did the United States, where reports of official
commissions headed by Nelson Rockefeller and Gordon Gray foreshadowed the possibility of much enlarged development assistance in
the future. The Colombo Plan emerged in 1950 as part of the
architecture of the postwar Commonwealth.

The Korean War crosscut these hopeful developments by focusing
US foreign aid around military assistance and economic support for
countries judged to be militarily endangered around the periphery
of the Communist world. And in 1951, the terms of trade, which had
been improving for the South for almost twenty years, turned unfavourable. Standing at 118 in 1951 (1963 = 100) they bottomed out
at 99 in 1965. Despite the problems posed by this shift in relative
prices, a remarkable generation of progress in the South as well as
the North ensued.[13]

## VI

The great boom of the 1950s and 1960s is a unique phenomenon in modern economic history. The annual rate of growth of real income *per capita* for advanced industrial countries averaged 3.8 per cent for the period 1950–73—almost three times the highest previous level (1.4 per cent, 1870–1913).[14] In the 1960s the developing regions were growing at about 5.6 per cent, a higher rate than for the advanced industrial countries (4.9 per cent). For a while, the three contrapuntal themes operated in harmony—or at least as much harmony as economic history is likely to provide; that is, movements in the terms of trade and in technology conspired to make it possible for North and South to move forward rapidly through appropriate stages of growth.

Western Europe and Japan became caught up fully in the age of the mass automobile and durable consumer goods and, along with the United States and Canada, exhibited high income elasticity of demand for travel, and public and private outlays on education and health. In addition, they proved willing to expand transfer payments on behalf of the less advantaged within their respective societies and in the developing regions via official development assistance. As the 1960s wore on, there was also an increased sensitivity to environmental degradation and the allocation of substantial resources to contain or roll it back.

The leading sectors in the North were closely geared to goods and services with a high elasticity of demand. Momentum was thus strongly supported by the absolute decline of basic commodity prices from 1951 to the mid-1960s and by an approximately 25 per cent improvement in the terms of trade. The latter, of course, directly lifted real income to an extent dependent, in each country, on the relative importance of foreign trade. The absolute decline in imported basic commodity prices affected directly cost of living indices, damping inflation both directly and by tempering labour demands for higher money wages.

In the South, as noted earlier, the 1950s and 1960s were a time when a good many nations made the transition into Take-off or moved beyond into the Drive to Technological Maturity, including China and India. Their average growth rates were relatively low; but for the first time in their recorded history a self-sustaining rise in real income *per capita* seemed under way. By the end of the 1960s, Latin American countries containing most of the region's population had also moved into the Drive to Technological Maturity as well as Turkey, Taiwan, and South Korea.

The effects of relative price movements on the South were more complex. The absolute and relative fall of basic commodity prices after 1951 hit hard the foreign exchange earning capacity of many developing countries, as one would expect with an average 10 per cent deterioration in the terms of trade.[15] This burden was mitigated by three factors. First, cheap energy, food, and raw materials stimulated industrial and urban development within the more advanced of the developing countries. Second, from the late 1950s the decline in the terms of trade for the developing regions decelerated and then ceased at levels far above those of 1930 and generally higher than in 1948. Third, flows of official development lending from the North began to increase quite dramatically in the late 1950s, easing, at least marginally, the foreign exchange constraint on development.

Technologically, the majestic boom in the North drew on two reasonably distinct sources. As noted earlier, there was the backlog of technologies associated with the mass production of the automobile and durable consumer goods, quite fully exploited in the United States, familiar but not yet fully exploited in western Europe and Japan. In addition, there was a group of technologies, being developed in the 1930s and in some cases accelerated during the war, which came on stream as rapidly expanding commercial innovations accepted by virtually all the advanced industrial countries from the 1950s; notably, synthetic fibres, plastics, television, new rounds of pharmaceuticals, the commercial jet aircraft. The two groupings are linked, for example, by the expanded use of plastics, synthetic fibres, and synthetic rubber in motor vehicles, aircraft and durable consumer goods. The developing countries moving into the Drive to Technological Maturity in this period quickly absorbed a good many of these technologies; e.g. plastics, synthetic fibres, and pharmaceuticals.

As price, relative price and technological factors were driving the world economy along at quite a merry pace, most mainstream macro-economists were living in something of a dream world. This was the case because mainstream macro-economics—Keynesian and monetarist—is structured so as to exclude, to fix, or to overaggregate critical dynamic variables. The excluded variables include large, persistent relative price changes and the ebb and flow of technologies. Thus, neither the sources of the boom nor the causes of the great turning point of the mid-1960s were clearly perceived at the time; for it was after 1965 that the pillars of the boom began to erode.

Specifically, the decline of basic commodity prices which had been going on at a decelerating rate since 1951 (Figure 2.5A) gave way to a gradual increase. The terms of trade remained approximately steady for the industrialized North down to the end of 1972; but inflation became more difficult to control as labour sought higher money wage settlements to compensate for a rising cost of living, no longer damped by falling basic commodity prices.

The effects of this process on unit labour costs was exacerbated by a deceleration from the mid-1960s in the rate of productivity increase in all the major advanced industrial countries.[16] The average deterioration was about 20 per cent between 1965 and 1970; for the United States about 30 per cent. The reason for this phenomenon was mainly the quite normal waning of potentialities for productivity increase in the leading sectors of the postwar boom; motor vehicles, steel, plastics, synthetic fibres, etc.

But even bigger trouble was building up. It was during the second half of the 1960s that conditions were developing which explain the grain and oil price explosions which shook the world economy in 1972–4.[17]

Grain reserves, measured in days of global grain consumption, fell from 95 in 1961 to 55 at the worst of the Indian food crisis of 1967. After a brief recovery, the figure was down to 51 in 1971. The global grain market was clearly vulnerable to the bad harvest year which came in 1972. That event produced not only the grain price explosion of 1972–4 but also drove the reserve level down to 37 days in 1973.

A similar attenuation of the underlying reserve position was going on in the world's oil markets, notably in the United States. Between 1965 and 1969 US oil consumption increased at 4.5 per cent per annum, while proved oil reserves declined at 2.3 per cent. After decelerating rapidly from 1966, US oil production began its absolute decline in 1971. The United States was importing 8 per cent of its energy consumption in 1965, 17 per cent in 1972 when, in the autumn, the Organization of Petroleum Exporting Countries judged that it had sufficient leverage to quadruple oil prices.

Only in a limited sense, then, were the explosive increases in grain and oil prices of 1972–4 exogenous events.

## VII

The reversal of relative prices had somewhat different effects on the movement through the stages of growth in the North and in the South.

In the North, progress promptly decelerated, halted or reversed, depending on the adjustments made or not made in the various advanced industrial countries. In general, these were the effects of the approximately 13 per cent unfavourable shift in the northern terms of trade:

Figure 2.6. *Petroleum Prices, 1972–1983: Current and Real*

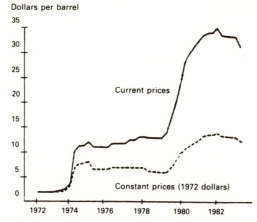

Dollars per barrel

*Source: World Development Report, 1983* (New York, 1983), p. 8.

Its real income effect flattened the already decelerating automobile-durable consumer goods boom.

The price elasticity of demand effect, via a disproportionate rise in the price of energy, reinforced the damping real income effect on the former energy-intensive leading sectors.

The impact of the sharp rise in import prices on the cost of living yielded the following sequence: accelerated money wage increases; a passage of double-digit inflation; strong measures of monetary restraint; and a deep recession in 1974–5.

This slow-down or reversal of growth, set against the built-in expansion of social expenditures, further heightened by the sharp rise in outlays for the unemployed, set in motion in virtually every advanced industrial country a protracted and difficult effort to discipline the rate of growth of social expenditure.

By 1974–5 the great boom was clearly over; but there was an interval of remission. The real price of oil levelled off in the recession and actually declined for those countries whose currencies were gathering strength against the dollar in which the international oil price was denominated (see Figure 2.6). The world economy recovered down to 1978; but inflation and unemployment rates remained high by the standards of the two previous decades, and average growth rates in the North were markedly lower. Average *per capita* GDP, which had been increasing at 3.8 per cent in 1950–73, fell to 2.0 per cent in 1973–9.[18]

The ending of a full generation's rapid growth based on the expansion in automobiles, durable consumer goods, and consumer

Table 2.5. *Performance of World Economy During First and Second United Nations'*
*Development Decades*

|  | Developed Market Economies (annual average Rates of Growth) | | Developing Market Economies (annual average Rates of Growth) | |
|---|---|---|---|---|
|  | 1960-9 | 1970-9 | 1960-9 | 1970-9 |
| Gross Domestic Product | 5·2 | 3·3 | 5·5 | 6·0 |
| Gross Domestic Product per capita | 4·1 | 2·5 | 3·0 | 3·7 |
| Total Industrial Output | 5·9 | 3·6 | 5·3 | 5·0 |
| Production of food per capita | 1·3 | 1·3 | 0·2 | 0·2 |
| Production of Energy | 3·9 | 1·3 | 9·8 | 4·2 |
| Consumption of Energy | 5·0 | 2·0 | 6·9 | 7·1 |
| Imports | 9·0 | 5·5 | 5·1 | 7·5 |
| Exports | 8·4 | 6·5 | 6·3 | 5·2 |

*Source: Statistical Yearbook, 1981* (New York, 1983), p. 17.

services, raised in the North some basic questions about the future. Among them was anxiety that, after two centuries, diminishing returns had at last set in with respect to science and invention. Indeed, some argued explicitly that the advanced industrial countries faced secular stagnation; and they did so in terms that recalled almost precisely the same argument in the 1930s.[19]

In the phrase commended by Stephen Potter in his classic *Gamesmanship*, to divert cocktail party conversations: it was different in the South. The price explosion of 1972–4, which extended to raw materials other than energy, briefly lifted the terms of trade for many developing countries, aside from oil exporters. Excluding energy, the prices of basic commodities relative to manufactures (1970=100) stood at 113 in 1974.[20] There was an interval of exhilaration in the South at the spectacle of the successful extraction of enormous rents from the North by a group of developing countries and of hope that the process could be repeated in other basic commodity sectors. This mood suffused the special session of the United Nations General Assembly in the spring of 1974.

A year later the atmosphere had changed as the oil importers of the South felt the full weight of both the rise in the oil price and the deep recession in the North. The terms of trade turned sharply against the oil importers of the South in 1975. Nevertheless, the leading growth sectors in the more advanced countries of the developing world, rooted still in the unapplied backlog of mainly capital goods technologies, were less damaged by the turn of events than the leading sectors of the North. The latter were linked to consumers' outlays and therefore dependent on a continuing rise in consumers' real income. By and large, the South maintained its momentum remarkably well in the 1970s, as Table 2.5 suggests. The prolongation in the South of high growth rates well into the 1970s was accomplished in some cases by structural readjustments involving sharp increases in exports (including the export of labour) to oil-exporting countries. In others, there was resort to large-scale borrowing from private markets to sustain the level of imports.

The oil exporters handled their vast accretion of external resources with various degrees of balance and good sense. For oil exporters with substantial populations and acute problems of development still to solve, it was difficult to avoid plunging ahead with greatly accelerated levels of investment, encouraged as their governments were by expert predictions of further increases in coming decades in the real price of oil. The economic and social distortions caused by such inflamed efforts to achieve targets beyond current absorptive capacity were compounded by the inescapable "gold-rush" effect; that is, the drawing of labour out of agriculture and other relatively low-income activities towards the higher-paying jobs linked to the expenditure of the oil revenues—a process to be observed, for example, in the nineteenth-century Californian and Australian gold rushes. At the margin there was Iran, where the distortions produced by over-ambitious efforts to achieve extraordinarily high development goals in a short period of time rendered old tensions in the society explosive. The Iranian revolution brought with it a radical decline in oil exports. In an excessive reaction of the international oil market, a further doubling in the oil price occurred in 1978–9 opening a second difficult phase of the fifth Kondratieff upswing.

## VIII

The second oil shock, to a degree, caused a repetition of phenomena familiar from the first: a sharp deterioration in the terms of trade, in this case for the oil importers of the South as well as the North; a phase of double-digit inflation, severe unemployment and a continued downward trend in productivity in the North; a subsidence during 1980 in the real oil price and the beginnings of some general economic recovery in 1980–1.

There were, however, three significant differences in the North as compared to the first oil shock and its aftermath; and these had important implications for the South.

First, with the agreement of President Carter, on 6 October 1979 the Federal Reserve Board launched a major experiment: a decision to govern monetary policy strictly in terms of the rate of increase in the money supply, permitting interest rates to move as they would. The result was a rise in both nominal and real rates of interest to levels never before experienced in the United States. The experiment was continued by President Reagan, although significantly modified in August 1982 to ease the extremely severe recession then under way. But as of early 1984 real interest rates in the United States were still about 7 per cent as opposed to an average of 2 per cent for the period 1953–78. This experiment had profound effects on the world economy as a whole as well as on the domestic economy of the United States. It not only made more difficult a sustained economic recovery, but also generated an artifically strong dollar as capital flowed to the United States to exploit the interest rate differential. The pathologically strong dollar helped damp inflation in the United States but constituted a substantial barrier to US exports, thus assisting the exports of other advanced industrial countries. The result was a mounting trade and, subsequently, overall US balance of payments deficit that threatened a crisis in the international trade and financial system at some point.

Second, the electorate of Britain in 1979 and of the US in 1980 brought to power governments committed to reversing the inflationary trend of the previous decade, cutting back social expenditures, and expanding the role of the private sector relative to government. Although more explicitly counter-revolutionary in rhetoric and mood than most other governments in the advanced industrial countries, they reflected political forces quite generally at work in the North. So far as the world economy was concerned the most significant results of this phenomenon flowed from two decisions of President Reagan in 1981. First was his decision to experiment with the theory of monetarist gradualism in the summer of 1981, a theory that promised to reconcile economic expansion with a simultaneous reduction in the rate of inflation. The result was a sharp recession at a time when the world economy was uncertainly recovering from the recession which had accompanied the second oil shock. Second, there was Reagan's tax cut of 1981 which greatly enlarged the structural element in the US federal budget deficit. That deficit was running at about 2 per cent of GNP in the depressed year 1981 (0.6 per cent in 1979); over 5 per cent in early 1984. Without a radical cut in expenditure and/or increase in taxes, the conventional expert view was that deficits of this relative order of magnitude would persist. Lacking an effective incomes policy (as in Japan, which managed its affairs quite successfully with deficits of this relative order of magnitude), the prospect of the US deficit contributed a strand of profound uncertainty to the international financial markets.

The third distinctive strand in the North in this period was the arrival in the second half of the 1970s of the Fourth Industrial Revolution. Concern about secular stagnation gave way to anxieties about the possibility of high chronic technological unemployment, puzzlement about the best methods for participating in the revolution or exploiting its products, and uncertainty about its ultimate effects on various sectors of the economy.

In the South, the chronic recession of 1979–82 was more acute and difficult to manage than its predecessor after the first oil shock. The purposefully deflated performance of the North brought about by unprecedentedly high real interest rates, struck the South in five ways: exports to the North were reduced; export prices fell; protectionist barriers against the manufactured exports of the South rose; official development aid was constrained by governments in the North facing their own difficult social problems; and the high interest rates generated in the North complicated the already acute debt problems of many nations in the South. The North co-operated to roll over the debts that could not be financed by normal means, but at the cost of commitments in the South to restrained growth in the future— a restraint socially and politically dangerous for societies with the demographic structures of most in the South. Only a strong sustained expansion in the North appeared capable of preventing the emergence of even more acute crises than those experienced by the South in the period 1979–84.

Meanwhile, the South as well as the North became increasingly aware that a new technological revolution was under way. The new technologies generated interest, concern, and a sense of frustration bordering on anger. Concern centred around the possibility that the new technologies would yield such increased productivity in older basic industries of the North (e.g., steel, motor vehicles, machine tools) that their drift to new industrial countries with relatively low wage rates would slow down or cease. An awareness of this possibility was particularly marked in the Pacific basin as Japan moved vigorously to install robots and other high-technology devices in some of the industries of the Third Industrial Revolution.

In fact, the position in the South was not set back as sharply as was widely feared. In Latin America, North Africa, the Middle East, and developing Asia the expansion of the pool of competent scientists, engineers and entrepreneurs had been proceeding more rapidly than was generally understood on the spot. For what the World Bank called "middle income countries" the proportion of those aged 20–24 enrolled in higher education rose from 3 per cent in 1960 to 11 per cent in 1979.[21] One can debate the quality and functional distribution of this revolutionary transformation; but it is increasingly clear that for a good many developing countries the problem of absorbing the new technologies does not lie in an insufficient pool of competent personnel but in the effective organization of the domains of science, engineering, and business in relation to each other. This linkage has been achieved in a few sectors in some of the more technologically advanced developing countries. But it is not a general phenomenon in the South. If the problem of this three-way linkage were solved, the lag induced by the arrival of the Fourth Industrial Revolution might well prove shorter and less formidable for the South than it appeared at first sight; and the brain-drain from South to North is likely to reverse.

## IX

This brings us to some issues of policy. In a paper prepared for fellow economic historians there is evidently no need to introduce problems that lie before us and lines of action that might mitigate or solve them. I could simply close and leave us to contemplate a somewhat dishevelled world economy, its leaders and citizens hoping, but not quite believing, that the present revival would move forward in something like the steady, low-inflationary environment of the period 1951–65.

But it is difficult to do that in a lecture honouring R. H. Tawney. Tawney belonged squarely in the tradition of the eighteenth-century founding fathers of modern economics who insisted that history and theory, moral values and policy, be inextricably bound together in what they called political economy—a tradition from which we have strayed in recent decades at considerable cost to our discipline and to the societies that discipline was created to serve.

On the other hand, it would be highly inappropriate to launch at this stage into a second paper on the policy implications of this historical sketch.[22] I shall, therefore, merely pose rather dogmatically three critical questions on which the outcome for the world economy is likely to depend in the generation ahead and relate them to some strands in our heritage from Tawney. As befits the design of this paper, the critical questions link directly to the three themes: stages of growth, relative prices, and technology.

The first question is: Can the North master inflation in ways consistent with reasonably low real interest rates, low unemployment and high growth rates? Without a positive answer to that question, vigorous forward movement in the stages of growth is doubtful in the South as well as the North, given the intense and even heightened interdependencies which exist and can be expected to continue between them. And a positive answer, in turn, depends, I am convinced, on the emergence of a capacity in the Northern societies to sustain effective long-term incomes policies combined with conventional devices of fiscal and monetary policy.

But the long-term control of inflation as well as the continuity of growth itself depends on a positive answer to a second question: Can North and South cooperate effectively to provide the resource foundations for continued high growth rates in both regions? Specifically, such cooperation is required to maintain high levels of investment in agriculture, energy, raw materials, reforestation, and other aspects of environmental protection. Those investment levels are needed to assure a moderately priced flow of resources capable of permitting the growth process to proceed in both North and South. The need is particularly acute for the South where, under normal circumstances, growth rates higher than in the North would be expected over the next generation and where growth is likely to be more resource-intensive than in the North.

A glance at the figures for food production *per capita* and energy production and consumption in Table 2.5 suggests the relevance of this question. Food production *per capita* is, overall, barely keeping up with population growth in the South, and, in fact, is falling progressively behind in a good many countries. A gap opened up in the 1970s between the rate of increase in energy production and consumption in the South, the latter figure running at a rate which required a doubling of energy consumption per decade. Data on raw materials and environmental degradation in the South also suggest that extremely large investments will be required to provide a resource base for continued southern growth, if the world economy returns to normal growth paths in the 1980s and 1990s. In short, a sustained revival of the world economy is likely to yield a reversal of the recent phase of decline in the relative prices of basic commodities.

And, finally, the third question: Can the societies of North and South bring together in close working partnership scientists, creative engineers, entrepreneurs and the working force to generate and diffuse efficiently the potential products of the Fourth Industrial Revolution? As noted earlier, the question arises because the technologies of the evolving revolution, much more than those which preceded them, are linked to areas of basic science which themselves are undergoing rapid evolution.

Now, a final word about Tawney. Suppose for a moment that these are, in fact, three critical questions for the future. What do they have to do with Tawney? In one sense, the answer is: nothing at all. Tawney belongs in history just where he wished to belong: a substantial figure in the moral, intellectual, and political struggle to bring about in Britain, not only the cushions against adversity which make up much of the welfare state, not only greater equality of opportunity in education, but also, to a significant degree, a social status of greater dignity for the British working man. Social welfare policies and resource outlays are, evidently, now under considerable pressure; but I would guess that throughout the advanced industrial countries they are likely to be more endangered by economic stagnation or slow growth than by counter-revolutionary politicians. The results of the widespread consensus in immediate postwar British society, reaching far beyond the Labour Party, were, like the New Deal, Great Society and civil rights reforms of the 1960s, essentially irreversible. And, in Britain, Tawney made a distinctive contribution to the building of the consensus.

But there was much in the social and political struggles which led to the welfare state victories on both sides of the Atlantic that is now inappropriate to our problems. Tawney felt, for example, that he was fighting an essentially zero-sum game on behalf of the British worker against the British capitalist. Indeed, as a man embedded in the seventeenth as well as the twentieth century, he contemplated a no doubt symbolic "cutting off the heads of our industrial Lauds and Straffords" even if the price were a century or so of "political jobbery and ineptitude."[23] Only a few would now put the faith Tawney did seventy years ago in the virtues of the government ownership and operation of the means of production. But in matters of economic, social, and political policy one should look back at a man in his time and place and not ask him to prescribe for times he never saw or felt.

Now, if I am more or less correct, the task before the North is not to continue *à l'outrance* with single-minded zero-sum struggles over the distribution of resources but to contain such inevitable friction and negotiations by common efforts to enlarge the pool of resources. The injunction to co-operate holds for the disciplining of inflation, North-South co-operation with respect to the global resource base, and the generation and diffusion of the new technologies. Indeed, the fate of the welfare state itself ultimately hinges on the success of such common efforts. But as I read Tawney, he also stood for two propositions which transcend his generation; and these propositions remain relevant to our time, to the tasks that must be taken in hand, and to the communal spirit that must inform the effort.

The first proposition was his unswerving insistence on the moral character of public policy. As he read detailed pre-1914 studies of social conditions, proposals for new legislation and new institutions, he argued that all these familiar instruments of a reform movement were not enough: "The direction in which we are moving is deter-mined," he wrote, "by quite other, moral and intellectual causes whose springs lie deeper. We ought to turn [to] these for strengthening and refreshment more often than we do".[24] Tawney attacked some of those in the labour movement for being "bought off by instalments of 'social reform'. It has become not a question of right and wrong, but a question of more and less".[25]

In this matter surely Tawney was correct. Many in Britain threw their support behind the labour movement when they were convinced it was fighting for what was right, but they took their distance when they thought it was fighting simply for more and more resources and/ or political power. In the societies of western civilization large public enterprises require a moral base which commends itself to a substantial majority of the people. In the end, it is one of the glories of our democratic societies that government policies and governments are judged in the light of a fuzzy, non-quantifiable question not susceptible of cost-benefit analysis or computer manipulation: Are they fair? At the end of the day the welfare state, including remarkable widening in health care and educational opportunity, was finally accepted in Britain not because post-1945 Cromwellian Roundheads were about to take over the corporate board rooms, but because a substantial majority of the British electorate had come to judge it wrong for rich, comfortable societies not to provide these basic services for all.

This brings us to a second relevant strand in Tawney's thought; and there is something of a paradox in it. Tawney was thoroughly prepared to inveigh against the capitalist, like an Old Testament prophet (or a product of Rugby and Balliol); but he also never wholly lost faith in the possibility of human beings—and, quite particularly, Britons—working together in communal harmony for large common purposes (again like a product of Rugby and Balliol). Writing of Tawney's reaction to the First World War, the editors of his *Commonplace Book* conclude:[26]

. . . Tawney's war experience was formative. The fact the nation virtually with one voice had committed its material and human resources to the prosecution of a just cause convinced him that the conflict had altered the internal development of British political and social affairs in a positive way. He saw in the national mobilization for war the faint outline of a future stable society in which men were bound together for the moral and physical betterment of all. This spiritual unity which the Allied cause generated in its first months fulfilled what Tawney defined as the necessary precondition for institutional action. He believed that all political associations are inherently mechanical bodies, capable of effective action only when animated by ideas which exist outside and grown independently of them. Tawney was convinced that the First World War had uncovered and developed such a progressive movement in mass political and social attitudes.

No doubt Britain's response to the Second World War—and the substantial area of consensus that existed in British politics in the immediate postwar years—vindicated this assessment in Tawney's mind.

Tawney's vision is relevant now because useful response to the three questions I posed will require more than institutional and legal blueprints for income policies, North-South investment programmes in basic resources, and new working arrangements between the research universities and the business community. The Austrian Finance Minister, Hans Seidel, captured something of what is required when speaking to the Joint Economic Committee of the American Congress on 2 June 1981. In explaining the institutional arrangements for an incomes policy in his country, he broke through the complexities by saying that, ultimately, what was required was a social partnership: "Social partnership does not just mean that we all sit in the same boat. It also means that we are willing to steer the boat in a direction upon which most of us agree." Tawney understood that history included the possibility of social partnership as well as zero-sum games.

But right now the critical unanswered question is: What is the direction upon which most of us must agree? Towards what goal must the social partnership work? It is surely not a return to a mid-Victorian obsession with material progress, nor a dismantling of the welfare state, nor a vast extension of the powers of the state over economic and social life. The argument implicit in this historical sketch of how we got to where we are suggests that the goal is: in the North, to maintain economies of sufficient vitality to permit its citizens to move forward in search for lives and societies of higher quality; in the South, to permit the movement through the stages of growth to proceed in conformity with the cultures and ambitions of its peoples without Malthusian or Ricardian tragedies; and for North and South to work together with an understanding of the profound common interest in the success of both ventures.

To carry forward these enterprises effectively in the 1980s and 1990s we in the North—to evoke Tawney's phrases—shall have to seek strength and refreshment in moral principles and intellectual concepts which would heighten our sense of community. Although we have not yet brought them to bear, they will remain deeply rooted in our culture and historical experience until we, as citizens, insist on political leadership which would evoke them once again.

## NOTES

I wish to acknowledge with gratitude the generous support of the administration and staff of the Institute of Economics and Statistics at Oxford while I was preparing this paper in the Hilary Term, 1984. I was also assisted by my colleagues in Austin, Texas, Miss Lois Nivens and Dr. Pedro Fraile, the latter organizing for this occasion highly relevant data from Project Mulhall, which he supervised. Prof. George Kozmetsky supplied the high technology data for Figure 1. Sir Alexander Cairncross, Lord Franks and Prof. D.C.M. Platt commented usefully on an early draft. The text was greatly improved by an acute and constructive critique by Prof. Elspeth Davies Rostow.

1. Paper presented to Section B3 of the Eighth Conference of the International Economic History Association, Budapest, August 1982.

2. I recognize, of course, that the stages of economic growth has been the subject of protracted debate to which I have responded in W. W. Rostow, ed. *The Economics of Take-off into Sustained Growth* (New York: St. Martin's, 1963); Appendix B of the second edition of *The Stages of Economic Growth* (Cambridge, 1971); *The World Economy: History and Prospect* (Austin, University of Texas Press, 1978), especially Part 4 and pp. 777–9. A recent retrospective view of the debate is to be found in W. W. Rostow, 'Development: The Political Economy of the Marshallian Long Period', in Gerald M. Meier and Dudley Seers, eds. *Pioneers in Development* (New York, 1984), especially pp. 229–40.

3. This elaboration is presented in my *World Economy: History and Prospect*, especially pp. 561–3; and *Why the Poor Get Richer and the Rich Slow Down* (1980), ch. 6. The latter presentation takes fully into account the cross-sectional findings, relating real income *per capita* to rate of growth, of Thorkil Kristensen, *Development in Rich and Poor Countries* (New York, 1974), and Hollis Chenery and Moises Syrquin, *Patterns of Development, 1950–1970* (Washington, D.C., 1975).

4. My view of trend periods (or Kondratieff cycles) can be traced through my *The British Economy of the Nineteenth Century* (Oxford, 1948), especially ch. 1; A. D. Gayer, W. W. Rostow and Anna Jacobson Schwartz, *Growth and Fluctuation of the British Economy, 1790–1850* (Oxford, 1953), especially Vol. 2, chs. 4 and 5; *The Process of Economic Growth* (Oxford, 1960), especially Part 3 and chs. 6, 8 and 9; *Why the Poor Get Richer*, especially chs. 1 and 2. *The Barbaric Counter-Revolution: Cause and Cure* (1984), especially pp. 8–11, 62–9, and 102–15, deals with recent phases of Kondratieff cycles and their policy implications.

5. The First Industrial Revolution is conventionally taken to centre on factory-manufactured textiles, Watt's steam engine, and the manufacture of good iron from coke. All emerge as viable innovations in the 1780s. The Second centred on the railroads and the cheap steel they induced due to the rapid obsolescence of iron rails. That powerful sequence begins in the 1830s, although it was in the 1840s that major railway booms occurred in Great Britain, the American northeast, Belgium, France and Germany. The third embraced the internal combustion engine, electricity, and a new round of chemicals. 1900 is a convenient bench mark although the innovational stage for these inventions starts on either side of that date. The existence of three pre-1914 periods when particularly important innovations entered the economy, long recognized by economic historians and dramatized in Joseph Schumpeter's

*Business Cycles,* is part of the intellectual framework for Part 3 of *The World Economy.* The emergence of a new major grouping of technologies is discussed in W. W. Rostow, *Getting from Here to There* (1979), ch. 9, especially pp. 158–66. I apply to them the notion of a Fourth Industrial Revolution in *The Barbaric Counter-Revolution,* especially pp. 54–60 and 89–94.

6. See *Politics and the Stages of Growth* (Cambridge, 1971), 6, and earlier discussion in *Stages of Economic Growth,* pp. 90–2 and 156. For a useful review of the expansion of social expenditures in advanced industrial countries, broken down by components, see 'Social Expenditure: Erosion or Evolution?' *OECD Observer,* No. 126 (January 1984), pp. 3–6. For more detail see especially Morris Beck, 'The Public Sector and Economic Stability', in *The Business Cycle and Public Policy,* A Compendium of Papers submitted to the Joint Economic Committee, Congress of the United States (Washington, D.C.: G.P.O., November 28, 1980), pp. 105–28.

7. Historically, as well as in contemporary cross-section, growth rates tended to be at their maximum in the Drive to Technological Maturity, but at lower absolute levels. See *Why the Poor Get Richer,* pp. 265–9.

8. W. Arthur Lewis, *Growth and Fluctuations, 1870–1913* (1978), especially pp. 69–111, 188–93.

9. Joseph Schumpeter, *Business Cycles* (New York, 1939), Vol. 1, p. 213.

10. It was to cope with the (to him) quite unexpected favourable shift in British terms of trade after 1920 that Keynes, in his debate with Beveridge, invented what later came to be called the income terms of trade in which an index for the value of exports is divided by the price index for imports. After 1920 the favourable effects for Britain of a radical favourable shift in the net barter terms of trade were out-balanced by the fall in export sales to food and raw material producing countries injured by low export prices. After the Second World War unfavourable relative price movements down to 1951 were out-balanced in their effects on the British economy by expanded exports plus the fact that Marshall Plan aid was calculated in terms of dollar rather than over-all balance of payments deficits. This permitted Britain to liquidate with expanded exports the sterling balances accumulated during the Second World War by some basic commodity exporters. For discussion of various terms of trade concepts, see *Process of Economic Growth,* pp. 170–5.

11. For deceleration in the critical automobile and durable goods sector, see *The World Economy,* pp. 565–7; in synthetic materials and electronics, see Christopher Freeman, John Clark and Luc Soete, *Unemployment and Technical Innovation* (1982), chs. 5 and 6; in rates of increase in total industrial production, *The World Economy,* p. 359. For rise in capital-output ratio in this period, see: *Why the Poor Get Richer,* pp. 286–7. The British slowdown in output and productivity is noted and measured in R.C.O. Matthews, C. H. Feinstein and J. C. Odling-Smee, *British Economic Growth, 1856–1973* (Stanford, 1982), pp. 23–5 and 547.

12. I elaborate this point in 'India and the Fourth Industrial Revolution', Vikram Sarabhai Memorial Lecture, 18 October, 1983, Ahmadabad: Indian Institute of Management, 1984 [reprinted here as Chapter 8].

13. *Statistical Yearbook, 1953*, United Nations (New York, 1953), p. 34.
14. Angus Maddison, *Phases of Capitalist Development* (Oxford, 1982), p. 44.
15. *Statistical Yearbook, 1972* (New York, United Nations, 1973), p. 42.
16. See data and analysis in *Why the Poor Get Richer*, pp. 284–8. Also references in n. 11, above.
17. For a more complete analysis of the pre-1973 developments in grain and energy markets, see Rostow, *World Economy*, pp. 247–59.
18. Maddison, *Phases of Capitalist Development*, p. 44.
19. See, for example, the views of Edward Renshaw summarized and discussed in Rostow, *Getting from Here to There*, pp. 138–46.
20. *Statistical Yearbook, 1981* (New York, United Nations, 1983), p. 51.
21. *World Development Report, 1983* (New York, 1983), Table 25, pp. 196–7.
22. In effect, my *The Barbaric Counter-Revolution* constitutes such an exercise.
23. J. M. Winter and D. M. Joslin, eds., *R. H. Tawney's Commonplace Book* (Cambridge, 1972), p. 11.
24. Ibid., p. 68.
25. Ibid., p. 80.
26. Ibid., p. xxii.

# THREE

# The Rich Country–Poor Country Problem: From the Eighteenth to the Twenty-first Century

*This chapter, which flows directly from work on my book about theories of economic growth, was delivered in shortened form at Louvain-la-Neuve, Belgium, on May 29, 1986. The occasion was a symposium in honor of Professor Albert Kervyn de Lettenhove, upon his retirement. We are friends going back almost forty years to the days when we served together as special assistants to Gunnar Myrdal, then executive secretary of the United Nations Economic Commission for Europe in Geneva.*

*This chapter should provide reasonably full background for later, recurrent references to the rich country–poor country problem.*

## I. INTRODUCTION

My theme is the dynamic relationship between technologically more- and less-advanced countries—past, present, and future. I have chosen this theme because I believe it is destined to become the central issue in both international and domestic affairs over, say, the next half century; and its wise handling will be critical to the maintenance and consolidation of peace. This relationship, in all its diverse ramifications, should become the central focus of political economy. Its exploration will require much more than narrowly mathematical theoretical formulations and econometric exercises; but, if conducted with a judicious sense of their limitations, they can contribute to this exploration.

## II. THE EIGHTEENTH CENTURY

Historians of economic theory and doctrine pride themselves on tracing the first articulation of a proposition further and further back in time, and there is understandably no consensus among them on who should be regarded as the first modern economist. But certainly David Hume belongs among the candidates. Philosopher, psychologist, historian, he wrote only about a hundred pages of economics incorporated in essays each sharply focused on an issue of public policy. However, as one of Adam Smith's biographers wrote, "but for Hume, Smith could never have been."[1] In any case, Hume was the first to articulate "the rich country–poor country problem."[2] I shall devote a good deal of space to Hume's and Smith's treatment of the problem because, in a rather paradoxical way, these two pioneers dealt with almost all its major dimensions better than any of their successors and foreshadowed the issues likely to dominate the several generations ahead.

The setting was the mid-eighteenth century world economy full of commercial vitality, clashing mercantilist ambitions, and chronic warfare—some thirty years before major technical innovations transformed the British cotton and iron industries and James Watt's improved steam engine began quite rapidly to diffuse. On balance, England (and Scotland) of the 1750s was still a grain surplus area. England was probably enjoying a slow expansion in real income per capita, certainly a more rapid expansion of manufacturing, and a still more rapid expansion in foreign trade. The global commercial revolution and related imperial developments since the end of the fifteenth century had acquainted interested observers with the state of economic affairs and, in a rough-and-ready way, with the dynamics of a spectrum of economies, including those of China and India, North and South America; and it led them to reflect on the relative levels of real income per capita within their own region.

In Europe the seventeenth century economic primacy of the Dutch had given way to the eighteenth century clash of Great Britain and France for leadership. The British were conscious that two centuries earlier they had lagged behind France, Italy, and Spain. In short, thoughtful observers understood that real income per capita varied widely among nations and regions and that relative positions in the queue were subject to change. It was, therefore, natural, in their mercantilist world, that the appropriate posture of the richer to the poorer nations was a living issue of public policy.

Meanwhile, Scotland, having settled the terms for union with England in 1707, had acquired some momentum of its own during the eighteenth century, although it still lagged behind the colossus of the South; and Scotland was where most of the British economists were. It was there that Hume, as part of the grand effort to shift the Heavenly City to "earthly foundations"[3]—to identify the natural and just laws that should govern the behavior of national societies and the international community—came to address the rich country–poor country problem in the context of his challenge to the conventional mercantilist wisdom of his day.

Hume's analysis of the rich country–poor country problem can only be understood in a larger context as part of his systematic contention against three doctrines of his time:

- That virtue in societies was associated with austerity if not poverty; luxury and wealth, with corruption and decay.[4]
- An influx of bullion, derived from a favorable trade balance, would assure the strength and trading advantage of a rich country.
- The economic rise of poor countries could only be at the expense of rich countries.

Hume's response can be summarized as follows.

1. Wealth is the friend of virtue. The process of developing "luxuries," requiring the systematic exploitation of comparative advantage, is central to economic growth; and economic growth and prosperity are fundamental to the security of the state, a civilized social life, political liberty, and, above all, to the creative fulfillment of individual talents and of other legitimate sources of human satisfaction.

2. The demonstration of the possibility of economic growth sets in motion both within societies and among them "a fermentation" that yields similar efforts to cultivate commerce, industry, and refinements in the mechanical arts.

3. In particular, poor nations have the capacity to catch up with the rich nations because they enjoy, in their period of transition, the advantage of lower money wages.

But what of the fate or rich nations in the face of the rise to riches of the poor? Before the debate was finished, Hume would produce several answers, but here is the most fundamental, building up to what was, at a time of chronic mercantilist confrontation between Great Britain and France, a rather dramatic climax.

It ought . . . to be considered, that, by the encrease of industry among the neighbouring nations, the consumption of every particular species of commodity is also encreased; and though foreign manufactures interfere with them in the market, the demand for their product may still continue, or even encrease. And should it diminish, ought the consequence to be esteemed so fatal? If the spirit of industry be preserved, it may easily be diverted from one branch to another; and the manufacturers of wool, for instance, be employed in linen, silk, iron, or any other commodities, for which there appears to be a demand. We need not apprehend, that all the objects of industry will be exhausted, or that our manufactures, while they remain on an equal footing with those of our neighbours, will be in danger of wanting employment. The emulation among rival nations serves rather to keep industry alive in all of them. . . . I shall therefore venture to acknowledge, that, not only as a man but as a British subject, I pray for the flourishing commerce of Germany, Spain, Italy and even France itself. I am at least certain, that Great Britain, and all those nations, would flourish more, did their sovereigns and ministers adopt such enlarged and benevolent sentiments towards each other.[5]

But Hume's full treatment of the problem did not conclude on so unambiguously confident a note. His further discussion of the catching-up process included some observations that plunged him into controversy; for he was too good a historian not to note that prosperity of countries and regions could prove transitory: "Manufactures . . . gradually shift their places, leaving those countries and provinces which they have already enriched, and flying to others, whither they are allured by the cheapness of provisions and labour; till they have enriched there also, and are again banished by the same causes."[6]

When challenged on this apparently gloomy prospect for the rich by two able contemporaries (James Oswald and Josiah Tucker), Hume argued that this flying about was sectoral. What he had in mind was a division of manufacturing according to comparative advantage— that is, the rich would concentrate on production of capital- and skill-intensive manufactures; up-and-coming countries and provinces would concentrate on simpler and more labor-intensive manufactures.[7] As Tucker perceived, Hume's clarification left dangling the question whether this division of effort would persist, or whether relative wages and prices would move to equality between a rich and formerly poor country when the "fermentation" had yielded a full exploitation of comparative advantage. And in a phrase in a letter of 1758 to Lord Kames, Hume did, indeed, indicate that poorer nations would be expected to move on from "coarser" manufactures to the "more elaborate" with the passage of time.[8]

But major technological innovations do not appear in Hume's system. He did not, therefore, believe in unlimited growth. His final dictum on the limits to growth, within the technological possibilities he could perceive, clearly acknowledged that a limit did exist. "The growth of everything, both in arts and nature, at last checks itself."[9] But one gets the impression that Hume was not much interested in driving this argument about the long-run future of the various economies of the world to a dogmatic conclusion. As a historian and philosopher, he understood well the complexity and impenetrability of the forces that would determine the ultimate outcome in a world subject to endless change. And besides, he was conscious that one could project man's fate only on the basis of an inadequate few thousand years of recorded history. The opening passage in "Of the Populousness of Ancient Nations" probably reflects most accurately his net judgment.

> There is very little ground either from reason or observation to conclude the world eternal or incorruptible. The continual and rapid motion of matter, the violent revolutions with which every part is agitated, the changes remarked in the heavens, the plain traces as well as tradition of an universal deluge, or in general confusion of the elements; all these prove strongly the mortality of this fabric of the world, and its passage, by corruption or dissolution, from one state or order to another. . . . The arts and sciences . . . have flourished in one period, and have decayed in another: But we may observe, that, at the time when they rose to greatest perfection among one people, they were perhaps, totally unknown to all the neighbouring nations; and though they universally decayed in one age, yet in a succeeding generation they again revived, and diffused themselves over the world.[10]

But this mild, long-run philosophic pessimism about the staying power of greatness in a single country does not capture Hume's inherently cheerful and activist temper. He was primarily concerned to use his qualities of mind and character to move the world and time of which he was a part toward more civilized policies; and this he did.

Adam Smith's position on the rich country–poor country problem was close to Hume's but not identical.

1. A rich country had a number of inherent advantages over a poor country, which ought to permit it to retain its lead, barring failure to conduct correct policies.

2. These advantages included lower unit labor costs, despite higher real wage rates, resulting from the greater division of labor, in turn made possible by the abundance and cheapness of capital. They included also a more elaborate and efficient transport system, reducing the relative prices of basic commodities.

3. Therefore, a rich country could afford to move toward a free trade where it would enjoy the advantages of a large and productive commerce with its partners in the world economy, even with its potential military adversaries.

The flavor of Smith's view is well captured in the following two quotations.

The more opulent therefore the society, labour will always be so much dearer and work so much cheaper, and if some opulent countries have lost several of their manufactures and some branches of their commerce by having been undersold in foreign markets by the traders and artisans of poorer countries, who were contented with less profit and smaller wages, this will rarely be found to have been merely the effect of the opulence of one country and the poverty of the other. Some other cause, we may be assured, must have concurred. The rich country must have been guilty of some error in its police [policy].

*    *    *

A nation that would enrich itself by foreign trade, is certainly most likely to do so when its neighbours are all rich, industrious, and commercial nations. A great nation surrounded on all sides by wandering savages and poor barbarians might, no doubt, acquire riches by the cultivation of its own lands, and by its own interior commerce, but not by foreign trade.

The question then arose, as with Hume, of what would happen in the long run if there were limits to growth. Would not the poor late-comers catch up with the initially richer nations if the latter came to a steady state?

Smith, unlike most of his successors, drew a clear distinction between incremental improvements in technology, done on the job as the market expanded, and major discontinuous changes brought about by "philosophers." But he was not quite capable of envisaging that his specialized philosophers could generate a flow of profitable major inventions and innovations over long periods of time that the rich could exploit in a forehanded way to maintain their place at the front of the queue. There were, therefore, limits to the extent that the expansion of the capital stock could expand the market and reap for nations the benefits of the progressive division of labor. In a famous passage, he explicitly acknowledged that there was for each country a ceiling on population and real output.

In a country which had acquired that full complement of riches which the nature of its soil and climate, and its situation with respect to other countries, allowed it to acquire; which could, therefore, advance no further, and which was not going backwards, both the wages of labour and the profits of stock would probably be very low. In a country fully peopled in proportion to what either its territory could maintain or its stock employ, the competition for employment would necessarily be so great as to reduce the wages of labour to what was barely sufficient to keep up the number of labourers, and, the country being already fully peopled, that number could never be augmented. In a country fully stocked in proportion to all the business it had to transact, as great a quantity of stock would be employed in every particular branch as the nature and extent of the trade would admit. The competition, therefore, would every-where be as great, and consequently the ordinary profit as low as possible.

But perhaps no country has ever yet arrived at this degree of opulence. China seems to have been long stationary, and had probably long ago acquired that full complement of riches which is consistent with the nature of its laws and institutions. But this complement may be much inferior to what, with other laws and institutions, the nature of its soil, climate, and situation might admit of. A country which neglects or despises foreign commerce, and which admits the vessels of foreign nations into one or two of its ports only, cannot transact the same quantity of business which it might do with different laws and institutions.[12]

In Smith's judgment, Holland, which did not neglect or despise foreign commerce, was nearer to its full complement of riches than China.[13]

Again, like Hume, Smith did not try seriously to resolve the logical contradiction between the short- and medium-run mutual advantages of free trade between rich and poor countries (and regions) and a long-run prospect of steady state stagnation. The latter concept could not exclude the poor achieving levels of wealth and productivity that might challenge the rich when all had achieved their "full complement of riches" and, according to his analysis of this steady state (and the case of China), wages declined. Smith could and did argue that with sound policy, the rich ought to be able to look after themselves; but, in fact, his interest was not in the long run but in his "very violent" attack on current British and Continental economic policy. In a world where market forces were permitted (with a few specified exceptions) to work their will, colonies permitted to go their way, and investment in agriculture (as well as manufactures and commerce) not discouraged, the prospects were good that a high level of income per capita could be sustained in Great Britain and elsewhere. At this point, as Istvan Hont noted, wealth and virtue are brought together by Smith's central proposition that high productivity (low unit labor costs) induced by the widening of the market can reconcile high wages and low costs in manufactures.[14] That is the indecisive stage of the debate when Great Britain went into take-off in the 1780s.

### III. THE TARIFF DEBATE IN THE PERIOD OF BRITISH PRIMACY: 1783–1870

Economic theory and doctrine have evolved over the centuries in a curious two-level contrapuntal manner. On one level, there is a dialectical continuity among the professionals. We can examine and debate how the theory of value, of interest, of rent, or whatever has evolved over the better part of three centuries. We can observe how each generation picked up where the last left off and tried its hand at challenging, radically modifying, or marginally refining its inheritance with respect to what has emerged over time as the grand core issues of the science (or art) of political economy. But this in-house continuity, common to virtually all intellectual disciplines, has interacted with the shifting agenda imposed by developments in the active world. Unlike the U.S. Supreme Court, economists may not follow the election returns; but they have systematically reflected in their work the great practical issues of their day, notably those that were paramount when they defined their governing (usually youthful) "visions."[15]

In any case, the primal take-off of the 1780s sharply reduced attention in Great Britain to the rich country–poor country problem for about a century, shifted its locus, and transformed its terms. Great Britain's leadership in demonstrating that invention and innovation had widened from a thin, mainly incremental, stream to a majestic flow, and that large discontinuous technological change was possible— creating, in effect, new industries and radically transforming old ones— caused virtually all British economists to stop worrying about a stationary state in a time period worth worrying about. This optimism was heightened by the radical fall in grain prices after 1812. The real costs to Great Britain of the French Revolutionary and Napoleonic wars undoubtedly slowed growth below the rate that would otherwise have been attained; and there was an interval of postwar economic and social distress with two particularly difficult years (1816 and 1819). But it was also palpable that the technological gap between Great Britain and its rivals and potential rivals had substantially widened as compared to the situation in 1793. There was something farsighted, principled, and even noble in Hume's assertion that as a loyal British subject, he wished well the economy of the chronic adversary, France.[16] This was also true of Smith's attack on Great Britain's effort to maintain a monopoly of trade with the American colonies.[17]

But to those who lagged behind Great Britain in the new technologies of manufacture there was something self-serving, even ominous, in the rising pressure out of London for free trade. The question that lay at the center of the policy debate over the rich country–poor country problem from the 1780s forward was the legitimacy of tariff protection for infant industries in a country lagging technologically behind the front-runner. The seriousness of the issue was heightened by the perception of Alexander Hamilton in 1791 that more than money was at stake: "Not only the wealth but the independence and security of a country appear to be materially connected with the prosperity of manufactures."[18] By and large, Hamilton's formula, with its security as well as welfare strand, was to be the primary rationale for industrialization in relatively underdeveloped countries over the subsequent two centuries. It was first accepted in countries of the Atlantic world conscious by 1815 of the widened technological gap with Great Britain. Thus the U.S. and Continental tariffs of the post-Napoleonic period.

The tradition of classical economics had, of course, been strongly in support of free trade. But it had not been a blind and rigid support. Hume, for example, thought that some taxes on imports might be justified;[19] Malthus had a good word for some agricultural protection;[20] and even Ricardo believed transitional tariffs might be envisaged en route to free trade in grain.[21] J. S. Mill did not, of course, originate the case for transient protection for infant industries, but he stated it with clarity and elegance.

> The only case in which, on mere principles of political economy, protecting duties can defensible, is when they are imposed temporarily (especially in a young and rising nation) in hopes of naturalizing a foreign industry, in itself perfectly suitable to the circumstances of the country. The superiority of one country over another in a branch of production, often arises only from having begun it sooner. There may be no inherent advantage on one part, or disadvantage on the other, but only a present superiority of acquired skill and experience. A country which has this skill and experience yet to acquire, may in other aspects be better adapted to the production than those which were earlier in the field. . . . But it cannot be expected that individuals should, at their own risk, or rather to their certain loss introduce a new manufacture, and bear the burden of carrying it on until the producers have been educated up to the level of those with whom the processes are traditional. A protecting duty, continued for a reasonable time, might sometimes be the least inconvenient mode in which the nation can tax itself for the support of such an experiment. But it is essential that the protection should be confined to cases in which there is good ground of assurance that the industry which it fosters will after a time be able to dispense with it; nor should the domestic producers ever be allowed to expect that it will be continued to them beyond the time necessary for a fair trial of what they are capable of accomplishing.[22]

Something like Mill's formulation of the case for asymmetry survives in mainstream economics textbooks (and in international agreements) to the present day.

## IV. THE SECOND GRADUATING CLASS
## CATCHES UP WITH THE LONELY LEADER:
## ALFRED MARSHALL AND THORSTEIN VEBLEN

Great Britain was the only nation to move into take-off in the first graduating class in the last quarter of the eighteenth century (see Figure 3.1). The next graduating class of, say, the second quarter of the nineteenth century included the United States, Belgium, France, and Germany. It was the movement of this second class to the drive to technological maturity—the stage beyond take-off—that revived the rich country–poor country anxiety in Great Britain. In the last quarter of the nineteenth century, post–Civil War America drove its railroads to the Pacific, rounded them out with feeder lines, and pushed its population to the limits of the frontier. Bismarck consolidated his empire and exploited fully its potentialities in the age of coal and steel, surpassing Great Britain in steel production in the 1890s. Great Britain became conscious that its time of lonely primacy was passing and that late-comers did indeed command the potentiality of catching up with early-comers. Alfred Marshall was one of the most thoughtful commentators on the process.

Marshall began his most detailed consideration of the problem in *Industry and Trade* with three chapters that are, in effect, analytic essays in British history.[23] They cover elements in the past that prepared the foundations for British pioneering of what Marshall called "massive industry," which he dated proximately from the mechanization of the cotton industry in the late eighteenth century to 1873. He then considered the subsequent challenge to Great Britain's primacy and the British response. Chapters follow on the special characteristics of French, German, and U.S. industrialization. The genius of each he found, respectively, in "fine goods, embodying some artistic feeling and individual judgment"; industries that can be nurtured by "academic training and laboratory work"; and "massive multiform standardization." He closed with "some slight speculations as to future homes of industrial leadership."

The first edition of *Industry and Trade* was published in 1919, the fourth and final edition in 1923. But, typical of Marshall's long periods of gestation, a good deal of the book had been set in type as early as 1904. His analysis of Great Britain's relative position and the intensity of the challenge it confronted better reflected the mood of 1904 than 1919 or 1923. The point is germane because Marshall's recommendations to his countrymen were modest, and like his analyses of France, Germany, and the United States, they did not capture the major economic consequences of the First World War and its aftermath.

Figure 3.1. *Four Graduating Classes into Take-off: Stages of Economic Growth, Twenty Countries*

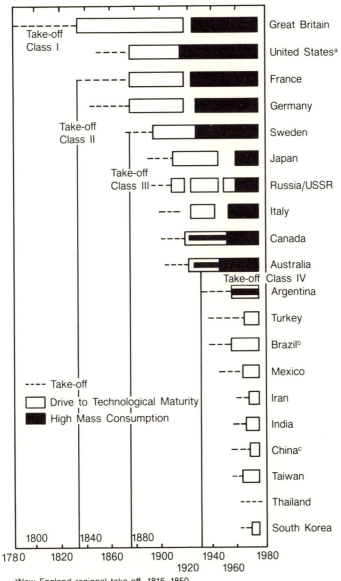

[a]New England regional take-off, 1815–1850.
[b]São Paulo regional take-off, 1900–1920.
[c]Manchuria regional take-off, 1930–1941.

*Source:* See W. W. Rostow, *The World Economy: History and Prospect* (Austin: University of Texas Press, 1978), p. 51 and Part 5.

Marshall did insert references, however, to wartime developments and noted that "Britain surprised the rest of the world, if not herself, by the energy which she has shown in the World-War: and the English speaking peoples of four continents have proved themselves to be united in spirit and truth."[24]

Specifically, Marshall commended to his countrymen an intensification of measures already belatedly under way: an expansion and improvement of popular education, a need recognized and acted upon starting in 1904;[25] an improvement of university education for "the well-to-do classes in England";[26] an expansion of training in science and engineering as well as increased allocation of public resources for scientific research laboratories;[27] improved information about overseas markets and less conservative methods of industrial financing.[28]

Despite his sense that Great Britain was responding to the industrial challenge in appropriate directions and his evident pride in its redoubtable wartime performance, the general tone of Marshall's view of the future is not unlike Hume's long-run philosophic acceptance that manufactures tend to shift from countries and provinces they have already enriched and fly to others.

Marshall looked to some of the British Dominions assuming, in time, degrees of industrial leadership but noted that they were likely to be more influenced by the experience of the United States than Great Britain.[29] His concluding reflections went beyond the Atlantic and English-speaking world and, on the whole, are prescient:

Passing away from European races, we find in Japan a bold claimant for leadership of the East on lines that are mainly Western. Her insular position, contiguous to a great Continent, is almost as well adapted for the development of industry and trade as that of Britain. She has learnt so much during the last thirty years, that she can hardly fail to become a teacher ere long. It seems indeed that stronger food than they now have will be required to enable her people to sustain continuous, severe, physical strain: but the singular power of self-abnegation, which they combine with high enterprise, may enable them to attain great ends by shorter and simpler routes than those which are pursued where many superfluous comforts and luxuries have long been regarded as conventionally necessary. Their quick rise to power supports the suggestion, made by the history of past times, that some touch of idealism, religious, patriotic, or artistic, can generally be detected at the root of any great outburst of practical energy.

India, though less agile, is developing renewed vigour and independence in industry as in thought. She is the home of some of the greatest thoughts that have ever come to the world; and the originator of many of the subtlest and most artistic manual industries. She has suffered in the past from lack of unity, and a scarcity of power for manufactures and transport. But she may yet be found to have considerable stores of coal: and some of her regions may be enriched by electrical energy derived from water power. The rapid recent rise of her larger industries is a source of just pride to her, and of gladness to Britain.

Great futures may also await Russia and China. Each is large, continuous and self-contained: each has enormous resources, which could not be developed so long as good access to ocean highways was a necessary condition for great achievement. Their populations differ in temperament; the persistence of the Chinese being complementary to the quick sensibility of the Russian: each has inherited great powers of endurance from many generations of ancestors who have suffered much. . . .

. . . it may be concluded that there is no sure ground for thinking that industrial leadership will remain always with the same races, or in the same climates, as in recent times; nor even that its general character will remain unaltered.[30]

Marshall did capture, in this passage, some of the principal actors (e.g., China and India) in what might be called the coming third round of adjustment of the advanced industrial countries to the challenge of maturing late-comers—the first having been Great Britain's adjustment to the maturing of countries whose take-offs began in the second quarter of the nineteenth century (Belgium, France, the United States, and Germany); the second, the adjustment of Western Europe and the United States to the maturing of countries whose take-offs began in the 1880s and 1890s (Japan, the USSR, and Italy).

At about the same time, the same phenomenon—the catching up and surpassing of Great Britain by Germany and the United States with a precocious Japan in the wings—caught the imagination of Thorstein Veblen. His *Imperial Germany and the Industrial Revolution*[31] was published in 1915. Veblen focused more sharply than Marshall on Great Britain and Germany, and his study is marked by three further distinguishing features. First, he explored the cultural characteristics of the two national societies at much greater length; second, as a major theme, he linked culture, the economy, and war; and third, he examined the costs as well as benefits of being first in industrial development and the distortions as well as advantages of being a late-comer.

Taken as a whole, Veblen's study is a reminder of the power implications and military dangers that can flow from the catching up of poorer countries with the rich—in my vocabulary, as they move beyond take-off to complete the drive to technological maturity when they have in hand all the then relevant technologies.[32]

## V. THE PERSPECTIVE FROM 1945:
## FOLKE HILGERDT

In the more than two centuries since Hume generated a lively discussion among his contemporaries of the rich country–poor country problem, one of the most important empirical studies bearing directly on the economic issues it poses is, clearly, *Industrialization and Foreign Trade.*[33] Mainly the work of Folke Hilgerdt, it was published in 1945 by the League of Nations, a final product of its distinguished Economic, Financial and Transit Department. Hilgerdt's study ranges more widely than its title implies. It includes in Chapter 4, for example, a consideration of "The Conditions for Industrial Development," which clearly belongs among the pioneering analyses of development policy.[34] For our narrow purposes in this essay, it constitutes, in effect, a systematic analytic test of some of Hume's basic propositions, based on statistical data covering the years 1870 to 1938. The three major findings were

> *first,* that until about 1930 the growth of manufacturing, far from rendering countries independent of foreign manufactured goods, stimulated the import of such goods;
> *secondly,* that again up to about 1930, those countries in which manufacturing developed most rapidly as a rule increased their imports of manufactured goods more than did other countries; and
> *thirdly,* that after the breakdown of multilateral trade early in the "thirties," this relationship between the growth of industry and of trade in manufactured goods was severed.[35]

By 1945, an analyst of industrialization and foreign trade clearly had available a wider body of data than, say, Marshall and Veblen. The third graduating class, which had moved into take-off in the last quarter of the nineteenth century, was on the scene and part of the world trading system (e.g., Sweden, Japan, Italy, the Soviet Union, and the more advanced parts of the old Austro-Hungarian Empire). But Hilgerdt's story was distorted by the pathology of the interwar years as well as by the autarchic economic policies of the Soviet Union. Nevertheless, the process of mutual adjustment envisaged by Hume went on and is well captured in Hilgerdt's conclusion on the changing composition of manufactures as "poor countries" industrialize and on the related problem of "adaptation" in "rich countries." It is well worth quoting.

> While normally the import from older industrial countries is thus not likely to decline as a result of industrial growth elsewhere, these imports

are likely to change in character, for the countries in which industry develops will diversify their demand for consumption goods and increase their demand for manufactured capital goods. Different supplying countries will thus be differently affected; and even those able to raise their sales may experience some difficulty in affecting the necessary adaptation. Under normal conditions, however, time for adapation is likely to be afforded, for in the majority of countries, particularly those with a dense population, there are strong forces resisting the industrial development which is accordingly, as a rule relatively slow.[36]

The resistance to industrial development within developing countries appears to have diminished sharply in the second half of the twentieth century.

## VI. 1945–1986: THE INITIAL IMPACT OF THE FOURTH TAKE-OFF GRADUATING CLASS

The take-offs of the major Latin American countries and Turkey, beginning in the 1930s, inaugurated the fourth graduating class. They were joined in the 1950s and 1960s by India and China as well as by the extraordinarily dynamic smaller countries along the western rim of the Pacific. It would be helpful if the United Nations or the World Bank, with data on the forty post–World War II years in hand, were to test Hilgerdt's conclusions systematically against the larger body of comparable evidence now available. Nevertheless, easily accessible data make it clear that, by and large, the now familiar process has proceeded, although, as always, with some special features.

Although strongly affected by the rise and subsidence of the relative price of oil, the data in Tables 3.1 and 3.2 broadly validate the three basic Hilgerdt propositions for the period from the early 1960s to the early 1980s:

* The period down to 1981 was marked by an extraordinary expansion in manufactured exports from developing countries;
* this surge was accompanied by continued high (but lesser) rates of increase in exports of manufactures to developing countries;
* there was an evident sensitivity of exports from developing countries to the rate of growth of advanced industrial countries; but the shift toward manufactured exports altered the relationship.

As stated in the *World Bank Development Report, 1984,*

This diversification away from primary products does not mean that foreign demand no longer matters. Developing countries depend on

Table 3.1. *Growth of Exports, 1963–1984*

| Country Group and Commodity | Average Annual Change in Export Volume (percent) | | | | | |
|---|---|---|---|---|---|---|
| | 1965–73 | 1973–80 | 1981 | 1982 | 1983[a] | 1984[b] |
| *Export volume, by commodities* | | | | | | |
| Developing countries | | | | | | |
| Manufactures | 13.8 | 11.0 | 14.1 | 1.0 | 11.5 | 15.0 |
| Food | 2.2 | 5.4 | 12.4 | 11.8 | 4.6 | 4.8 |
| Nonfood | 3.6 | 1.6 | 0.7 | -3.9 | 1.3 | -1.8 |
| Metals and minerals | 5.7 | 5.5 | -2.4 | 5.9 | -5.2 | 3.9 |
| Fuels | 3.9 | -1.0 | -12.9 | 1.6 | 1.6 | 5.1 |
| World, excluding nonmarket industrial economies | | | | | | |
| Manufactures | 10.7 | 5.8 | 6.0 | -2.1 | 4.4 | 11.7 |
| Food | 4.5 | 9.0 | 7.2 | 9.9 | 6.0 | 7.0 |
| Nonfood | 3.2 | 3.6 | 3.1 | -0.9 | -9.7 | 0.2 |
| Metals and minerals | 6.8 | 7.2 | -15.7 | -4.0 | -5.7 | 0.5 |
| Fuels | 9.5 | 0.7 | -7.9 | -11.2 | -5.7 | 2.5 |
| *Export volume, by country group* | | | | | | |
| Developing countries | 5.2 | 4.1 | 3.3 | 3.2 | 5.8 | 8.9 |
| Manufactures | 13.8 | 11.0 | 14.1 | 1.0 | 11.5 | 15.0 |
| Primary goods | 3.6 | 1.3 | -3.4 | 4.8 | 1.8 | 4.2 |
| Low-income countries | 3.1 | 5.2 | 7.0 | 6.6 | 3.6 | 11.4 |
| Manufactures | 5.3 | 6.5 | 17.0 | -4.8 | 6.2 | 23.5 |
| Primary goods | 2.0 | 4.4 | -0.1 | 16.1 | 2.3 | 2.9 |
| Asia | 2.3 | 7.2 | 13.0 | 8.1 | 5.6 | 12.8 |
| Manufactures | 5.2 | 6.7 | 20.7 | -3.8 | 6.5 | 24.0 |
| Primary goods | -0.1 | 7.8 | 5.6 | 21.4 | 4.8 | 2.8 |
| Africa | 5.1 | -0.5 | -14.8 | -0.7 | -5.3 | 3.2 |
| Manufactures | 5.6 | 3.1 | -33.4 | -30.5 | -7.3 | 2.5 |
| Primary goods | 5.0 | -0.9 | -12.1 | 2.7 | -5.1 | 3.2 |
| Middle-income oil importers | 7.3 | 8.3 | 12.5 | 4.5 | 7.3 | 9.1 |
| Manufactures | 17.0 | 12.2 | 13.8 | 1.6 | 11.1 | 13.2 |
| Primary goods | 3.1 | 4.3 | 10.8 | 8.7 | 2.0 | 3.1 |
| Major manufacturing exporters | 10.0 | 9.7 | 13.7 | 4.0 | 8.0 | 9.6 |
| Manufactures | 17.4 | 12.6 | 13.8 | 1.4 | 10.9 | 12.9 |
| Primary goods | 5.1 | 5.5 | 13.6 | 9.2 | 2.6 | 2.8 |
| Other middle-income oil importers | 1.6 | 3.4 | 7.2 | 7.0 | 3.9 | 6.9 |
| Manufactures | 13.5 | 7.6 | 13.9 | 5.2 | 14.5 | 17.1 |
| Primary goods | 0.3 | 2.4 | 5.3 | 7.6 | 0.7 | 3.5 |
| Middle-income oil exporters | 4.2 | -0.4 | -11.6 | -0.5 | 3.6 | 7.4 |
| Manufactures | 11.5 | 6.9 | 13.5 | 5.0 | 27.5 | 24.5 |
| Primary goods | 4.1 | -0.7 | -13.2 | -0.9 | 1.6 | 5.5 |
| High-income oil exporters | 15.9 | 1.1 | -7.3 | -25.5 | -15.8 | -7.6 |
| Industrial market economies | 9.5 | 5.6 | 2.9 | -1.1 | 2.5 | 10.0 |
| World, excluding nonmarket industrial economies | 9.1 | 4.7 | 2.0 | -2.5 | 1.9 | 8.7 |

[a]Estimated
[b]Projected

Source: *World Development Report, 1985* (New York: Oxford University Press for the World Bank, 1985), p. 152.

Table 3.2. *Destination of Manufactured Exports: 1962, 1982 (percentage of total)*

|  | Industrial Market Economies | | East European Non-market Economies | | High-income Oil Exporters | | Developing Economies | |
|---|---|---|---|---|---|---|---|---|
|  | 1962 | 1982 | 1962 | 1982 | 1962 | 1982 | 1962 | 1982 |
| Lower-income economies | 57 | 48 | 9[a] | 5 | 2[a] | 10 | 37 | 36 |
| Lower middle-income economies | 53 | 52 | 8 | 2 | 1 | 5 | 38 | 41 |
| Upper middle-income economies | 50 | 48 | 5 | 5 | 1 | 5 | 44 | 42 |
| Industrial market economies | 63 | 64 | 3 | 3 | 1 | 5 | 33 | 28 |
| Specifically: | | | | | | | | |
| United Kingdom | 58 | 62 | 3 | 2 | 2 | 8 | 37 | 29 |
| France | 63 | 63 | 4 | 3 | 1[a] | 4 | 33 | 30 |
| FRG | 74 | 72 | 8 | 4 | 1[a] | 4 | 21 | 26 |
| Japan | 45 | 48 | 4 | 3 | 1 | 8 | 50 | 41 |
| United States | 48 | 53 | — | 1 | 1 | 6 | 51 | 40 |

[a]1965

*Sources:* 1962, *World Development Report, 1984* (New York), pp. 242–243; 1982, *World Development Report, 1985* (New York), pp. 198–199.

developed-country markets for their manufactured exports; short-run fluctuations in the demand for their exports due to fluctuations in growth in industrial countries can still be important. But the diversification of exports toward manufactures has changed the medium- and long-run competitive position of developing-country exports in developed-country markets. Their manufactured exports account for less than 5 percent of apparent consumption in developed countries, and are substitutes for goods produced within advanced countries. As long as markets for developing countries' manufactured exports remain relatively free of protective barriers, external demand constraints will not limit developing-country exports.

The experience of the 1960s and 1970s bears this out. There has been no stable statistical relation between the volume of developing-country exports and real income in developed countries in the 1960s and 1970s. Developing-country exports increased twice as fast in relation to developed-country income in the 1970s; for each 1 percent change in real income in developed countries, the volume of developing-country exports increased by only 0.9 percent in the 1960s but by 1.7 percent in the 1970s.[37]

Thus far one can conclude that the advanced industrial countries of the non-Communist world and the countries of the fourth take-off graduating class moved after the Second World War into an exceedingly intimate interacting process in which each group became highly dependent on the continued high growth rates of the other; a structural process was actively at work in which developing countries were competing successfully in certain manufacturing sectors within advanced countries, expanding their imports of more sophisticated manufactures and forcing the more advanced industrial countries to alter the composition of their industrial output. Down to 1914 a similar interdependence existed; but it was based on an exchange of basic commodities from the developing countries for manufactures from the more advanced. This was the system that was fractured during the interwar years. Its successor system operated (except for the less-developed oil exporters) with a progressively larger component of exchange of less sophisticated for more sophisticated manufactures, as Hume initially envisaged. Manufactured exports from developing countries rose from about 10 percent of their total exports to 46 percent between 1960 and 1980.[38]

At the moment, the international trading and financial system is, as we all know, in a phase of uncertain recovery, shadowed by the unresolved debt situation, the two-edged oil price decline, the outcome of the downward readjustment of the dollar, and other familiar problems. Evidently the world economy faces a difficult and potentially precarious adjustment if dynamically stable growth patterns are to be established in both the advanced industrial and developing regions.

In this essay I shall look beyond that readjustment and address three large questions posed for the more distant future by this brisk historical survey of the rich country–poor country problem.

First, is the fourth take-off graduating class likely, over the next half century, to move into industrial maturity, absorbing along the way the advanced technologies now rapidly expanding in the advanced industrial world—notably, microelectronics and genetic engineering?

Second, if this outcome is likely, what are the implications for domestic policy of the presently advanced industrial societies?

Third, if this outcome is likely, what are the major implications for foreign policy and the arena of world power?

## VII. CAN THE FOURTH TAKE-OFF GRADUATING CLASS ACHIEVE TECHNOLOGICAL MATURITY?

With all the cautions with which one ought to surround predictions, I am prepared to argue that the United States and Western Europe (and the Soviet Union and Eastern Europe as well) face a progressively intensified competitive challenge in the several generations ahead.

We currently tend to regard Japan as the foremost competitor; however, South Korea, Taiwan, and other Southeast Asian states preparing to go high-tech, closely followed by India, China, Brazil, and other Latin American countries.

I make this prediction because of a virtually unnoticed revolution in the technologically more advanced developing countries. In "lower middle-income" countries, the proportion of the population aged 20 to 24 enrolled in higher education rose from 3 to 10 percent between 1960 and 1982; that for "upper middle-income" countries increased from 4 to 14 percent.[39] In India, which has low income per capita but a vital educational system, the increase was from 3 to 9 percent. In comparison, in 1960 the proportion for the United Kingdom was 9 percent and that for Japan was 10 percent.

Moreover, the educational emphasis recently shows a radical shift toward science and engineering. In India, for example, the number of scientists and engineers has grown from 190,000 in 1960 to 2.4 million in 1984—a figure exceeded only in the United States and the Soviet Union. In Mexico, from 1957 to 1973 the annual average increase in the number of graduates in natural science was about 3 percent, in engineering 5 percent. From 1973 to 1981 the comparable figures were 14 percent to 24 percent, respectively—an almost fivefold increase.

Even if we take into account the problems of educational quality, the more advanced developing countries have a high potential absorptive capacity for the new technologies. Their central problem—like that of most advanced industrial countries—is how to utilize the skills of the increasingly number of scientists and engineers. They also must develop an ability to create and maintain effective and flexible partnerships among scientists, engineers, entrepreneurs, and the working force. As the more advanced developing countries build more and more of these interactive partnerships, I predict that the brain drain from these countries would be reversed.

## VIII. CAN THE PRESENTLY ADVANCED INDUSTRIAL COUNTRIES REMAIN "INDUSTRIOUS AND CIVILIZED"?

Although the United States and Western Europe will surely enjoy enlarged export markets if technological virtuosity diffuses in the manner I suggest as likely, but will these old industrial societies of the Atlantic "remain industrious and civilized"? Or, in the language of economics, will they exhibit a sufficiently high elasticity of substitution to make Hilgerdt's "necessary adaptation" in good time?

On present evidence, a general dogmatic answer to that question is not justified. The outcome depends, I believe, on whether we of the Atlantic world generate a vital new generation of political economists and practitioners of political economy for what might be called the third century of modern economic growth.

During the first century of political economy—from Hume and Smith to J. S. Mill and Marx—the focus was on the potentialities and limits of economic growth and their implications for relative prices and distribution. In Great Britain, the central policy issue became free trade; on the Continent and the United States, tariffs, public support for transport, and other methods for encouraging industry. But although they had their roots in the older tradition, Mill and Marx also opened the second century of political economy. They assumed the existence of an ongoing system based on expanding technological possibilities, and they identified the inequities and elements of harshness of that system. In effect, they both asked how the system could be rendered humane and civilized in terms of the abiding values of Western culture and its religions. Alhtough their answers were, of course, very different, they launched a century and more in which the political economy centered on one question: How should the resources be allocated from an expanding pie? Should they go to welfare or for private consumption and investment? Bismarck can be said to have begun the shift to welfare with his reforms of the 1870s and 1880s. And that phase ended rather dramatically in the slowdown of the world economy of the 1970s after welfare outlays had risen from an average of about 14 percent to 24 percent of GNP in the major OECD countries between 1960 and the mid-1970s. I believe that the fate of the social and physical infrastructure of the advanced industrial countries depends today not on the balance between conservative and liberal politicians but on the response of political process to the new age of intensified technological competition—an age that the United States and Western Europe have not yet faced and dealt with. That response or the lack of response will determine whether the pie can continue to expand and whether it can sustain and refine the amenities thus far achieved.

To meet the challenge of meshing the new technologies in the world economy, the United States and Western Europe must radically alter their politics. They must shift their primary emphasis from a zero-sum conflict over the allocation of a presumably automatically expanding pie to long-term cooperation to ensure that the pie will, in fact, continue to expand.

In the United States one can observe at the state and local level considerable evidence of a shift toward communal cooperation.[40] Henry Cisneros, the young mayor of San Antonio, spoke for a good many of his contemporaries in both political parties in many parts of the United States in defining the correct political strategy for these times as follows: "The real answers are not found in confrontation, obstruction, or denying access, but rather in inclusion, co-operation, providing facts, and trying to build a common stake in the future."[41] Something like this spirit is beginning to suffuse some sectors of the business-labor relations. Optimists can observe that new patterns of national politics are often foreshadowed at state and local levels. Skeptics can observe that Washington still seems firmly gripped by anachronistic concepts and battle cries and the United States is still a long way from paying its way in the world; although historians may regard the 1986 action in the Senate in the direction of tax reform as the beginning of the assertion of communal over parochial interests in national politics.

Seen from a distance, Western Europe projects across the Atlantic a similarly indecisive set of more and less hopeful signals. It is, thus, too soon to be confident that the graduates of the first two take-off classes will be capable in the next several generations of the "industrious and civilized" performance Hume counseled. What we can say is that the outcome will depend on the emergence of new patterns of domestic politics underpinned by a political economy focused on a quite different set of problems than those that have dominated the agenda in the past century.

## IX. CAN THE WORLD COMMUNITY MAKE THE NECESSARY ACCOMMODATION PEACEFULLY?

Tables 3.3 and 3.4 and Figure 3.1 tell a suggestive story—or perhaps three stories. They provide a rough measurement of the remarkable diffusion of industrial power away from Great Britain and France between 1870 and 1913 as the United States, Germany, Russia, Italy, and Japan gained ground at the expense of the older industrial states of Western Europe. They demonstrate the interwar surge of Japan, of the USSR (after 1929), and of Germany (after 1933) relative to Great Britain, France, and the United States, and they show the initial postwar dominance of the United States and the Soviet Union (combined weight, Table 3.4, 1950, 65 percent), gradually declining to a combined figure of 43 percent in 1983 as economic power diffused not only to Western Europe and Japan but also to the developing

Table 3.3. *Distribution of World's Industrial Production, 1870–1983 (in percentages)*

| Year | Total | Europe | | | | | | | | |
|---|---|---|---|---|---|---|---|---|---|---|
| | | UK | France | Germany | Russia | Belgium | Scandinavia | Italy | Rest of Europe |
| 1870 | | 32 | 10 | 13 | 4 | 3 | a | 2 | |
| 1881–1885 | | 27 | 9 | 14 | 3 | 3 | 1 | 2 | |
| 1896–1900 | | 20 | 7 | 17 | 5 | 2 | 1 | 3 | |
| 1906–1910 | | 15 | 6 | 16 | 5 | 2 | 1 | 3 | |
| 1913 | | 14 | 6 | 16 | 6 | 2 | 1 | 3 | |
| 1913[b] | | 14 | 7 | 14 | 4[c] | 2 | 1 | 3 | |
| 1926–1929 | | 9 | 7 | 12 | 4[c] | 2 | 1 | 3 | |
| 1936–1938 | | 9 | 5 | 11 | 19[c] | 1 | 2 | 3 | |
| 1963 | 53 | 5 | 4 | 6[d] | 19[c] | 1 | 2 | 2 | 14[e] |
| 1968 | | 5 | 3 | 4[d] | 16[c] | 1 | 2 | 2 | |
| 1971 | | 4 | 3 | 5[d] | 16[c] | 1 | 2 | 2 | |
| 1983 | 40 | 3 | 3 | 4[d] | 18[c] | 1 | 2 | 2 | 7 |

[a]Less than 0.5 percent
[b]The second line for 1913 represents the distribution to the frontiers established after the First World War
[c]USSR
[d]Federal Republic of Germany
[e]Eastern Europe, 10 percent; other European, 4+ percent

Table 3.3. *Cont.*

| Year | North America | | | Central America | | South America | | | Latin America |
|---|---|---|---|---|---|---|---|---|---|
| | Total | USA | Canada | Total | Mexico | Total | Brazil | Argentina | |
| 1870 | 24 | 23 | 1 | | | | | | |
| 1881–1885 | 30 | 29 | 1 | | | | | | |
| 1896–1900 | 31 | 30 | 1 | | | | | | |
| 1906–1910 | 37 | 35 | 2 | | | | | | |
| 1913 | 38 | 36 | 2 | | | | | | |
| 1913[b] | 38 | 36 | 2 | | | | | | |
| 1926–1929 | 44 | 42 | 2 | | | | | | |
| 1936–1938 | 34 | 32 | 2 | | | | | | |
| 1963 | 34 | 32 | 2 | 1[f] | 1[f] | 3 | 1[g] | 1[g] | 4 |
| 1968 | 37 | 34 | 3 | 2 | 1 | 2 | 1[h] | 1[h] | 4 |
| 1971 | 36 | 33 | 3 | 2 | 1 | 2 | 1[h] | 1[h] | 4 |
| 1983 | 28 | 25 | 3 | — | — | — | — | — | 5 |

[f]Central American weight is 0.74, of which Mexico is 0.64
[g]Brazil's weight is 0.85; Argentina's, 0.72
[h]For Brazil, the 1968 percentage is 0.66; for Argentina, 0.55. In 1971, the two figures were 0.67 and 0.59, respectively

Table 3.3. Cont.

| | | Rest | | | | | | | |
|---|---|---|---|---|---|---|---|---|---|
| Year | Middle East | Rest of Asia | Japan | India | China | Africa | Oceania | Other Countries | World |
| 1870 | | 2 | 1 | | | | | 11 | 99 |
| 1881–1885 | | 2 | 1 | 1 | | | | 12 | 101 |
| 1896–1900 | | 2 | 1 | 1 | | | | 12 | 100 |
| 1906–1910 | | 2 | 1 | 1 | | | | 12 | 99 |
| 1913 | | | | 1 | | | | 12 | 100 |
| 1913[b] | | | | 1 | | | | 14 | 99 |
| 1926–1929 | | 4 | 3 | 1 | | | | 13 | 99 |
| 1936–1938 | | 5 | 4 | 1 | | | | 12 | 101 |
| 1963 | [a] | 6 | 4 | | | 1 | 1 | | 99 |
| 1968 | 1 | 7 | 4 | 2 | | 2 | 1 | 15 | 100 |
| 1971 | 1 | 8 | 5 | 1 | | 2 | 1 | 15 | 100 |
| 1983 | 2 | 3 | 5 | 3[i] | 8 | 3 | 1 | 2 | 100 |

[i]This figure is for all of South Asia

Sources: 1870 to 1936–1938, Hilgerdt calculations; 1963–1971, United Nations calculations. Explanation of sources, 1870–1971, *World Economy: History and Prospect* (Austin: University of Texas Press, 1978), pp. 50 and 728. 1983 from *BP Statistical Review of World Energy* (London: 1984, British Petroleum Company), p. 28. Radical decline in "Other Countries" between 1971 and 1983 due to some differences in categories; e.g., 1983 use of South Asia for India. The rise in 1983 figure for the U.S.S.R., relative to 1971, may reflect lesser energy conservation measures in the 1970s, but the increase appears excessive.

Table 3.4. *World Energy Consumption by Major Regions: Percentage Distribution, 1950, 1960, 1970, and 1983*

| Region | Energy Consumption (percentage distribution) | | | |
|---|---|---|---|---|
| | 1950 | 1960 | 1970 | 1983 |
| North America | 48.0 | 39.3 | 34.7 | 27.7 |
| Canada | 3.5 | 3.1 | 3.3 | 3.0 |
| United States | 44.5 | 36.1 | 31.4 | 24.7 |
| Western Europe[a] | 22.8 | 21.0 | 22.3 | 17.6 |
| Oceania | 1.2 | 1.1 | 1.1 | 1.3 |
| Latin America | 3.1 | 4.0 | 4.3 | 5.0 |
| Asia (non-Communist) | 5.0 | 6.6 | 9.7 | 9.7 |
| Japan | 2.3 | 3.0 | 5.2 | 4.9 |
| Other Asia[a] | 2.7 | 3.7 | 4.5 | 4.8 |
| Africa | 1.7 | 1.7 | 1.7 | 2.7 |
| USSR and Communist | | | | |
| Eastern Europe | 16.7 | 20.9 | 20.9 | 28.0 |
| USSR | 11.0 | 14.4 | 14.9 | 18.6 |
| Eastern Europe[a] | 5.7 | 6.5 | 6.0 | 9.4 |
| Communist Asia | 1.6 | 5.3 | 5.3 | 8.0 |
| World | 100.0 | 100.0 | 100.0 | 100.0 |

[a]Yugoslavia is included in Western Europe in this table; Turkey appears in Other Asia

*Source:* J. Darmstadter and S. H. Schurr, "World Energy Resources and Demand," *Philosophical Transactions of the Royal Society of London,* Series A, vol. 276 (1974), p. 415.

regions, including notably the leading members of the fourth take-off graduating class. The rather dramatic shift between 1950 and 1983 is suggested by the rise in Table 3.4 of Asia (including the Middle East but less Japan), Africa, and Latin America from 11 percent to 25 percent of the total.

These tables and Figure 3.1 also capture the changing global economic framework that led to the First and Second World Wars; the cold war between the United States and the Soviet Union; and, finally, the declining relative positions of the United States and the USSR and the foreseeable problem of economic, political, and strategic adjustment to the rise to technological maturity of the fourth take-off class—the presently more technologically advanced developing countries.

There is, of course, a great deal more to the coming of the First and Second World Wars and the cold war than these numbers, and much more than the likely future trend in these numbers will determine the strategic shape of the global arena. But they do suggest why, in 1914, the German General Staff could conceive of victory if Great Britain and France could be swiftly disposed of, German power concentrated against Russia, and a self-isolated United States kept from mobilizing and bringing its potential power to bear in a relevant period of time; why Hitler could conceive of victory if he could neutralize the Soviet Union with the 1939 pact and then deal decisively with the West while, once again, the United States remained bemused and irrelevant to the swiftly achieved outcome; why the Japanese military could conceive of achieving regional hegemony in 1941 with Hitler neutralizing both Western Europe and the Soviet Union and the United States only beginning to mobilize its resources and committed to support beleaguered Great Britain and the Soviet Union; why the Soviet Union could conceive of hegemony in Europe in 1945–1946 with Western Europe and Japan prostrate and President Franklin Roosevelt predicting at the opening session in Yalta that the United States would not keep military forces in Germany for more than two years.

The tables also suggest the cost to the world as well as to the United States of the ambiguity it projected concerning the interests for which it was, in the end, prepared to fight. The temptations of various powers to seek hegemony in Eurasia would clearly have been tempered if the oscillation of the U.S. posture between determined neutrality and determined engagement had been avoided, for throughout the period the U.S. industrial potential palpably represented a decisive strategic margin when committed and mobilized.

Turning to the future, what, then, are the broad implications of the diffusion of industrial and technological virtuosity that appears to be under way?

In my view, the world economy and polity face an enormous adjustment over the next century. Although the population of the advanced industrial countries (including the USSR and those of Eastern Europe) is now about 1.1 billion people, or approximately 24 percent of the world's population, at least 2.6 billion people, or about 56 percent, live in countries that I predict will acquire technological prowess within the next century. Moreover, in the near future, the population in the emerging countries will increase more rapidly than that in the advanced. This will give rise to a great historical transformation.

The early-comers can benefit economically as the late-comers move toward technological equivalence. But the process could eventually generate all types of frictions and dangers. The presently advanced industrial nations will require strength, unity, poise, and inner confidence to maintain their vitality and to help the world community, as a whole, through this complex and potentially explosive adjustment.

Although I cannot present the case fully here, I believe that an effective mechanism to smooth the adjustment between more and less advanced nations is greatly strengthened regional organizations containing societies at different degrees of modernization. The size of the United Nations, acting as a whole, forces the membership into sterile and oversimplified political polarization. The smaller regional organizations are closer to day-to-day pragmatic problems and may be tempered by a sense of neighborhood.

Specifically, strengthened enterprises should be encouraged in the Pacific Basin, the Western Hemisphere, and Euro-Africa. In happier times, a Middle East regional organization might be envisaged and one for South Asia, the basis for which already exists. The advanced industrial countries might work with all these groupings, although their relative roles would evidently vary with their location and historic and current interests.

It may well be that a second type of intensified economic collaboration will come to make sense. The generation and absorption of the new technologies is, evidently, a critical part of the task of remaining "industrious" and making the rapid "adaptation" required in the advanced industrial societies. A sufficiently high elasticity of substitution may, in turn, require heightened cooperation within Europe, across the Atlantic, and, ultimately, with Japan, for the latter, while at the moment challenging with vigor Western Europe and the United States, is quite aware already that it, too, will be increasingly challenged by the fourth take-off class. In short, new forms of West-West (or North-North) as well as North-South cooperation may be a natural outcome of the process under way.

But what about East-West? Where does it fit in this way of looking at the sequence of generations ahead? I have been arguing since the late 1950s that the most powerful underlying force at work in the world arena is the diffusion of effective power away from both Washington and Moscow. The data I have just cited and the trend they apparently foreshadow strengthen this long-held conviction. For example, I made the following observation toward the end of a Pugwash conference in Moscow in December 1960:

Faced with this fact [the diffusion of power], there are three choices open to the Soviet Union and the United States. We can stumble into a war and destroy a large part of what man has built on the face of the earth and a large part of the world's population. We can continue the cold war until the diffusion of power removes the capacity to decide from Moscow and Washington. Or, working constructively together, we can [strongly influence] the terms on which power will become diffused.

This is the limit of the historical powers of the Soviet Union and the United States. I would hope that we could choose the third path. This is the historical responsibility we owe to our peoples.

In short, the cold war is already an anachronism. If rationality were to prevail, the inherently deadend character of the arms race, the profound economic challenges the Soviet Union faces along with the other advanced industrial powers, the rise of nationalism and thrust for human freedom in the Soviet empire, and the prospect for a relative rise in economic power and technological virtuosity, as well as national assertiveness in the developing regions, should lead the Soviet Union to seek safety not only in its own great defensive capability but also by working with others to render peaceful the inevitable further diffusion of power.

Thus, the task of the West remains essentially what it was forty years ago: to try to make rationality prevail. Despite all our frustrations and disappointments over these four decades, I believe the chance of success is greater now than then if, as that wise Scotsman counseled a while back, we remain industrious and civilized.

## NOTES

1. R. B. Haldane, *Life of Adam Smith* (London: Walter Scott, 1887), p. 9.

2. See, notably, Istvan Hont's account of the eighteenth century debate over this problem in "The 'rich country–poor country' debate in Scottish classical political economy," Chapter 11 in Istvan Hont and Michael Ignatieff, eds., *Wealth and Virtue: The Shaping of Political Economy in the Scottish Enlightenment* (Cambridge: at the University Press, 1983).

3. The image is from Carl L. Becker, *The Heavenly City of the Eighteenth-Century Philosophers* (New Haven: Yale University Press, 1932), p. 49.

4. Hont traces this strand in western thought back to Aristotle and Machiavelli, op. cit., p. 272.

5. *David Hume: Writings on Economics*, edited and introduction by Eugene Rotwein (Madison: University of Wisconsin Press, 1955), pp. 80–82.

6. Ibid., pp. 34–35.

7. Ibid., pp. 190–205, for textual reflections of the debate, including letters to Lord Kames, the recipient of communications from both Hume and Tucker. Also Istvan Hont, op. cit., pp. 275–276.

8. Rotwein, ed., op. cit., p. 200.

9. Ibid., p. 198.

10. Ibid., pp. 108–109.

11. The quotations are to be found, respectively, in Istvan Hont, op. cit., p. 300 (where original sources are provided), and Adam Smith, *The Wealth*

*of Nations,* Edwin Cannan (New York: Random House, 1937), p. 462. It might be noted in passing that in the discussions within the United States government on post-1945 economic policy, one strand was articulated (notably by Will Clayton) in terms almost identical with the second quotation. Clayton argued that the United States could not live in either prosperity or safety as a rich man on the hill surrounded by impoverished peoples. He deployed this argument against those who asserted, in a mercantilist spirit, that U.S. assistance to Europe would only foster strong trading rivals.

12. Smith, pp. 94–95.

13. Smith, p. 96. Holland was experiencing the expected decline in interest rates, which, in Smith's view, had the wholesome effect of driving rentiers into commerce or manufactures where profits were higher than the safe rate of interest. But, unlike China, Holland was not yet experiencing the expected decline in wages to a subsistence minimum that accompanied movement to a "full complement of riches."

14. Ibid., p. 300.

15. Joseph Schumpeter, *History of Economic Analysis* (New York: Oxford University Press, 1954), pp. 41–42.

16. Rotwein, ed., op. cit., p. 82.

17. Smith, pp. 557–558.

18. Alexander Hamilton, "Report on Manufactures (1791), in *Alexander Hamilton's Papers on Public Credit Commerce and Finance,* edited by Samuel McKee (Columbia University Press, 1934), p. 227.

19. Rotwein, ed., op. cit., p. 76, and Rotwein's comments in Introduction, pp. lxxvi–lxxviii.

20. *Essay on Population,* sec. ed. (London: J. M. Dent, 1914, 1952), vol. 2, p. 79.

21. P. Sraffa, ed., with the assistance of M. Dobb, *The Works and Correspondence of David Ricardo* (Cambridge: at the University Press, 1951) vol. 1, pp. 265–267.

22. J. S. Mill, *Principles of Political Economy* (London: Routledge & Kegan Paul, 1965), pp. 918–919.

23. A. Marshall, *Industry and Trade* (London: Macmillan, 1919; reprinted New York: Augustus M. Kelley, 1970, Reprints of Economic Classics), Chapters 3–5, pp. 32–106.

24. Ibid., p. 104.

25. Ibid., pp. 95–98.

26. Ibid., p. 98.

27. Ibid., pp. 99–102.

28. Ibid., pp. 102–103.

29. Ibid., pp. 104–105 and 157–159.

30. Ibid., pp. 161–162.

31. See most accessibly the August M. Kelley Reprints of Economics Classics edition, Joseph Dorfman, ed. (New York, 1964). As Dorfman's introduction points out, there are important references to the United States and Japan, despite the primary focus on Germany and Great Britain.

32. For a systematic discussion of the relation of this process to major struggles for continental hegemony, see my *Stages of Economic Growth* (Cambridge: at the University Press, 1960, 1971), pp. 114–121. Another more narrowly economic impression of the transience of economic leadership in the world economy was evoked by Simon Kuznets in his *Secular Movements in Production and Prices* (Chicago: Hart, Schaffner, and Marx, 1930), pp. 3–4: "This picture of economic development suffers a curious change as we examine it first in a rather wide sphere, then in a narrow one. If we take the world from the end of the eighteenth century, there unrolls before us a process of uninterrupted and seemingly unslackened growth. We observe a ceaseless expansion of production and trade, a constant growth in the volume of power used, in the extraction of raw materials, in the quality and quantity of finished products. . . . Some nations seem to have led the world at one time, others at another. . . . Great Britain has relinquished the lead in the economic world because its own growth, so vigorous through the period 1780–1850, has slackened."

33. League of Nations, *Industrialization and Foreign Trade* (New York: distributed in the United States by International Documents Service, Columbia University Press, 1945), with a Preface by A. Loveday, director of the Economic, Financial and Transit Department, dated July 1945.

34. In his "Summary of Findings" (Chapter 7, pp. 116 ff.), Hilgerdt devotes 9 of his 22 conclusions to "Conditions for Industrial Development."

35. Ibid., p. 5. This summary passage is from Loveday's Preface.

36. Ibid., p. 117.

37. *World Development Report, 1984* (New York: Oxford University Press for the World Bank, 1984), p. 43.

38. Ibid. The quoted data exclude major exporters such as Korea, Hong Kong, and Singapore, but include India, Mexico, Brazil, and Egypt.

39. *World Development Report, 1984* and *1985* (New York: Oxford University Press for the World Bank, 1984 and 1985), Table 25, pp. 266–267 and 222–223, respectively. For evident reasons, I have chosen to dramatize here accelerating technological absorptive capacity rather than relative rates of increase in GNP. Nevertheless, a comparison of proportions of global GNP is instructive. The unique calculations of Herbert Block suggest that the combined totals of the United States and the Soviet Union declined from 44 percent to 33 percent of the world total output of goods and services between 1950 and 1980; those for the developing countries rose from 20 percent to 25 percent. The extraordinary increase of Japan over this interval was from 3 percent to 8 percent. These data are to be found in Block's *The Planetary Product in 1980: A Creative Pause?* (Washington, D.C.: Department of State, 1981), Table 1, pp. 30–31.

40. This point is elaborated in "My Life Philosophy," *The American Economist* (Pace University, Fall 1986) [reprinted here as Chapter 1].

41. From "Mayor Henry Cisneros: Putting a Smile on San Antonio," in *United* (United Airlines, March 1986).

# FOUR

# Long Cycles and Policy

*This essay was presented on December 6, 1984, at a conference in an unlikely setting: the headquarters of the Duke of Wellington at Waterloo, now a rather vivid museum evoking details of the battle, hour by hour. The building is also used as a conference center by the Centre d'Études Européennes de Waterloo, which sponsored the gathering.*

*Analytically, this essay goes beyond my earlier writing on long cycles in two respects. First, I speculate briefly on a possible reason for the tendency of major new innovations to cluster. Second, I provide some examples of interaction between the supply of food and raw materials and the dynamics of technology—these being the two principal candidates to explain Kondratieff cycles.*

## I

The theme of this conference—which I take to be the possible policy implications of long cycles—is in the tradition of economics at its best. That tradition accepts economics (or, better, political economy) as an instrument of analysis designed to improve the lives of men, women, and children.

In that spirit, I shall first define the two major hypotheses that aim to explain the existence of long cycles; then consider the interplay between the forces that underlie these hypotheses; and conclude with some policy implications of the analysis.

## II

Nicolai Kondratieff, as we all know, did not produce a long-cycle theory of his own. He identified long cycles (or waves, as he called them) in commodity prices, interest rates, and money wages reaching back from the 1920s to the 1790s; tried, but failed, to establish concurrent cycles in real growth rates; asserted five empirical characteristics of long-cycle upswings and downswings, some challengeable; and then speculated tentatively on the possible role of four variables in relation to the statistical phenomena he had isolated. Those variables were new technologies, war and revolutions, the opening up of new countries, and gold discoveries.

Looking back from the 1980s—with the advantage of a further sixty years beyond Kondratieff's working horizon—only two of his four variables still justify serious consideration as explanations for long-cycle behavior over the whole span since the last decade of the eighteenth century. The first still relevant hypothesis centers on the ebb and flow of technological innovation and is associated with Joseph Schumpeter's *Business Cycles*.[1] The second is related to Kondratieff's opening up of new countries but is more accurately formulated as cycles in the prices of basic commodities relative to manufactures; that is, the intersectoral terms of trade. This is the case because, as Kondratieff was aware, the opening up of new territories has been generally associated with periods of rising or high relative prices for basic commodities. I developed this hypothesis during the 1930s, in my work on trend periods in the British economy, first published in systematic form in 1948.[2] W. Arthur Lewis has also viewed the Kondratieff long cycle as primarily a phenomenon induced by relative price movements stemming from phases of relative scarcity and overabundance of basic commodities;[3] and, still earlier, Colin Clark had published suggestive analyses in this vein.[4]

Put another way, since the 1920s the case for the other two Kondratieff hypotheses has weakened: Gold discoveries have clearly ceased to be a significant factor in determining movements in the value-denominated series on which Kondratieff focused; and, although wars and revolutions have certainly affected the movement of such a series in recent decades, those political events were generally not caused by the upswing of long waves, as Kondratieff suggested.[5]

Thus, the question before us narrows to cycles in technological innovation and/or in the relative prices of basic commodities; the links between such cycles; and their contemporary relevance, if any, to the world of policy.

III

Schumpeter tried to link cycles in innovation with the price (not relative price) cycles on which Kondratieff focused. Schumpeter evoked an early, inflationary stage of innovation, when resources were borrowed and spent inefficiently, followed by a phase of falling prices when the innovation had reached a phase of rapidly increasing efficiency and widespread diffusion. He thus viewed cycles as the outcome of a dynamic race between demand and supply curves in certain key innovational sectors, with supply curves moving more slowly downward and to the right in upswings than in downswings. I have explained elsewhere the four reasons why this imaginative concept, linking innovation in key sectors to the macro performance of the economy, doesn't work very well when confronted with historical data.[6] Nevertheless, Schumpeter's hypothesis has been quite influential, and properly so. He did not explain the price, interest rate, and money wage Kondratieff presented, but he dramatized effectively a phenomenon of which economic historians had long been aware; namely, that between the 1780s and 1914 a good many major innovations took place in three clusters. Cotton textile machinery, Watt's steam engine, and iron fabricated with coke came on stage in the 1780s; the railroad in the 1830s and 1840s, helping induce the steel revolution in the next generation; and electricity, the internal combustion engine, and an array of new chemicals round about the turn of the century. Contemporary long-cycle analysts in the Schumpeterian tradition have generally dropped his effort to link the rhythm of innovations to price behavior. They concentrate on the believed effects of the ebb and flow of innovations on the demand for capital, level of employment, rate of productivity increase, growth rate, and other real factors.

But Schumpeterians have only recently reemerged. The extraordinary success of post-1945 recovery and growth in both the Atlantic and Pacific communities led most economists to set aside issues of this kind. Macroeconomics—Keynesian, monetarist, or hybrid—dominated the perspective of mainstream economists, on the explicit or implicit assumption that the unexpectedly high rate of growth in the world economy was the result of a sophisticated manipulation of the level of aggregate demand. But, as the historically unique boom of the 1950s and 1960s gave way to the troubled 1970s and 1980s, propositions much like the secular stagnation hypothesis of the 1930s began to be reasserted;[7] and in academic life, as the present occasion suggests, there was a revival of research and theoretical debate on the historical and contemporary process of innovation.

One intellectual issue arose of some relevance to policy: Where does the world economy stand in terms of the rhythm of innovation— if, indeed, there is a rhythm? Accepting Schumpeter's three pre-1914 technological revolutions, Christopher Freeman and his colleagues identified a post-1945 "Fourth Long Wave."[8] It peaked in the mid-1960s and is linked to plastics, synthetic fibers, and pre-microchip electronics, including television—sectors analyzed by Freeman in an original and fruitful way. He was quite aware of the extremely important role of motor vehicles and durable consumers goods in the great postwar boom; and these sectors were (excepting television) evidently far beyond an innovational stage, clearly belonging with the Third Industrial Revolution. But Freeman chose to dramatize the rise and deceleration of a batch of technologies, long germinating, which clearly did emerge into large-scale production after 1945.

I am inclined to regard the leading sectors of the postwar boom (including plastics, synthetic fibers, and television) as the rounding out of the Third Industrial Revolution, placing more emphasis than Freeman on the diffusion in the 1950s and 1960s of the automobile and durable consumers goods revolution to Western Europe and Japan, sectors that, incidentally, absorbed significant proportions of the output of synthetic materials and light electronics.

The point I would make here is not that my view is correct and Freeman's incorrect: It is that while the phenomenon of bunching is a feature of modern economic history, our groupings and dating are inherently arbitrary. They should be taken seriously but not too seriously, as we recall that many important innovations occurred outside the intervals of cluster and that the clusters can be grouped in different ways.

I would, however, offer somewhat tentatively a reason why major innovations should have grouped themselves as they did over the past two centuries. As I note in *The Process of Economic Growth* (pp. 83–86), the scale of inventions and innovations in a modern society is a function of noneconomic as well as economic variables, but the composition of the stream of invention and innovation is determined by profit incentives. There is a good deal of truth in the old proposition that necessity is the mother of invention if one takes into account the fact that invention does not always respond to necessity (e.g., the persistence of the common cold) and that serendipitous accidental discoveries and inventions are possible. Further, if one assumes that the yield on refinements to individual inventive breakthroughs is subject to diminishing returns, the profitability of concentrating creative R&D talent in a given direction will gradually diminish. This means the incentive will increase with the passage of time for R&D talent to be drawn in new directions of more profitable creative activity, as diminishing returns operates in the sector where it is currently engaged.[9] Some such process may explain why, with appropriate time lags, new profitable inventions and innovations emerge as old leading sectors decelerate. Such engagement, disengagement, and reengagement in new directions is, of course, similar to that of the pattern of investment in general; and, as I argue in *The Process of Economic Growth*, it is one reason for treating basic research, invention, development, and innovation as part of the investment process.

I would side, however, with Freeman in his questioning of Gerhard Mensch's particular hypothesis about invention, innovation, and the profit motive; namely, that depressions systematically provide the breeding ground for the major innovations of the next upswing. The economic history of the past two centuries simply does not support that proposition. I would suggest that deceleration of an old leading sector and diminishing returns to refinements of its technological base—rather than cyclical depression—is the mechanism by which R&D talent is freed to create in new directions, concentrating in leading sectors at a relatively early, high-growth rate stage.

Where I would differ with Freeman is in underlining the rather dramatic and distinctive path of innovation that opened up from about the mid-1970s: the microchip, genetic engineering, the accelerating diffusion of lasers and robots, the emergence of new industrial materials, and revolutionary developments in communications. I am inclined to regard this complex as the Fourth Industrial Revolution (see Figure 2.1), and with its arrival concern about secular stagnation has given way to anxieties about the possibility of high chronic technological unemployment.

The Fourth Industrial Revolution has some distinctive characteristics as compared to its predecessors, which, as we shall later see, bear on issues of policy. It is more intimately linked to areas of basic science, which are themselves undergoing rapid revolutionary change. This means the scientist has become a critical actor in the drama; and the successful linkage of the scientist, engineer, and entrepreneur has become crucial to the generation and diffusion of the new technologies. The new technologies are also proving ubiquitous, progressively suffusing the older basic industries, agriculture, animal husbandry, and forestry, as well as all manner of services from education and medicine to banking and communications. And the new technologies are, in different degree, immediately relevant to the economies of the developing regions, depending on their stage of growth, absorptive capacity, and resource endowments.

We can conclude this part of our analysis with the following propositions.

- There have been over the past two centuries four (or, if you like, five) major innovational clusters, spaced 50 to 70 years apart.
- No generally accepted theory now exists that suggests why the clustering should have been what it has proved to be either with

respect to its composition or timing, although several candidate propositions are up for examination. I am inclined to believe that the process of invention, as well as innovation, responded, by and large, to the believed locus of profitability, and the normal decelerating path of profitability in a leading sector could help account for the observed clustering, once the First Industrial Revolution occurred.

- We are now living in the early stages of an extremely powerful and pervasive technological revolution with evidently profound implications for the future of our societies and of the world economy as a whole.
- Like its predecessors, the current technological revolution is raising what Keynes called the expected marginal efficiency of capital; but it is also generating a debate on whether it will yield, for the first time in modern economic history, high chronic technological unemployment—an issue relevant to policy to which we shall return.


## IV

We consider now the second possible hypothesis about long cycles, focused on the prices of basic commodities relative to manufactures. Here the data are more easily quantifiable, and a quite lucid theoretical basis for a long cycle can be outlined.

Figure 2.4 exhibits fluctuations in the ratio of primary to manufactured goods in the world economy from 1876 to 1982; that is, by my reckoning from the second Kondratieff downswing to the fifth Kondratieff upswing.[10] The relative price movements in the United States since 1951 (see Figure 2.5) also exhibit this cyclical process, which runs, with many irregularities, over two centuries.[11]

The question is: Why should the relative prices of crude materials and manufactured goods have moved in a cyclical pattern with a rhythm longer than, say, the classic nine-year business cycle? Here we have a clear-cut answer. Historically—and, indeed, down to the present— the period of gestation of investment to expand output of energy, food, and raw materials has often tended to be longer than that required to expand output of manufactures. And, as in all feedback mechanisms, the length of the lag (along with the length of life of the capital instrument) helps determine the length of the cycle. The implications of that proposition have been set out in formal mathematical terms; reasonable parameters inserted in the equations; and a model set in motion. This model yields a 40-year cycle within which relative price movements and shifts in the direction of the investment induce movements in real wages, rents, inflation rates, and overall growth rates that fairly well match typical long-cycle behavior.[12]

The model is presented, as it should have been, as an oversimple version of reality. Many other forces were at work in history—and are at work in the contemporary world—aside from the long cycle conceived as an overshoot-undershoot feedback mechanism induced by the effect of relative price changes on basic commodity sectors with long gestation periods. Moreover, I have tried to underline from the beginning of my work in this field that all basic commodity prices did not move together.[13] Nevertheless, there is an important element of reality in the relative price approach to long cycles.

There is also an intriguing analytic question that relates to policy and bears a family relation to the question I posed earlier about where we stand in the rhythm of innovational clusters based on new technologies. The question is: What are the prospects for relative prices for the rest of the 1980s and 1990s?

The fifth Kondratieff upswing, conceived in relative price terms, began at the close of 1972 with an explosion of grain prices, followed by a quadrupling of oil prices the next year. In both cases, exogenous events played a role—that is, the poor harvests of 1972 and 1973 and the Middle East war of October 1973. But a deeper examination makes clear that strong endogenous forces were at work in the late 1960s that decreed, in time, a reversal of post-1951 relative price trends.[14]

Despite various government efforts to suppress or mitigate the impact of the energy price rise on consumers, the Kondratieff upswing process worked to a degree; that is, energy-related investment sharply increased. In the United States, for example, conventional energy investment rose from 1.8 percent of GNP in the mid 1960s to about 3.5 percent in 1981. This excludes large investments in energy conservation, which may have amounted to 3 percent of all capital outlays in 1981.

As of late 1984, of course, energy, food, and raw material prices were soft compared to their levels, say, two or three years ago; and it is wholly fair to ask if the fifth Kondratieff downswing has begun after a much shorter upswing than in the historical past. After all, the length of the upswings was primarily determined in the pre-1914 world by the time it took to open up new territories and bring them into large-scale, efficient production. Now much of the expansion will come from increases in productivity and the exploitation of already accessible resources. Moreover, the increase in energy prices was so extreme by historical standards that it might have induced more rapid compensatory adjustment—both conservation and increased non-OPEC

(Organization of Petroleum Exporting Countries) output—than in the historical past.

On the other hand it may well be that the fifth Kondratieff upswing will reassert itself in the late 1980s and 1990. Consider, for example, the following.

- In diminishing degree, geared to income elasticities of demand, the softening of raw materials, energy, and agricultural prices has been caused by the severe recession of 1979 to 1982, which has not yet given way to a robust and general expansion in the world economy.
- Even then, near the bottom of the recession (September 1982), crude material prices (1967 = 100) in the United States stood at 317, total finished goods prices at 283. The real international price of oil, despite the recent decline, is still more than three times higher than in 1972 (see Figure 2.6). A revival in the world economy is likely to reverse, in some degree, the recent relative price shift in basic commodities and weaken the U.S. terms of trade, now artificially supported by abnormally high real interest rates, capital imports, and a grossly overvalued currency.
- With respect to agriculture, the inescapable increase of population in the developing regions, due to age structure, despite current declines in birthrates, may add something like two billion human beings to the planet in the next generation; and, overall, the rate of increase in agricultural production in those regions is not yet matching the rate of increase in the demand for food, inducing a rate of growth in grain imports of more than 3 percent per annum. In addition, there is the apparently intractable pathology of agriculture in most of the Communist states.
- As for raw materials, there is evidence of underinvestment in recent years and distorted patterns of investment. In Latin America, for example, the tension between an understandable desire of foreign investors for stable and reasonable terms for their outlays has resulted in reduced rates of raw material development in a number of countries. If the world economy revives, we may encounter raw material bottlenecks.

There is another major resource problem to be dealt with; that is, the need to roll back degradation of the environment and maintain for the long pull supplies of clean air and water, arable land, the forests, and irreplaceable areas for recreation and wildlife. These are tasks for both advanced industrial and developing countries.

Considerations of this kind lead me, without dogmatism, to believe that the fifth Kondratieff upswing is not over if the world economy revives strongly in the 1980s. If that view is correct, the current period of recession in basic commodity prices will, in retrospect, emerge as one more example of a countertrend, middle cycle of the kind referred to earlier (see note 11).

With respect to the relative-price Kondratieff hypothesis, I conclude that we have a sounder historical and theoretical basis for a long cycle than in the case of technological clusters; but I, at least, cannot assert that we are still in the midst of the fifth Kondratieff upswing with quite the confidence that I am prepared to assert that we are caught up in the early stage of the Fourth Industrial Revolution.

## V

Putting aside the fun and games of defining, counting, and measuring one kind of long cycle or another over the past two centuries, I turn now to examine a related issue rooted in the fundamentals of economic analysis as far back as the eighteenth century. In terms of the argument of this paper, the issue can be posed as follows: How, if at all, do our two contesting concepts of the long cycle relate to each other? Were the cycles in relative prices and the clusters of major innovations linked? If so, how? In a larger sense, the question is: Why, for two centuries, was the analysis and prediction of the founding fathers of modern economics proved wrong when they envisaged that the production of food and raw materials would be governed by diminishing returns, the production of manufactures by increasing returns? From Adam Smith's *The Wealth of Nations* to, say, *The Limits of Growth*, this proposition runs through the literature of economics like the theme of a symphony; but the assumption about the relation of technology to the two sectors that underlies the proposition has thus far proved false.

The simple historical fact is that for more than two centuries the dynamics of the supply of food and raw materials has interacted intimately with the dynamics of technology. The net result of this interaction has been that, by and large, diminishing returns has been held at bay and the globe's population has increased (since 1750) by almost 6 times, industrial production by, perhaps, 430 times, and real GNP per capita, as a global average, by something like 10 times. Clearly, in an era when the rate of population increase is only slowly decelerating from unprecedented levels, and the peoples and governments of virtually all of the nations of Latin America, Africa, the Middle East, and Asia are determined to move forward in industrial growth, the creative interaction of food and raw material supply on the one hand, technology on the other, will have to continue into the future if large-scale Malthusian and/or Ricardian crises are to be avoided.

How, then, did this creative interaction work in the past? Here it may be useful to cite, briefly, a few major examples of interaction before offering any generalizations.

1. *Mining and Watt's Steam Engine.* Thomas Newcomen's steam engine had existed since the beginning of the eighteenth century, a response to the need in Great Britain to pump water out of mines. It was inefficient and costly in fuel to operate. The potential profitability of a more efficient steam engine was evident. Thus, the remarkable partnership of James Watt and Matthew Boulton and the final success of Watt's vastly more efficient engine, with its separate condenser, double-acting rotative engine, and governor. Once created, the steam engine found many more uses than initially envisaged and its efficiency was incrementally but rapidly improved.

2. *The Timber Price and Iron from Coke.* From the early eighteenth century it was known that good pig iron could be made from coke, and, for certain purposes, such iron was made on a relatively small scale. Between 1750 and 1790, however, the proportion of pig iron made from coke rose in Great Britain from 5 percent to 86 percent of the total. This change in industrial technology flowed directly from a change in the relative price of a raw material; that is, the rise in price of timber and charcoal relative to coal. The process of transformation from charcoal to coke was completed with Henry Cort's method for using coke to puddle and roll iron, permitting the concentration of the fabrication stage of the industry. The use of the steam engine proved essential to Cort's major innovation.

3. *Cotton Machinery, the Cotton Price, and the Cotton South.* As the new cotton textile machinery began to diffuse rapidly after 1785, there was a mighty expansion of production in Great Britain. A sixfold increase in raw cotton imports took place between the average for 1775 to 1784 and 1795 to 1804. Raw cotton output responded in several parts of the world to this remarkable shift in demand; but the price of raw cotton (varying with the harvests) tended to rise. The financial incentive to solve the problem of removing the seeds from U.S. long staple cotton by machine sharply increased. Responding to this incentive, Eli Whitney, teaching in the South, fresh from undergraduate life at Yale, created the cotton gin in 1793. Its use spread rapidly (without the benefit of patent royalties to Whitney), yielding a surge in production in the American South and, tragically, an increased demand for slaves.

4. *The Railroads, Agriculture, and Raw Materials.* The first railroads were induced by the possibility of cheaper transport from coal pithead to canal or river. Animal power was used to pull the carts on rails. When the commercial use of steam-powered railroads began in the 1830s, the initial links were between existing commercial and industrial centers; e.g., Manchester-Liverpool, Boston-Lowell, Washington-Baltimore. But again, the cheapened transport of a bulky raw material (cotton) remained an important incentive.

As the use of the railway spread, however, it became, on a worldwide basis, a principal instrument for expanding the supplies of agricultural products and raw materials: in Europe to the Urals, and beyond; in Canada and the United States, Mexico, Brazil, Argentina, and elsewhere in Latin America; in Australia, India, China, and other parts of Asia and the Middle East. With all due respect to the counter-factual railroad revisionists, the globe's geography did not permit canals, horses, and wagons to substitute effectively for railroads in this critical function.

5. *Railroads, Steel Ships, and Freight Rates.* The rapid diffusion of railroads, notably in the 1840s and 1850s, dramatized a problem: the high rate of obsolescence of iron rails. The incentive rose to find a way to produce cheap, high quality steel. The inventors broke through in the 1860s, and the steel industry emerged rapidly in the 1870s with the railroads their major customer. By the 1880s, as railway building decelerated, the steel industry seemed overbuilt; but new uses for steel were soon found in shipbuilding, machinery, bridges, and urban construction. The new steel ships, with more efficient steel engines, at last supplanted sailing vessels on long-distance routes. Freight rates were about half the level of the early 1870s in the mid-1890s, thus cheapening for Europe the prices of imported agricultural products and raw materials.

The array of complex interactions between industrial innovation and the supply of basic commodities could be indefinitely extended; electricity, modern dairy farming, and the refrigerator ship; chemistry, chemical fertilizers, and pesticides; the internal combustion engine and the tractor; space flight and photovoltaic cells; and so on.

What we have here is a fundamental process of far greater significance than the question of whether long cycles or waves existed in either innovations or relative prices. What we observe over the past two centuries are inventions and innovations that responded initially to an agricultural or raw material requirement (often in a phase of rising or high relative prices for basic commodities), which then were applied to other highly productive industrial or transport uses. But we also observe inventions and innovations that responded initially to an industrial or transport requirement, which then found other highly productive applications in expanding the supply of basic commodities.

This is the interacting process that explains why, for two centuries at least, that old devil Diminishing Returns has been more or less frustrated. Put another way, no analysis of long cycles is satisfactory if it does not take into account the forces at work in technological innovation, the forces at work on the relative prices of basic commodities, and the interactions between these two sets of forces. That is why I structured Part 3 of my *World Economy: History and Prospect,* which deals with long cycles, to embrace all these factors in a rather ecumenical way; and, in setting up an array of long cycle models, in Chapter 2 of *Why the Poor Get Richer and the Rich Slow Down,* I included both technological and relative price variants.

In narrower, more technical economic terms, the linkage can be stated as follows. Barring the opening up of new lands and other natural resources and barring the introduction of new technologies, diminishing returns would apply to the progressive exploitation of both existing natural resources and existing technologies. Diminishing returns have been kept at bay by both the opening up of new natural resources and the invention and innovation of new technologies. The two processes interacted intimately over the past two centuries. But the outcome differed with respect to natural resources and technologies.

The relative prices of natural resources tended to move in an irregular long cycle because of the relatively longer period of gestation of investment in these commodities than in manufactures. These long cycles had their impact not only on the price level, interest rates, and money wages, as Kondratieff detected, but also on the international and interregional terms of trade, and on income distribution between the urban worker on the one hand and those deriving their income primarily from natural resource rents or interest.

Because (*inter alia*) of diminishing returns to any given technological complex, the path of a leading sector incorporating a given technology tended to decelerate and profit possibilities to diminish. Like other forms of investment, investment in research and development tended, therefore, systematically to shift its focus, concentrating in the early, high-growth rate, high-profitability stage of a leading sector, shifting in other directions as creative possibilities (and profitability) become attenuated with the passage of time. Something like this process accounts for the tendency of innovations to cluster.

There is no logical reason for the rhythm of long cycles in relative prices and in the clustering of major innovations to conform; and, in fact, over the past two centuries their timing differs significantly.

## VI

This way of looking at long cycles suggests a few lessons for public policy. Following the structure of this analysis as a whole, I shall group them under these headings: the new technologies; food, raw materials, and the environment; and interconnections.

### Policy and the New Technologies

Like the great technological clusters of the past, railroads excepted, the bulk of the task of generating and diffusing the fourth Industrial Revolution can be left to the private sectors in the advanced industrial countries of the non-Communist world. But there are at least six areas of public policy where the new technologies pose problems or present opportunities that only governmental action can solve or fully exploit.

1. *Education and Personnel Retraining.* It is apparent that societies suffused with the new technologies will require major changes in emphasis and method from elementary education on to the research universities and institutes. The diffusion of the new technologies is already creating, in the United States and elsewhere, shortages of engineers, leading, in turn, to a drain of engineering teachers from universities.

The evident requirement for personnel retraining is, on the basis of past experience, best left to the private sector, with perhaps some incentive from public funds; but a margin of retraining in public institutions may be required, notably for older members of the work force. As education is, in virtually all societies, in large part a public domain, action on these matters is generally a matter of public policy.

2. *Linking the Research Universities to Engineering and the Production Process.* Perhaps the most striking aspect of the Fourth Industrial Revolution is the need to build regular, interacting working relations among the scientist, engineer, and entrepreneur. The working force should, in effect, be a fourth member of the partnership. As the nature of the new technologies becomes clear, the political leadership in one country after another has come to perceive the central character of this task and to perceive also that significant institutional changes will be required if the necessary linkages are to be made and sustained.

The particular changes required vary country by country, sector by sector. In a good many countries, for examples, the linkages are fairly well established in military production, space, and nuclear energy; but elsewhere, the links are weak or do not exist. The structure of the research universities and institutes, the attitudes they generate toward the production process and, indeed, toward business professionals, and the flexibility afforded faculty members to move back and forth from academic and production domains emerge as major general issues to which each society will have to fashion responses consistent with its heritage from the past and with future goals. Because research universities and institutes are public institutions or subsidized by government in most societies, this array of issues is, inevitably, part of the political agenda.

3. *Entrepreneurship in the Older Sectors.* A related but narrower issue arises in the older industrial sectors of many advanced industrial economies, but it can be observed also in Latin America, India, and China. The issue is: How to induce entrepreneurship not comfortable with the R&D process to make the most of the new technologies in their sectors. Take the United States, for example. Three sectors are, evidently, quite viable on an international basis despite the tariff imposed on U.S. exports by high U.S. interest rates and a grossly overvalued exchange rate. Those sectors are: electronics, chemicals, and aerospace. All three industries arose, in a sense, from laboratories, and the vital connection was never lost. The same can be said for modern agriculture in the United States where the Morrill Act of 1862 evoked the land grant colleges. The Department of Agriculture was created in the same year. Toward the end of the nineteenth century the movement toward the application of science to farming gathered momentum. And, in time, research conducted in the land grant colleges was linked to the farmer by county agents of the Department of Agriculture, who, in turn, closed the circle by bringing the farmer's problems back to those doing agricultural research. On the other hand, there are (among others) three sectors where the entrepreneurs who emerged in recent decades were notably awkward and ill-equipped in dealing with the R&D process: motor vehicles, steel, and machine tools. These sectors have been under great international pressure, their difficulties compounded by low average U.S. growth rates since 1974 and a punitive exchange rate for the 1981 to 1985 period.

It is, of course, not easy for governments to influence constructively the character and quality of entrepreneurship in private sectors of the economy. In the United States, a president can, in Theodore Roosevelt's phrase, use his "bully pulpit"; and Congress can investigate almost anything. Operationally, taxes can be used as stick-and-carrot to try to push things in a desired direction; and where government subsidies and loans are employed, leverage exists, which, quite legitimately, can take into account management's ability and will to introduce efficiently the new technologies, when relevant.

The scope for government influence on the quality of entrepreneurship in the old basic industries varies, of course, from country to country and includes in some cases direct control when government owns and operates plants or sectors of the economy. No general prescriptions are, therefore, possible. Nevertheless, the issue is important to recognize because conventional microeconomics, with its oversimple profit maximization hypothesis, conceals the nature and reality of the problem of maximizing profits over time in a world of rapidly changing production functions and the special entrepreneurial qualities required.

4. *Public R&D.* R&D expenditures in the early 1980s are running in the range of 1.8 to 2.5 percent of GNP for the major OECD countries, except Italy; there the figure is under 1 percent. In all cases government is a major source of R&D funds, 47 percent in the United States (1982); and governmental institutions are substantial performers of R&D (13 percent, 1982).

The scale of private R&D is also strongly influenced by federal tax policy in the United States as elsewhere. Evidently, as a major investor in R&D, governments cannot avoid the responsibility of allocating scarce financial and human talent and are, therefore, major actors in the Fourth Industrial Revolution. Among their tasks is that of assisting actively in the commercialization of potentialities generated by military and other classified R&D, a matter discussed further below.

5. *High Chronic Technological Unemployment?* It is widely asserted that the new technologies will yield high chronic structural unemployment. Given the impact of the second oil price shock of 1979 and 1980 and the deflationary macro-policies conducted by a good many governments since 1979, it is impossible to establish to what extent, if any, the high average unemployment levels in the Atlantic community can be attributed to the new technologies as opposed to deflationary macro-policies. For the United States, at least, I am convinced that, thus far, the new technologies, like their predecessors, have posed certain transitional employment problems but have, on balance, increased total employment. I would guess that this pattern would continue. The likely large-scale diffusion of robots, however, poses questions we cannot answer confidently at the present time: Will they destroy more jobs than they create? If so, in what proportion?

The possibility of substantial chronic technological unemployment, notably in semiskilled and unskilled labor, elevates the priority of public investment in physical infrastructure and in the control of environmental pollution. The rehabilitation and improvement of roads, ports, bridges; the expansion of water and sewerage facilities; the replanting of forests; the cleaning of air and water (rivers, lakes, and seas) are, in Adam Smith's phrase, investments that "may frequently do much more than repay it [their expense] to a great society."[15]

A great backlog of unmet depreciation in these areas grew up in the United States of the 1970s and early 1980s. The backlog in Western Europe may be less but is evidently large. Outlays to make good this depreciation belong in special investment budgets separated from military, social, and other conventional categories of public expenditure. Given the typically high level of unemployment benefits in the Atlantic community, the net cost of such infrastructure investment is not likely to be high so long as substantial levels of unemployment persist.

6. *North-South Relations and the New Technologies.* As noted earlier, the technologies of the Fourth Industrial Revolution appear immediately relevant to all the developing countries in different degree. Leaders in both the public and private sectors are intensely interested in the new technologies and concerned to establish what they must do to exploit them. In any serious effort to create a working economic partnership between the advanced industrial and developing countries—to supplant the evidently sterile negotiations centered on the New International Economic Order—the implications of new technologies should be high on the agenda. Indeed, Indonesia may have set in motion the first movement in that direction in July 1984. The occasion was the Association of Southeast Asian Nations (ASEAN) meeting in Djakarta. After such meetings, it is now a convention that the countries of the ASEAN, acting collectively, meet bilaterally with representatives of the European community, Japan, Canada, the United States, Australia, and New Zealand. On this occasion, Indonesia, acting for ASEAN as a whole, proposed what may well turn out to be a historic first meeting of the Pacific Basin countries; that is, a collective meeting with all its bilateral partners except the European community. At that session, Indonesia proposed that collective work be started in the Pacific Basin on human resources development. It is inevitable, in any serious action in that area, that the subject be linked to the long-term requirements of the new technologies. The potentialities for productive action, of great interest to the developing countries of the region, would be substantial. A Pacific Basin program that proves useful is likely to induce other regions to launch similar North-South enterprises in the field of human resources development in the context of the Fourth Industrial Revolution.

*Policy Toward Food, Raw Materials, and the Environment*

Public policy toward the new technologies is likely to consist of highly selective actions, mainly designed to strengthen the hand of the private sector, or to supplement its efforts. For good or ill, policy toward agriculture, raw materials, and the environment, in a good many nations, operates more directly, inevitably so with respect to the environment. The key policy problems differ substantially with respect to each of these three broad sectoral categories.

Agriculture is caught up in a political pattern that to a cosmic observer would no doubt be regarded as an occasion for laughter but, viewed from on the planet, contains elements of tragedy. In order to appease a politically influential minority of farmers, the advanced industrial countries are subsidizing agriculture and generating surpluses, which are almost impossible to dispose of commercially. In order to appease a politically influential minority of urban dwellers, a good many developing countries impose artificially low prices on farmers, thus dampening the motive to produce and generating demands for food imports difficult to finance. There are some developing countries that have, with difficulty, managed to move toward agricultural systems incorporating strong production incentives for the farmer, and many have come to invest heavily to increase agricultural productivity, notably by the expanded use of chemical fertilizers. The somewhat erratic result is exhibited in Table 4.1. Clearly, the poorer regions of the developing world, notably Africa and South Asia, are in a precarious marginal situation as the world moves into a generation of perhaps maximum strain between population pressure and the food supply.

The problem with respect to raw materials (including energy) is somewhat different. We simply do not know the extent to which the present softening of relative prices is the result of lower growth rates in the world economy or structural changes of a permanent character brought about by the radical increase in the relative price of energy and technological changes in the field of raw materials. What we do know is that, if the world economy reachieves reasonably high and steady growth rates, the demand for energy and raw materials is likely to increase, and a resumed rise in the relative prices of basic commodities is possible. Behind this assessment is a simple fact: At this stage of history the requirements for energy and raw materials are likely to increase more rapidly in the developing regions than in the advanced industrial countries. Table 4.2 suggests the scale of the process over the 1973 to 1983 period with respect to energy consumption, a decade during which energy consumption declined slightly in the advanced industrial regions but increased at an annual average rate of 4.7 percent in the developing regions. Between 1973 and 1983 the proportion of total energy consumed in the developing regions rose from 17 percent to 22 percent of the global total. If these rates

Table 4.1. *Growth Rates of Food Output by Region, 1960–1980 (average annual percentage growth)*

| Region or Country Group | Total | | Per Capita | |
|---|---|---|---|---|
| | *1960–70* | *1970–80* | *1960–70* | *1970–80* |
| Developing countries | 2.9 | 2.8 | 0.4 | 0.4 |
| Low-income | 2.6 | 2.2 | 0.2 | −0.3 |
| Middle-income | 3.2 | 3.3 | 0.7 | 0.9 |
| Africa | 2.6 | 1.6 | 0.1 | −1.1 |
| Middle East | 2.6 | 2.9 | 0.1 | 0.2 |
| Latin America | 3.6 | 3.3 | 0.1 | 0.6 |
| Southeast Asia[a] | 2.8 | 3.8 | 0.3 | 1.4 |
| South Asia | 2.6 | 2.2 | 0.1 | 0.0 |
| Southern Europe | 3.2 | 3.5 | 1.8 | 1.9 |
| Industrial market economies | 2.3 | 2.0 | 1.3 | 1.1 |
| Nonmarket industrial economies | 3.2 | 1.7 | 2.2 | 0.9 |
| World | 2.7 | 2.3 | 0.8 | 0.5 |

[a]Excludes China

Note: Production data are weighted by world export unit prices. Growth rates for decades are based on midpoints of five-year averages except that 1970 is the average for 1969–71.

*Source: World Bank Development Report, 1984* (New York: Oxford University Press for the World Bank, 1984), p. 90, where primary sources are given.

persisted for an additional twenty years the proportion would be 41 percent.

History does not, in fact, proceed in any such simple linear way. But the process determining the high energy consumption growth rates of the developing regions is likely to persist for some time. That process includes these elements: higher average real GNP growth rates than for the advanced industrial countries; more rapid flow of population from rural areas to more energy-intensive cities; the continued absorption of such energy-intensive technologies as steel, metalworking, and chemicals, at a time when expansion in the advanced industrial countries is mainly in less energy-intensive, high-technology sectors and services; and more rapid expansion of the pools of motor vehicles in the developing regions. The sectoral character of economic expansion is also likely to decree higher rates of increase in demand for industrial raw materials.

Finally, there are the problems of gross environmental degradation. In the advanced industrial countries these are primarily matters of national policy, although a good many European environmental prob-

Table 4.2. *Primary Energy Consumption: 1973–1983*

| | Million Tons Oil Equivalent | Annual Average Growth Rates | |
|---|---|---|---|
| | | 1973–1983 | 1983/1982 |
| North America | 2004–1917 | −0.4% | −1.3% |
| Western Europe | 1241–1222 | −0.2 | −0.2 |
| Japan | 348–341 | −0.2 | — |
| Latin America | 237–349 | 3.9 | −1.2 |
| Middle East | 87–131 | 4.2 | 2.8 |
| Africa | 98–190 | 6.8 | 3.2 |
| Southeast Asia | 92–158 | 5.0 | 4.4 |
| South Asia | 104–173 | 5.2 | 5.9 |
| China | 363–553 | 4.2 | 5.8 |
| USSR | 874–1287 | 3.8 | 3.5 |
| OTHERS | 400–518 | 1.6 | 0.1 |
| Total centrally planned economies | 1637–2358 | 3.6 | 3.2 |
| WORLD | 5913–6929 | 1.6 | 1.0 |
| Advanced industrial countries | 3593–3480 | −0.3 | — |
| Developing regions (inc. China) | 986–1554 | 4.7 | — |
| Centrally planned economies (less China) | 1274–1805 | 3.5 | — |

*Source:* Derived from *BP Statistical Review of World Energy* (London: British Petroleum Company, June 1984), p. 28.

lems are likely to be best dealt with on a regional basis. In the developing regions national and regional programs are also called for; but the scale of the investment effort required to reverse, for example, the destruction of arable land through deforestation is likely to require external assistance in the poorer developing regions.

The need to deal with severe environmental degradation is palpable. We are confronted, *ex post facto*, with the results of prior failure to provide adequate levels of investment to meet the depreciation of fixed assets. But a dilemma exists with respect to agriculture, energy, and raw materials, which should be made explicit. It is by no means easy to predict future price levels for such commodities, and there is a strong prima facie case for letting current market prices and profitability as judged by competitive markets determine the flows of capital to basic commodity sectors. But the lead times for such investments are generally long. With respect to energy in the United States, for example, lead times range from, say, four years to open a surface coal mine on private lands to, say, nine to thirteen years for a nuclear or hydroelectric power station or synthetic fuel plant. Under such circumstances, investment solely on the basis of current market indicators of profitability can prove rather unsatisfactory. The long lead times can cause gross overshooting and undershooting of requirements, accompanied by price movements of disturbing amplitude; and, quite specifically, if periods of shortage are encountered, the time required for correction by enlarged investment may be incompatible with desired levels of growth and unemployment.

Although mistakes can be and have been made, both private and public authorities have usually chosen to operate on the best estimates of future requirements they can muster, when lead times are long, rather than on short-run market criteria. There is wisdom in that calculus as well as risk.

The policy upshot of this view can be stated simply. Quite aside from national efforts to provide adequate supplies of food, energy, and raw materials in the developing regions, and to redress environmental degradation, there is scope for a major North-South collaborative effort. It should form an important component of the long-delayed partnership, which the increasing interdependence of the advanced industrial and developing countries makes rational.[16] The partnership should aim to generate supplementary international capital flows—private and public—to assure adequate resource foundations for continued growth in the world economy; it should be organized regionally and centered around the Latin American, Asian, and African development banks but with the active participation of the World Bank in all the regions, as well as the United States, Western Europe, and Japan.

### Policy to Encourage Interactions

A U.S. expert in technologies and their diffusion recently wrote: "America's future comprehensive security, defense and economic, depends on our abilities to support R&D diffusion through innovative commercialization of the technologies of the 1980s."[17] This statement was made in relation to the task of linking military R&D to the normal commercial activities of the U.S. economy; and the study of which it is a part concludes with a substantial group of public policy recommendations, including changes in law and taxation. The scale of military R&D makes the problem particularly important in the United States, but it is, in fact, a matter relevant to most of the advanced industrial countries.

The exploitation for civil purposes of technology developed for military purposes is, of course, only part of the larger problem briefly discussed earlier and illustrated with examples from history; that is, technologies developed to solve a problem in one sector of the economy can prove useful in others.

On this broader front, the European governments and Japan have taken a wide range of initiatives to stimulate the diffusion of new technologies. In the United States it has been the state governments that have thus far been most active. Looking to the future, a conference was held in Dallas, Texas, on February 5–7, 1984, on "Technology Venturing: American Innovation and Risk-Taking." The conference and the consensus at which it arrived are reported in two volumes.[18] The conference rejected a direct federal industrial policy but identified fourteen desirable initiatives in public policy, of which ten are commended to the federal government, four to state governments. The substance of these proposals need not concern us here; but they do illustrate vividly the general proposition that the new technologies are driving our societies toward a network of new linkages: between the universities and the public sector, the universities and the private sector, and between the public and private sector. The theme of the consensus can, indeed, be found in a quotation in the *Technology Venturing Data Book:* "We shall have to abandon the sterile political rhetoric of 'public sector' versus 'private sector,' and learn instead the neglected arts of intersectoral harmony and collaboration."[19]

There is, evidently, a significant selective and supporting role for public policy in this area. But rapid exploitation of the new technologies depends ultimately on private entrepreneurs comfortable in the world of R&D and rapid technological change, capable of searching the horizon beyond their sectors for developments that may prove productive and profitable in their own firms.

## VII

The argument of this paper is, then, that long-cycle analysis suggests strongly that key policy tasks on the agenda of the Atlantic community and Japan are to nurture and diffuse the new technologies; to assure an adequate resource foundation for continued growth in the South as well as the North; and to encourage constructive interaction between these technological and resource tasks. The larger significance of this argument flows from the fact that effective action along these lines might contribute to a successful completion of the historical transition through which the advanced industrial countries are now passing in a rather halting and painful way.

The transitions arise because events in the world economy in the early 1970s broke up the consensus on domestic and international economic policy that had crystallized after the Second World War— a consensus that acquired legitimacy with the historically unique growth rates of the 1950s and 1960s. No viable successor consensus on domestic economic policy has yet emerged. And without consensus on domestic policy there can be no effective consensus on international policy.

This judgment stems from a particular view of where the Atlantic world stands in the sweep of modern political and social history. For the century since Bismarck's social legislation in 1883, the central question asked in the advanced industrial nations of Western Europe and North America has been, How can we build industrial societies that reconcile technical efficiency with humane values? In politics the debate often centered on balancing the resource allocations between welfare and private consumption and investment—between the less affluent and more affluent. A major achievement of the Western democratic process was that this muted class struggle proceeded relatively peacefully, reaching in the 1960 to 1976 period a remarkable apogee. The proportion of social outlays rose in seven major OECD countries from 14 percent to 24 percent of GDP between 1960 and 1980[20]—a truly revolutionary shift.

The expansion of social outlays at rates higher even than the extraordinary real growth rates of the 1950s and 1960s was bound to cease eventually. Pressures to contain these outlays increased sharply with the explosion of oil prices, exacerbated inflation, and reduced growth rates of 1974 to 1984.

Clearly, the central issue of domestic political life in the West can no longer be defined in terms of determining the allocation of social welfare. Western countries must work together to maintain their economic level amid an increasingly competitive world economy and to sustain the living standard they have created during two centuries of economic growth.

Three issues appear fundamental if the erosion of the social and physical infrastructure of the advanced industrial countries is to be avoided.

> First, an issue not dealt with in this paper—the mounting of long-term policies capable of reconciling relatively high rates of growth with control over inflation. In my view this objective requires effective long-term incomes policies, as well as a judicious blend of fiscal and monetary policies.
>
> Second, the bringing together of scientists and engineers, entre-preneurs, and the working force to generate and absorb effi-

ciently—and across the board—the technologies of the Fourth Industrial Revolution.

Third, the generation of a North-South partnership to ensure the resource foundations for continued growth in the world economy over the coming period of acute strain.

The advanced industrial countries of the Atlantic world are in a transition between the resource allocation struggle characteristic of the welfare state and the communal cooperation needed if growth and control over inflation are to be reconciled, if the new technologies are to find an appropriate role in our societies, and if major Malthusian or Ricardian resource crises are to be avoided in the world economy.

In short, the policy meaning of this analysis is that we require, at home and abroad, a new political economy of cooperation and partnership, whether we lean to a technological or resource definition of long-cycle rhythms.

## NOTES

1. Joseph Schumpeter, *Business Cycles* (New York: McGraw-Hill, 1939).

2. *Essays on the British Economy of the Nineteenth Century* (Oxford: at the Clarendon Press, 1948), especially Chapters 1 and 2 where the analyses of both Kondratieff and Schumpeter are discussed. My subsequent work on long cycles can be found in A. D. Gayer, W. W. Rostow, and Anna Jacobson Schwartz, *Growth and Fluctuation of the British Economy, 1790–1850* (Oxford: at the Clarendon Press, 1953), especially vol. 2, Chapters 4 and 5 (actually written in 1939–1941); *The Process of Economic Growth* (Oxford: at the Clarendon Press, 1951 and 1960), especially Part 3 and Chapters 6, 8, and 9; *The World Economy: History and Prospect* (Austin: University of Texas Press, 1978), especially Part 3; *Why the Poor Get Richer and the Rich Slow Down* (London: Macmillan, 1980), especially Chapters 1 and 2. Chapter 1 discusses views of the Kondratieff cycle other than my own. It should be noted that the opening up of new areas with railroads could take place in a period of falling prices for mixed political-economic reasons, e.g., the Argentine Pampas and Western Canada. This point is discussed and illustrated in "The Terms of Trade and Development," my contribution to *Perspectives on Economic Development*, Essays in honor of W. Arthur Lewis, T. E. Barker, A. S. Downes, and J. A. Sackey, eds., (Washington, D.C.: University Press of America, 1982), pp. 256–258.

3. W. Arthur Lewis, *Growth and Fluctuations, 1870–1913* (London: George Allen and Unwin, 1978). Lewis's current views were foreshadowed in his *Economic Survey, 1919–1939* (London: Allen and Unwin, 1949). For a recent evocation of relative price cycles, see John Levi, "Omens from the Terms of Trade—Expectations about the Next Few Years," in *Inter-economics*, no. 3 (May–June, 1983):120–124.

4. Clark's interest in the relation between movements in the relative productivity of industry and agriculture, and the pattern and terms of world trade can be traced through *National Income and Outlay* (London: Macmillan, 1937); *The Conditions of Economic Progress* (London: Macmillan, 1940, 1931); and *Economics of 1960* (London: Macmillan, 1942). Clark discusses briefly his linkage of Kondratieff cycles to terms of trade movements in his retrospective essay, "Development Economics: The Early Years," in Gerald M. Meier and Dudley Seers, eds., *Pioneers in Development* (New York: Oxford University Press for the World Bank, 1984), p. 72. I track out this line of thought from still earlier beginnings, reaching back to Torrens, in "The Terms of Trade in Theory," Chapter 8, in *The Process of Economic Growth.*

5. The Iranian Revolution of 1978 is an interesting possible exception to that generalization if one accepts my relative price hypothesis about long cycles. The quadrupling of the oil prices in 1973–1974 set in motion an accelerated but extremely distorted process of economic development that heightened social and political tensions already present in Iranian society and thus contributed to the overthrow of the Shah and, of course, to the second oil price shock of 1978–1979. A less straightforward but even more important exception is the American Civil War. The explosive rise in the world wheat price in 1852–1854 led to the development of railroads in the U.S. Midwest and put the issue of transcontinental railroads on the national agenda; the prospect of bringing a large number of non-slave states in the Union and destroying the slave–non-slave state balance in the Senate helped lead southern leaders to contemplate secession as the only realistic alternative to permanent subservient status in the Union.

6. *Why the Poor Get Richer and the Rich Slow Down*, pp. 5–8. The four weaknesses in Schumpeter's hypothesis are the capital requirements in the early stages of innovation were not sufficient to impart the inflationary impulse Schumpeter's hypothesis requires; the cost-reducing effects of the innovations often came about quickly, operating to damp, rather than amplify other inflationary forces at work in Kondratieff upswings; the timing of major innovations does not fit easily the timing cycles Kondratieff identified in value-denominated series; and other inflationary cycles were clearly operating in the periods of rising price trends, which Schumpeter's analysis could not take into account. On the other hand, the periods of falling prices, primarily caused (in my view) by falling basic commodity prices were, in most cases, reinforced by reductions in cost linked to the diffusion of major innovations.

7. For references and discussion, see my *Getting from Here to There* (London: Macmillan, 1978), Chapters 8 and 9.

8. Christopher Freeman, John Clark, and Luc Soete, *Unemployment and Technical Innovation* (London: Frances Pinter, 1982), especially Chapters 6–8.

9. An interesting and original aspect of the study by Freeman et al. (op. cit.), especially Chapters 4–7, is their empirical analysis of the linkage of science and invention to the time path of certain major innovational leading sectors.

10. No single series covering earlier years exists that can be joined to the League of Nations–United Nations linked series for the period 1876–1982. The course of relative prices can, nevertheless, be traced out from various sources with reasonable confidence from, say, 1790 forward. See, for example, my *Process of Economic Growth*, Chapters 8 and 9, and *The World Economy: History and Prospect*, Chapters 8 and 9 and Part 3, "Trend Periods." For an even more detailed analysis of the first Kondratieff upswing and downswing, see A. D. Gayer et al. (op. cit.), vol. 2, pp. 623–658.

11. Kondratieff cycle irregularities—that is, deviations from smooth sine curve behavior—have, to a degree, been quite systematic. See, for example, *The Barbaric Counter-Revolution: Cause and Cure*, pp. 63–64. Specifically, a high proportion of the total price rise in Kondratieff upswings occurred in a brief interval close to the beginning of the upswings; Kondratieff downswings typically began with a sharp decline in the relative prices of basic commodities that subsequently decelerated; and both upswings and downswings were typically marked by a middle (Juglar) cycle when the trends abated or temporarily reversed. I raise the question at the end of this section as to whether we are not in the midst of such a countertrend middle cycle.

12. *Why the Poor Get Richer and the Rich Slow Down*, Chapter 2.

13. See, for example, *The Process of Economic Growth*, pp. 197–201, and *The World Economy: History and Prospect*, especially pp. 88–92.

14. These forces are traced out in some detail in *The World Economy: History and Prospect*, pp. 247–261.

15. Adam Smith, *The Wealth of Nations* (New York: The Modern Library, 1937), p. 651.

16. For an elaboration of this argument, see *The World Economy: History and Prospect*, Part 6; *Getting from Here to There*, Chapters 4, 5, 6, and 13; *Why the Poor Get Richer and the Rich Slow Down*, Chapter 7; "Latin America Beyond Take-Off," *Americas*, vol. 31, no. 2 (February 19, 1979); and "Working Agenda for a Disheveled World Economy," *Challenge* (March/April 1981).

17. Eugene B. Konecci, "Private/Public Ventures: National Commercialization Act," in Robert Lawrence Kuhn, ed., *Commercializing Defense Related Technology* (New York: Praeger, 1984), p. 59.

18. *Initiatives for Technology Venturing*, formulated by Eugene Konecci, J. R. Kirkland, George Kozmetsky, and Raymond W. Smilor (Austin: IC² Institute, 1984); and *Technology Venturing Data Book*, compiled by Konecci, Smilor, and Kozmetsky (Austin: IC² Institute, 1984).

19. Konecci et al., *Initiatives*, p. 31. The quotation is from Frank Davidson, chairman of the System Dynamics Steering Committee, Sloan School, M.I.T.

20. "Social Expenditures: Erosion or Evolution?" *OECD Observer*, no. 126 (January 1984):3–6. Detailed figures for thirteen countries of government expenditures, including transfer payments as proportions of GDP, are given for 1950, 1960, 1970, and 1977 in Morris Beck, "The Public Sector and Economic Stability," in *The Business Cycle and Public Policy, 1929–1980*, a compendium submitted to the Joint Economic Committee, Congress of the

United States, November 26, 1980 (Washington, D.C.: GPO, 1980), p. 128. Transfer payments as proportions of GDP rise in an arithmetic average for this sample from 10.2 percent in 1950 to 11.3 percent in 1960 to 19.5 percent in 1975 when deceleration or slight absolute decline begins for most countries, including the United States.

# FIVE

# A Perspective on the
# Global Economic Agenda

*With minor modifications, Chapter 5 is an essay presented at a conference at Stanford University on January 24, 1985. As the text indicates, the subject of the conference was U.S.-Mexican investment problems and prospects. My assignment was to put the subject in a global context from a U.S. perspective. Victor Urquidi had a similar assignment from the Mexican side. I used the occasion to reflect on some of the lessons I had drawn from my wife's and my* Wanderjahr *of 1983–1984.*

I

My task here is to help provide a global view to frame the highly detailed and professional question of U.S.-Mexican investment problems and prospects. The global economic issues now discussed everyday within, between, and among governments and in the media are, indeed, important and relevant to our task: for example, debts, interest rates, the dollar exchange rate, growth rate prospects in Western Europe and the United States, protectionism, the future of energy and raw material prices, perverse agricultural policies with different kinds of perversity in both the advanced industrial and developing regions, a peculiarly sterile North-South economic negotiation under United Nation auspices. And, of course, the list could be extended.

Although I shall refer to some of these matters I decided to present a somewhat different, more personal, somewhat eccentric perspective on the global economic agenda. It results from an adventurous year of travel undertaken by my wife and me between July 6, 1983, and July 1, 1984. We visited some thirty-four countries, about a hundred cities, delivered between us some two hundred lectures. We traveled through the Pacific Basin to the Asian mainland, thence to the Middle

East and Mediterranean Europe, and after three months of relative quiet at Oxford, we crisscrossed the continent from Paris to Moscow, Brussels to Budapest, Luxembourg to Izmir, Verona to Uppsala, with a final stop at Wimbledon before returning to Austin. Just about half the countries we visited were in what is called the developing South, the balance in the developed North.

What I shall describe here are four perspectives on the world economy that were somewhat different at the end of the year than they were when we took off from Austin for Honolulu:

- The increasingly explicit awareness in many developing countries that the dynamics of development since the 1950s has yielded an excessive role for government and that a new balance between the public and private sectors must be struck.
- An interest in the emerging new technologies that can properly be described as obsessive in both North and South.
- In the North, a growing awareness that an old economic and political agenda, familiar for a century and more, has run its course; but an equal awareness that no consensus has yet crystallized on a new agenda.
- Finally, out of these and other impressions, I am even more convinced than I was at the beginning of our journey that North-South economic negotiations should be launched on a wholly new basis.

## II

First, then, the state, the private sector, and the role of competitive markets. Let me begin by reading a description I came across during our trip of the situation in one developing country:

> The _____ economy bears the legacy of economic policies dating from the 1950's which were motivated by concern for equity and assistance to the poor. These policies were characterized by price regulation, subsidization of consumer goods, a dominant public sector and state control. Subsequently the government has tried to insulate the average citizen from many of the shocks in the international economy and has not adjusted prices over the years. . . . consumers have not faced world prices for energy or many basic commodities. Both prices and wages of government workers in particular have been held down significantly. As the gap between the market and the administered prices has grown, it has become more and more difficult and costly to maintain the current system.

That particular assessment was written about the Egyptian economy, and I used it to open a discussion of these matters at the National Bank of Egypt. But it applies more or less equally to knotty problems faced in many Latin American countries, in the People's Republic of China, India, and other parts of the developing world. Other problems can be added to the considerable list I read with wide application in the developing regions: for example, agonizingly slow reductions in the birth rate, insufficient domestic competition, and the emergence of "state bourgeoisie" often pursuing interests of their own not necessarily identical with those of the people as a whole.

I do not cite this rather formidable array of problems in a critical or sadistic spirit. On the contrary, my thirty-five years of association with the cause of the developing countries makes the identification of these problems rather painful. Moreover, it is important to note that governments are increasingly willing to talk about the excessive role of the public sector and the need to move in a different direction. During our travels we heard or read of high officials addressing this question in Indonesia, Thailand, China, South Korea, India, Egypt, and Morocco.

The bloated public sector must be viewed as the outcome of a historic complex process. It resulted from the convergence of what might be called technical economic and political forces and certain strongly held attitudes in the developing countries of the 1950s.

On the economic side, developing countries could not earn or borrow, at tolerable rates, sufficient foreign exchange to avoid highly protectionist import substitution policies. Because of these policies there was insufficient competition in domestic markets, and the entrepreneurial spirit of both private and public sectors was dampened. The policy of rationing foreign exchange required that large powerful bureaucracies decide the products to be imported. In many countries this process passed for economic "planning." On the political side, governments, fearing violence from the urban sector, exploited the farmers for the benefit of the city population. This strategy, of course, decreased the farmers' incentives and slowed the growth rate of agricultural production; as a result grain imports were increased at the expense of industrial development.

During the 1950s "capitalism" was an unpopular word whereas "socialism" was a popular word in the developing regions. Political leaders associated capitalism with colonial or quasi-colonial status because it involved an intrusive external power. At the same time considerable sentimental appeal was associated with socialism: Several European social democratic governments were proving successful; Mao

Zedong's Great Leap Forward and Chinese Communist policy in general were superficially appealing; and even Nikita Khrushchev's boast that the USSR would soon surpass the United States in total output seemed credible. On top of this many of the emerging political leaders were intellectuals or soldiers, suspicious of the market process but trustful of the powers of government administration.

I have gone into this brief and incomplete historical analysis of how some of the difficulties of the developing countries came about for the same reason that I shall shortly try to put in historical perspective some of the critical economic problems of the North. There can be, in neither case, a simple, antiseptic economic or technical cure. The solution or serious mitigation of this array of difficulties will require political, social, and institutional change. But in the South, as in the North, the beginning must be a candid recognition of where we are and how we got there.

Obviously, the answer is not and should not be a compulsive Friedmanesque reliance on the market process. But the time has come to examine afresh and skeptically the accumulated economic functions of government and to strike new balances between the public and private sectors—balances that would exploit the potentialities of private enterprise and competitive markets a good deal more than they are exploited at present.

There is a quite particular reason why such a shift of balance is appropriate at the present time. Most of the population in the developing regions now live in economies undergoing the drive to technological maturity. This is the stage beyond take-off when a society progressively demonstrates the capacity to absorb efficiently technologies of increased sophistication over a widening range of sectors. Production diversifies. The whole process is rooted in an increased absorptive capacity resulting from an enlarged corps of well-trained entrepreneurs and an increased proportion of the population with secondary and higher education. This increased pool of entrepreneurs and scientists reflects a truly revolutionary change in the productive potential of the developing regions.

Now, why is this transformation relevant to the public-private sector balance? The answer is that public authorities have proved everywhere peculiarly clumsy and inefficient in managing the production of the highly diversified manufactures characteristic of the drive to technological maturity; and today private entrepreneurs exist in the developing world who are capable of producing diversified industrial products competitively for world markets.

## III

The transformation of the developing societies, as they move through the drive to technological maturity, bears also, of course, on the question of the new technologies.

I had planned, when we left Austin, to spend some of my time in lectures trying to put the new technologies into historical perspective. But as word got about that I had something to say on the subject I was literally forced to lecture in one city after another on "Country X and the Fourth Industrial Revolution." And, I had to learn a good deal as we went along. Broadly speaking, my argument runs as follows.[1] The new technologies embrace the microchip, genetic engineering, the laser, robots, new communication methods, and new industrial materials. Although germinating for some time, the innovational stage of this technological revolution will be dated by historians, I believe, from, roughly, the second half of the 1970s.

I have arbitrarily designated this rather dramatic batch of innovations in the past two hundred years as the Fourth Industrial Revolution. The First Industrial Revolution of the 1780s, dated by innovation rather than invention, embraced factory-manufactured cotton textiles, good iron fabricated with coke, and Watt's more efficient steam engine. The second revolution started in the 1830s and became an extremely large-scale enterprise in Great Britain and the northeastern United States in the 1840s; it was dominated by the railroad, which within a generation induced the invention of cheap mass-produced steel. The third revolution, which began about the turn of the century, was driven by the utilization of electricity, the internal combustion engine, and a new batch of chemicals. In their various elaborations these innovations were in force until the second half of the 1960s, when the leading sectors of the Third Industrial Revolution decelerate markedly.[2]

The Fourth Industrial Revolution is more intimately linked to areas of basic science than were its predecessors, and these areas are themselves undergoing rapid revolutionary change. Thus the scientist has become a critical actor in the drama; and the successful coordination of the scientist, engineer, and the entrepreneur has become crucial to the generation and diffusion of the new technologies. The new technologies themselves are proving ubiquitous, and they are progressively entering into the older basic industries, agriculture, animal husbandry, and forestry, as well as into all sorts of services, including education, medicine, banking, and communications. In different degree, they are proving relevant to the economies of the developing regions, depending on their stage of growth, absorptive capacity, and resource endowments. I would stress that no concept is more misleading than that we are entering a post-industrial age.

The extraordinary range and diversity of the new technologies results, I believe, in another distinctive characteristic. I find it most improbable that any one nation will achieve and sustain across-the-board technological leadership in the Fourth Industrial Revolution or, indeed, leadership in a major area such as microelectronics or genetic engineering or new industrial materials. Each such area represents, in fact, a group of highly specialized and differentiated activities. Given the reasonably even distribution of scientific, engineering, and entrepreneurial talent among the advanced industrial countries—and the similar educational level and skills of their working forces—with the passage of time, specialized comparative advantage is likely to be distributed among a considerable range of countries; and one is likely to see a great deal of cooperation and trade in the new technologies, as well as competition. Indeed, if one examines the pattern of joint ventures across international boundaries and the expanding trade in high technology sectors, the process can already be seen to be under way, despite the somewhat slower start of Western Europe than Japan and the United States in exploiting the new possibilities.

The diffusion of virtuosity in the new technologies will be accelerated by their indirect impact on the developing regions. Over the next decade we are likely to see the new technologies vigorously applied in the motor vehicle, machine tool, steel, textile, and other industries rooted in the longer past. One result of this conversion to high technology along a broad front is that the more advanced developing countries will no longer be able to count on generating increased manufactured exports simply by exploiting their lower money wage rates. There is a lively awareness of this change in prospects in the Pacific Basin because of palpable Japanese progress in applying the new technologies to the older industries. In consequence, there is intense interest among the newly industrialized countries in acquiring the emerging technologies. The Republic of Korea, for example, is gearing its current Five-Year Plan to the rapid absorption of the new technologies, including quite radical changes in education policy.

Each developing country differs, of course, both in the extent to which the new technologies are relevant and in its capacity productively to absorb them. But, in general, potential absorptive capacity is higher than relative per capita levels of real income would suggest.

Consider the case of India, a country with an exceedingly low average real income per capita, conventionally measured. The World Bank calculates 1981 Indian GNP per capita at $260 as compared to $2,250 for Mexico. Nevertheless, the pool of scientists and engineers in India has increased from about 190,000 in 1960 to 2.4 million in 1984; and that pool is sustained by the fact that something like 9 percent of the Indian population aged 20 to 24 is now enrolled in higher education, three times the proportion twenty years earlier. Taken along with the large absolute size of India's population, this means that India is quite capable of assembling the critical mass of scientists and R&D engineers required to solve the kinds of problems increasingly posed by the Fourth Industrial Revolution and its efficient absorption.

The central question is whether Indian society can bring together its scientists, engineers, and entrepreneurs. Although it has accomplished this in the disciplines of atomic energy, space, and agriculture, it has not effected this linkage in many industrial sectors. I would guess that if these linkages began to firm up in one sector after another, the Indian brain drain would begin to reverse.

While the Indian case is rather dramatic, given the country's size and relatively low real income level, I have already noted that the revolutionary expansion of higher education over the past generation is quite typical of the developing world. It will certainly take time for these more advanced developing countries to bring about the partnership of scientists, engineers, and entrepreneurs that the absorption of the Fourth Industrial Revolution requires. (It is, indeed, taking quite a lot of time in Western Europe and the United States.) But I do believe it will happen, and the process will strengthen the diffusion of technological virtuosity within the world economy.

Mexico is in the midst of a revolutionary expansion of its pool of scientists and engineers (see Table 5.1). From 1957 to 1973 the average increase in Mexican graduates in natural science was about 3 percent per year; in engineering, 5 percent. From 1973 to 1981 the comparable figures were 14 percent and 24 percent, respectively. The number of graduates in mathematics and computer science rose from 490 to 1,033 between 1980 and 1981, and a high rate of increase continues. No doubt Mexico's basic problem in incorporating the new technologies will prove to be the effective organization of its human resources rather than a shortage of scientists and engineers.

All this bears directly, I believe, on the narrower issues of U.S.-Mexican investment relations. I shall put my conclusions tersely and bluntly in four propositions because, as you will quickly perceive, I am touching on some large, intensely debated questions.

First, like South Korea and a few other advanced developing countries, Mexico should reorganize its institutions and policies promptly to absorb progressively in all the relevant sectors the technologies emerging as the Fourth Industrial Revolution proceeds. This process

Table 5.1. Graduates in Science and Engineering in Mexico, 1957–1981

| Year | Natural Science | Mathematics and Computer Science | Engineering | Architecture and Urban Planning | Medical Sciences |
|---|---|---|---|---|---|
| 1957 | 389 | —[a] | 987 | —[a] | 1,641 |
| 1960 | 239 | — | 818 | — | 1,320 |
| 1961 | 422 | — | 992 | — | 1,912 |
| 1962 | 506 | — | 1,087 | — | 2,498 |
| 1963 | 586 | — | 1,002 | — | 2,290 |
| 1965 | 374 | — | 1,729 | — | 1,791 |
| 1969 | 463 | — | 2,619 | — | 2,665 |
| 1973 | 665 | — | 2,196 | — | 3,805 |
| 1980 | 1,395 | 490 | 14,272 | 2,384 | 18,051 |
| 1981 | 1,925 | 1,033 | 15,032 | 2,341 | 20,744 |

[a]Data unavailable.

*Sources:* Anuario Estadístico de Mexico, 1960–61; Anuario Estadístico 1981, Asociación Nacional de Universidades e Institutos de Ensenanza Superior (ANUIES); *UNESCO Statistical Yearbook 1964 to 1983.*

will have implications for a wide range of activities from education to tax policy. And, I would underline, it should revolutionize the old manufacturing industries as well as agriculture and services.

Second, the heart of the effort must be, as elsewhere, the linking of Mexico's scientific capacity to its engineering and entrepreneurial capacity. This new kind of partnership is essential not merely to generate contributions to the flow of new technology—which Mexico is quite capable of doing—but also to efficiently absorb new technologies from abroad. (It will be recalled that the wheat strains generated at the Chapingo research station could not be applied simply and automatically in other countries—not even in all parts of Mexico—without creative modification involving the same basic skills that went into creating new strains.) Contrary to much United Nations rhetoric, the heart of technology transfer lies in the scientific, engineering, and entrepreneurial capacity of the recipient country.

Third, do not believe those who argue that the new technologies are skill intensive, capital intensive, and involve no significant infrastructure outlays and will, therefore, not generate many new jobs. Even by the most narrow definition of job generation in the United States—the Standard Industrial Classification—calculating equipment employment (production and servicing) grew from 367,000 in 1972 to 847,000 in 1982, an annual average rate of growth of 4.3 percent. This compares with 690,000 engaged in manufacturing motor vehicles and equipment.

It is often forgotten that those directly engaged in manufacturing constitute only a modest proportion of the employment generated by a given technology. (For motor vehicles in 1972 the proportion was estimated at 16 percent.) The balance appears in various other input manufacturing industries and services. I know of no overall employment estimate for computers; but, as an exercise in casual empiricism, I counted the number of yellow pages in the Austin, Texas, telephone directory devoted to computers—their production, care, and feeding. The number was seventeen pages. Only a few entries represented manufacturing firms. I commend a similar exercise in the Bay area.[3] Statistically, it can have no standing, but it will suggest why a Department of Labor study concluded rather inelegantly, "Computers need an army-sized work-force to keep them armed, loaded and firing. The duties of these troops are so varied that almost any one can find a place in their ranks." The evidence now suggests strongly that the computer revolution, on balance, is substantially expanding employment in the United States.

Finally, it is a profound common interest of the United States that Mexico—and other developing countries—absorb the new technologies in all relevant sectors as fast as they can be efficiently transferred. In bilateral terms this area should be a major dimension of U.S.-Mexican investment cooperation, including in that category investment in education and training.

## IV

While the developing nations search for new balances in their domestic dispositions, and the world economy as a whole struggles to perceive and act on the possibilities and problems posed by the Fourth Industrial Revolution, the six months we spent in Europe impressed on us the fact that the advanced industrial societies of the Atlantic world are in the midst of a difficult historic transition. (One could say much the same for the Soviet Union and Eastern Europe; but, for the moment at least, Japan seems somewhat better geared to deal with the 1980s and 1990s.) Given the intense and inescapable character of North-South interdependence, the character of the transition of the Atlantic world is highly relevant to the developing regions and, quite particularly, to Mexico.

At the latest, the story begins in 1945. At the end of the Second World War the United States consciously accepted the responsibilities for economic leadership, including making large grants and loans to foreign governments. A widespread international consensus supported the U.S. role, and governments accepted domestic responsibility for both employment levels and the expansion of social services.

The circumstances that emerged in the world economy in the early 1970s broke up the consensus on domestic economic policy that followed World War II and acquired legitimacy with the historically unique growth rates of the 1950s and 1960s. No viable successor consensus on domestic economic policy has yet emerged. And it is the lack of an effective consensus on domestic policy in Western Europe and the United States that mainly accounts for the rise of protectionism, distorted real interest rates, precarious debt structures, a grossly overvalued dollar, and other pathological aspects of a disheveled world economy. Specifically, internationl economic policy is likely to remain ineffectual until the Atlantic world learns how to reconcile relatively full employment (and reasonably high and steady growth rates) with control over inflation and how to generate and absorb rapidly the technological possibilities inherent in the Fourth Industrial Revolution.

This judgment stems from a particular view of where the Atlantic world stands in the sweep of modern history. Since the 1870s when Bismarck formulated the first major social legislation, the advanced industrial nations of Western Europe and North America have faced a central issue: How can we build industrial societies that reconcile efficiency in a world of rapidly evolving technologies with the humane values of Western culture? In politics the process often assumed the form of debate and struggle within a zero-sum game that allocated resources between welfare and private consumption and investment, as between the less affluent and more affluent. One of the major achievements of the Western democratic process was that this muted form of class struggle proceeded in relative peace, reaching a culmination in the decades after the Second World War. The proportion of social outlays rose in seven major OECD countries from 14 percent to 24 percent of GDP between 1960 and 1980—a truly revolutionary shift.

Since trees do not grow to the sky, the expansion of social outlays at rates higher even than the extraordinary real growth rates of the 1950s and 1960s was bound to cease eventually. Pressures to contain these outlays increased sharply with the explosion of oil prices, exacerbated inflation, and high unemployment rates of 1974 to 1980. This time recession continued for a further two years, in part due to U.S. domestic economic policy. GDP per capita, which had grown at 3.8 percent per annum from 1950 to 1973 for the advanced industrial countries, decelerated to 2.0 percent for the 1973 to 1979 period, and averaged slightly negative over the next three years. Meanwhile, amidst these setbacks the Fourth Industrial Revolution asserted itself on the world scene with its potentialities, challenges, and dangers for those who lagged in its exploitation.

Clearly, the decision upon the amount to be allocated to social welfare was no longer the central issue of domestic political life in the West. Two strategies appeared necessary to avoid the erosion of the social and physical infrastructure of the advanced industrial countries: the implementation of long-term policies capable of reconciling relatively high rates of growth with control over inflation; and the coordination of scientists and engineers, entrepreneurs and the working force to generate and absorb efficiently the technologies of the Fourth Industrial Revolution. In my view, the former objective requires effective long-term incomes policies as well as a judicious blend of fiscal and monetary policies because incomes policies are essentially political, social, and institutional rather than narrowly economic arrangements.

In other words, the central issue facing advanced industrial countries is shifting their focus from the struggle over the allocation of resources in the welfare state to the development of sustained communal cooperation necessary (i) to reconcile growth and control over inflation and (ii) to find an appropriate role for the new technologies.

## V

I wish I could confidently predict a brisk, efficient passage of the Atlantic world through the transitional process it confronts, just as I would wish to see the developing nations escape quickly from the entrapments of the 1950s to new, more appropriate balances in domestic policy. In the end, each society will have to find its way in terms of its own unique history, institutions, and political processes. But it is important that we understand with historical compassion the difficulty of both transitions, generate a consensus on the appropriate directions of change, and seek to help each other.

And the fact is we could help each other a good deal more than we are now doing. One of the recurrent themes in our travels of 1983 and 1984 was the clash between the palpable intensification of North-South interdependence and the sterility of the New International Economic Order (NIEO) negotiations. In all the developing countries we visited I could not find one government official prepared either to defend those negotiations or to take them seriously. But they are serious, because their existence blocks alternative multilateral efforts to generate the North-South economic partnership solidly based on mutual interests. For example, at Cancun in October 1981 the leaders of the developing countries used their collective political capital to persuade President Ronald Reagan to resume NIEO negotiations rather than to pursue his suggestion that assistance from the North be focused, in part, on helping the South achieve self-sustaining positions in energy and food. In retrospect, it seems clear that it would have been wiser to have gone to work on energy, food, and in other functional areas. There has been no forward movement in North-South multilateral economic negotiations since Cancun.

But the fact that the developing countries, taken as a whole, are in the naturally high-growth stage of the drive to technological maturity has heightened economic interdependence for both sides—that is, the North's dependence on the South and the South's dependence on the North.

As for the North's increased dependence on the South, it can be simply stated: The proportion of the North's exports going to the South has rapidly increased since the early 1970s. For example, the proportion of U.S. exports to developing countries rose from 28 percent in 1972 to 38 percent in 1982. With the rise in the oil price, import dependence also rose from 27 percent of the value of imports from developing countries to 41 percent. And even if the North resumes higher growth rates, I would expect the trend to continue because of the naturally higher growth rates of the South at this stage of history.

The South's increased dependence on the North is reflected in the same figures seen from the South's perspective but also from two further characteristics of their present position and prospects. First, the drive to technological maturity is, as I suggested, the stage when the backlog of existing technologies is being absorbed rapidly over a much wider front than in the past. Most of those new technologies must, for the time being, be drawn from the North. This aspect of dependence has been recently heightened, of course, by the emergence of the Fourth Industrial Revolution. The second increasingly important element in the South's dependence on the North is that as countries move through the drive to technological maturity their case for concessional loans weakens and, not without some withdrawal pains, they become progressively more dependent on international private capital markets for external loans. With that increasing dependence comes the impact of interest rate fluctuations as decreed, among other things, by the domestic economic policies of advanced industrial countries, most notably the United States.

If a vivid demonstration of the reality of North-South interdependence was required, the debt problems of some major developing countries, partially (but only partially) caused by bad economic policies in the North and their playback effects on the northern banking system should suffice.

It is perfectly clear that each side has a large unambiguous interest in the success of the other, but no North-South partnership exists. What might a serious alternative to the NIEO be like? Its large objectives should be to assure supplies of food, raw materials, and energy in the world economy sufficient to support growth over the next several generations of maximum strain between population expansion and resources; to assure that gross environmental degradation is contained and rolled back by reforestation and other measures; and to accelerate the diffusion of the new technologies to the South.

The enterprise might be organized as follows.

1. It should be conducted primarily on a regional basis. The ultimate task is to examine sectoral investment requirements looking a decade or more ahead, and isolating projects to be financed domestically or with foreign private or official resources. This kind of technical activity does not lend itself to global gatherings, which now involve anywhere up to 150 governmental representatives.

2. The regional groups might center, in the Western Hemisphere, around the Organization of American States (OAS) and the Inter-American Development Bank (IADB); in Africa, around the African

Development Bank (AFDB) and the Economic Commission for Africa (ECA); in the Pacific Basin, around the Asian Development Bank (ADB). The World Bank would participate in all the regional enterprises as well as relevant global organizations; for example, the Food and Agriculture Organization (FAO). The United States, Western Europe, and Japan would also participate in the three regional ventures, although their degree of involvement might vary with their respective regional interests. India and China might well prefer, because of their size, to deal with this array of problems via the World Bank (and the kind of consortium arrangements the World Bank has managed) rather than in multilateral committees. But association of the World Bank and the ADB with the work of the recently formed association for South Asian regional cooperation might help move this potentially important grouping from a stage of creative but fragile diplomacy to serious business. And if China chose to work with a Pacific Basin organization, so much the better, so long as a formula was found (as at the Olympic Games) that would also permit the participation of Taiwan.

3. The participants would have to consist primarily of officials who bear serious responsibility domestically for policy toward the sectors under examination, not foreign office experts on United Nations rhetoric and resolutions.

Where appropriate, governments may wish to engage persons from their private sectors in the process.

## VI

The question I asked myself as I came toward the close of this paper was this: Are these four observations generated by a *Wanderjahr* relevant to the task of my hardworking colleagues or merely an ornamental distraction? Of course, only you can decide. But there may be a degree of relevance. Surely, investment possibilities in Mexico could widen if Mexico should decide it had come to a stage in its history when a somewhat different and easier balance between the public and private sectors should be struck; if the United States were to handle its affairs in ways that permitted drastically lower money and real interest rates and a higher noninflationary rate of growth; if Mexico should set about seriously and with vigor to organize its substantial scientific, engineering, and entrepreneurial talent to permit the rapid absorption of the Fourth Industrial Revolution and the United States would systematically cooperate with the venture; and if the United States and Mexico should demonstrate in their bilateral relations—and perhaps, later, in joint diplomatic initiatives—what a sensible North-South partnership for the second half of the 1980s and the 1990s should be like. But, as I say, this is for you to decide.

## NOTES

1. For a typical exposition see *India and the Fourth Industrial Revolution,* Dr. Vikram Sarabhai Memorial Lecture, delivered October 18, 1983 (Ahmedabad: Indian Institute of Management, 1984) [reprinted here as Chapter 7].

2. For further discussion, see W. W. Rostow, *The Barbaric Counter-Revolution: Cause and Cure* (Austin: University of Texas Press, 1983), especially pp. 54–60 and 88–94.

3. I should report that Mrs. Marilyn Smith, one of the organizers of the conference at Stanford, at which this talk was given, took up my challenge and reported the next day on the yellow page computer listings for Silicon Valley. As of March 1984, there were 26 total pages for San Jose and Santa Clara counties, of which wholesale listings and manufacturers filled 1⅔ columns and computer dealers claimed 19 pages. For Los Altos, Mountain View, and Sunningvale counties there were 18 total pages, 1½ columns for wholesalers and manufacturers, and 13 pages for computer dealers. The references included software, installation, repair, graphics, timesharing, etc.

# SIX

# Toward a New Hemispheric Partnership

*I was pleased to be among the nostalgic Latin and North American veterans of the Alliance for Progress who gathered at the Pan American building in Washington, D.C., on the twenty-fifth anniversary of President John Kennedy's March 1961 speech, which had launched the hemispheric venture. But, as my talk (delivered under the auspices of the Center for Advanced Studies of the Americas) argued, the operational agenda for the hemisphere in the next decade would have to differ radically from that of the 1960s if it was to be relevant.*

## I. INTRODUCTION: EIGHT STRANDS OF CONTINUITY

Many of us will, no doubt, observe on this occasion that we must look forward with realism, not backward with nostalgia, if we are to be helpful to the peoples of our hemisphere. After all, the concepts that generated the Alliance for Progress crystallized three decades ago in the 1950s. Here in the mid-1980s, on the basis of what we think we have learned and what we think we can discern over the next generation—we must prescribe for the future—down to, say, the year 2040, more than a half century from now.

The bulk of what I have to say will address the future. But some problems in history are more deeply rooted and slower to yield than others; and some principles, if not eternal, hold for long periods of time. There are, I believe, eight propositions that, with some modification, are just about as valid now in 1986 as they were a quarter century ago when President Kennedy addressed the Diplomatic Corps of the Latin American Republics.

First, the task of development in Latin America is overwhelmingly a task for Latin Americans. At the Punta del Este conference in

120

August 1961 it was roughly calculated that 80 percent of the investment for Latin American development in the 1960s would have to come from Latin America. The proportion turned out to be 90 percent or more. What the United States does or fails to do has been and is likely to remain a marginal factor in the equation of Latin American development, although sometimes a significant marginal factor. In any concerted effort at Latin American development, the United States will be a partner—but inevitably a junior partner.

Second, despite some decline in Latin American birth rates and overall rate of population growth, it will be extremely difficult for the Latin American governments to generate an adequate level of economic and social infrastructure for all their citizens—and jobs for all their working forces—until the rate of population increase is radically reduced. Whether we like it or not, the population problem remains high on the economic and social agenda for most Latin American countries.

Third, Latin economic integration remains as important as we thought it was in the 1950s and 1960s. Progress has been limited, and Latin American nationalism remains mighty resistant. As we shall see, the need to build up and organize critical masses of Latin American scientists and engineers to generate and absorb the technologies of the Fourth Industrial Revolution raises the potential payoff for progress in Latin American integration.

Fourth, there has been considerable progress in generating an expanding flow of diversified exports from certain Latin American countries; but, like its counterpart in the United States, Latin American industry, taken as a whole, still lacks the kind of determined orientation toward the world market that the times ahead demand.

Fifth, inflation is still an unsolved problem in most Latin American countries.

Sixth, Latin America shares a vital security interest with the United States; namely, that no substantial extracontinental military power emplace itself in this hemisphere. This is not a nationalist U.S. reassertion of the Monroe Doctrine. It is the multilateral doctrine of the OAS by which we have, by and large, lived in this hemisphere since 1962—and, indeed, earlier. One result is that Latin American military expenditures in 1980 were just about half the level of any other developing region: 1.5 percent of GNP, as compared to 2.9 percent for Africa; 12.5 percent for the Middle East; 3.6 percent for East Asia; 2.9 percent for South Asia.[1] Unless we continue to cherish this underlying, rarely acknowledged consensus, the hemisphere could easily become a strategic bear pit, with profound degenerative consequences for economic and social progress in Latin America, as well as extremely divisive political effects within our community.

Seventh, despite the great economic and social progress of Latin America over the past quarter century, and its enlarged economic and political ties across both the Atlantic and the Pacific, the areas of authentic common economic interest between the United States and Latin America remain substantial and justify a continued search for an agenda of heightened cooperation. About 35 percent of Latin American exports flow to the United States. If one also takes into account the intense financial interdependencies that exist in the hemisphere, it is clear we are, at this stage of history, locked in partnership. The question is, how wisely will we conduct this inescapable partnership?

Eighth, we badly need in the second half of the 1980s something we achieved for a time in the 1960s—that is, a hemispheric consensus among economists and political leaders on the nature of our common economic agenda and on what we ought to be doing together. The balance of this talk is an effort to contribute to the construction of such a new economic agenda for the generation ahead.

## II. LATIN AMERICA IN THE DRIVE TO TECHNOLOGICAL MATURITY

So much for familiar propositions that still hold.

The first and most basic difference of the present situation from that in 1961 is that Latin America, taken as a whole, is far along in what I call the drive to technological maturity—that is, the post-take-off stage when a country demonstrates the capacity to develop increasingly diversified industries and applies to its agriculture and services, as well as industry, increasingly sophisticated technologies. In most cases this stage is associated with levels of real output per capita that the World Bank designates as "upper middle-income." That is true, for example, of Mexico, Brazil, Argentina, Chile, and Venezuela. Colombia also belongs in this group. I shall first address some of the key present and foreseeable problems of these countries and turn later to the problems of the less advanced countries in the hemisphere.

In 1961 the more advanced countries of Latin America were generally suffering from a deceleration caused by a convergence of two forces: first, a loss of momentum as a take-off based on substitution for imported consumers goods—a strategy forced on Latin America by the Great Depression of the 1930s—reached its natural limits; second, a marked unfavorable shift in the terms of trade after 1951, following almost two decades of relatively favorable terms of trade. Looked at in this way, the Alliance for Progress was a method for helping Latin America bridge the awkward structural transition between the end of take-off and the achievement of high momentum in the drive to technological maturity. And that happened in the 1960s and for most of the 1970s.

But right now a set of forces operating within Latin America and on the world scene has slowed up or brought to a halt the drive to technological maturity. One way to define the task ahead—the task of the re-formed partnership now required—is to generate the hemispheric cooperation necessary to permit Latin America to complete the drive to technological maturity over the next generation.

In my view, that task has the following four dimensions as well as a fifth, which I will discuss later in this chapter.

- A shift in the balance between the public and private sectors in Latin America—a task only Latin Americans can undertake.
- The rapid absorption in Latin America of the technologies of the Fourth Industrial Revolution, a new, large area for cooperation both within Latin America and between Latin America and the United States, as well as with Japan and Western Europe.
- The assurance of adequate supplies of energy, food, and raw materials, as well as protection of the Latin American physical environment—another major potential area for intense hemispheric cooperation.
- Correction of the structural distortions in the U.S. economy, including the achievement of high sustained growth rates, reduced interest rates, and liberal trade policies, which would not only better serve the interests of the people of the United States but are also required to permit the Latin American debt burden to be reduced in an environment of rapid economic and social progress.

## III. SHIFTING THE BALANCE BETWEEN THE PRIVATE AND PUBLIC SECTORS

First, then, the state, the private sector, and the role of competitive markets. The existence of excessively powerful "state bourgeoisie"—pursuing interests that may differ from those of a majority of the citizens—is now acknowledged in every developing region, including the world's two most populous countries, China and India.[2] The phenomenon resulted from the convergence in the 1950s and 1960s of technical, economic, and political forces with certain strongly held attitudes in Latin America and other developing regions.

On the economic front, developing countries were unable to secure sufficient foreign exchange to avoid protectionist import substitution policies. These policies resulted in insufficient competition in domestic markets, discouraging entrepreneurs from both private and public sectors. Because of foreign exchange rationing, large powerful bureaucracies were needed to determine imports. On the political front, developing countries were threatened by fear of rebellion in the volatile cities, and, in effect, they chose policies that exploited the farmer to benefit the urban population. This approach reduced incentives in the agricultural sector and slowed the rate of increase of agricultural production; grain had to be increasingly imported at the expense of industrial development.

In developing regions in the 1950s, socialism, not capitalism, was the popular concept. The peoples of these regions associated capitalism with colonial or quasi-colonial status involving an intrusive external power. In contrast, socialism had considerable sentimental appeal: Some of the European social democratic governments were doing quite well; Mao Zedong's Great Leap Forward and Chinese Communist policy were attractive to those who did not study them deeply; and even Nikita Khrushchev's boast that the USSR would soon outstrip the United States in total output had some credibility. In addition many emerging political leaders were intellectuals or soldiers, types that are inherently suspicious of the market process, and they tended to have exaggerated confidence in the powers of government administration.

The convergence of these problems and attitudes has systematically slowed down economic and social development within Latin America and complicated necessary structural adjustments.

Obviously, the answer to the direction of economic policy is not found in compulsive Friedmanesque reliance on the market process. But countries must now reexamine the economic functions of government and rebalance the public and private sectors in a way that will more thoroughly exploit the potential private enterprise and competitive markets.

There is a particular reason why such a shift of balance is appropriate for Latin America at the present time. As I suggested earlier, most Latin Americans today live in economies developing toward technological maturity. Everywhere public authorities have proved clumsy and inefficient in managing the production of the highly diversified manufactures that characterize this stage of development; yet today's private entrepreneurs in Latin America are capable of producing diversified industrial products competitively for world markets. Such flexible private entrepreneurship is certain to be critically important in the Fourth Industrial Revolution.

## IV. LATIN AMERICA AND THE FOURTH INDUSTRIAL REVOLUTION

At first glance history appears to have played a dirty trick on Latin America as it was moving through the drive to technological maturity. I define that stage in terms of the degree to which a society has efficiently absorbed the pool of then existing technologies. Latin America in the 1960s and 1970s was in the process of learning to exploit efficiently the Third Industrial Revolution: metalworking, the internal combustion engine, electricity, the radio, and television; modern chemicals, including pulp and paper, synthetic fibers, plastics, and pharmaceuticals. Latin Americans had every reason to believe that they were rapidly closing the technological gap with the advanced industrial countries. Then, rather suddenly, a set of new technologies emerged: microelectronics, genetic engineering, the laser, robots, new communication methods, and new industrial materials. Although germinating for some time, the innovational stage of this technological revolution will probably be roughly dated from the second half of the 1970s.

I am inclined to regard this collection of innovations as the fourth such major grouping in the past two centuries. The First Industrial Revolution, which began in the 1780s, was characterized by factory-manufactured cotton textiles, good iron fabricated with coke, and Watt's steam engine. The second revolution began in the 1830s and became a large-scale enterprise in Great Britain and the northeastern United States in the 1840s; within a generation, utilization of the railroad led to the invention of cheap mass-produced steel. The third revolution, which encompassed electricity, the internal combustion engine, and a new batch of chemicals, started in 1900 and continued until the second half of the 1960s.[3]

Some characteristics distinguish the Fourth Industrial Revolution from the preceding three. It is more thoroughly linked to aspects of basic science that are likewise changing rapidly. Thus the scientist has become a critical actor in the revolution; and the successful cooperation of scientist, engineer, and entrepreneur has become crucial to the generation and diffusion of the new technologies. The new technologies themselves are infusing the older basic industries—agriculture, animal husbandry, and forestry—as well as services from education and medicine to banking and communications; and they are proving relevant to the economies of the developing regions to a degree dependent on their stage of growth, absorptive capacity, and resource endowments. In no way are we beginning a post-industrial age.

Because of the extraordinary range and diversity of the new technologies, it is very doubtful that a single nation will sustain technological leadership in the Fourth Industrial Revolution or even in a major area such as microelectronics or genetic engineering. Several highly specialized activities are involved in each major area. Because of the approximately even distribution of scientific, engineering, and entrepreneurial talent among the advanced industrial countries—and the similar educational level and skills of their working forces—a number of countries will likely share specialized comparative advantage; and a great deal of cooperation and trade in the new technologies will develop alongside the competition. Indeed, the pattern of joint ventures across international boundaries and the expanding trade in high technology sectors indicate that the process is already under way, even though its start was slower in Western Europe than in Japan and the United States.

The diffusion of skill in the use of new technologies will be enhanced by their indirect impact on developing regions. During the 1990s the new technologies will probably be vigorously applied in the motor vehicle, machine tool, steel, and textile industries. As a result of this conversion to high technology, the more advanced developing countries will no longer be able to count on generating increased manufactured exports simply by exploiting their lower money wage rates. Countries in the Pacific Basin are aware of this change because of the progress Japan has made in applying new technologies to older industries, and thus newly industrialized countries are very interested in acquiring up-to-date technologies. The Republic of Korea, for example, has incorporated into its current Five-Year Plan strategies by which it can rapidly absorb the new technologies, including radical changes in education policy. Latin America also should move in this direction.

Although developing countries differ in the relevancy of the new technologies, their absorptive capacities are generally higher than one might guess.[4] Because of major increases in the student population in secondary and upper-level schools between 1960 and 1981, the productive potential and technological absorptive capacity of the developing regions have experienced a revolutionary change.

For example, the World Bank calculated that in India—a country with an exceedingly low average real income per capita—the 1981 GNP per capita was $260 as compared to $2,250 for Mexico. Nevertheless, the number of scientists and engineers in India has increased from about 190,000 in 1960 to 2.4 million in 1984. That number is expected to be sustained because approximately 9 percent of Indian people aged 20 to 24 are now enrolled in higher education, three times the proportion twenty years ago. These figures, along with the large absolute size of India's population, mean that India has the capacity to assemble the scientists and R&D engineers necessary to solve the problems posed by the Fourth Industrial Revolution.

In a contrasting case, Mexico recorded from 1957 to 1973 an annual average increase in natural science graduates of about 3 percent; in engineering graduates, 5 percent. From 1973 to 1981 the comparable figures were 14 percent and 24 percent, respectively. The number of graduates in mathematics and computer science rose from 490 to 1,033 between 1980 and 1981. No doubt Mexico's basic problem with respect to the new technologies wil be the effective organization of its human talent rather than an absolute shortage of scientists and engineers.

All this bears directly on the appropriate agenda for future cooperation in the hemisphere on the issue of technology. First, Latin America should accelerate the reorganization of its institutions and policies—which is already beginning to happen—to absorb progressively in all the relevant sectors the emerging technologies. This process has implications for a wide range of activities from education to tax policy. And it should revolutionize the old manufacturing industries as well as agriculture and services. In the course of this effort, the considerable potentialities for intra–Latin American cooperation in science and technology should be exploited.

Second, the effort must focus on coordinating the capacities of Latin America's scientists with those of its engineers and entrepreneurs. This new kind of partnership is necessary not only to produce new technological advances but also to absorb new technologies generated elsewhere.

Finally, the United States and Latin America share an interest that Latin America absorb the new technologies in all relevant sectors as fast as possible. This process will enlarge trade within the hemisphere and strengthen the social and political bonds that need to be nurtured in years to come. The United States—both public and private sectors—should include in that cooperative effort intensified assistance to Latin America in education and training for the new technologies.

## V. ENSURING THE RESOURCE BASE
## FOR LATIN AMERICAN DEVELOPMENT

In 1980 I had the privilege of serving with a group of OAS appointed experts in an effort to define a hemispheric effort at cooperation for the 1980s.[5] Our chairman was Felipe Herrera. As in the Inter-American Committee on the Alliance for Progress (CIAP) in the 1960s, I was in my favorite role: the only gringo among a group of distinguished Latin Americans. Our deliberations occurred in the midst of the second great surge in oil prices, a time of powerful inflationary pressure. We devoted a good deal of our report to the need for enlarged investment in energy, food, raw materials, and the protection of the environment.

Right now, as we all know, oil prices are falling, as are most prices of agricultural products and raw materials. An important question is whether that downward trend will continue as it did from 1951 to the mid-1960s.

One can argue, for example, that the 1979 to 1980 doubling of the oil price was a grossly excessive response to the loss of Iranian oil exports; that the oil cartel is irretrievably shattered; that enormous reserves that are cheap to exploit exist in the Middle East, notably in Saudi Arabia; and that habits of conservation are now deeply ingrained in the oil importing areas. One can also argue that vast stockpiles in the United States and Western Europe overhang the agricultural markets; that China and India have moved successfully to increase domestic output and to reduce imports; and that other developing countries are likely to follow their lead. As for raw materials, a whole range of substitutes are proliferating—optical fibers, plastics, ceramics—likely to break the link between industrial output and certain older raw materials, e.g., copper, steel, aluminum.

On the other hand, one can argue that the interest of oil producers in preventing a free fall in the oil price is great; the fall itself is rendering a good deal of marginal production unprofitable. It is still to be demonstrated whether India and China have achieved a steady long-term upward trend or a remarkable short-term lift in the level of agricultural output. Above all we must take into account, on the demand side, that real output in the world economy since 1979 has averaged only about half its trend growth rate in the 1950s and 1960s.

The fact is that even with the most sophisticated computers and a vast array of equations, we economists are exceedingly poor at predicting.

With two exceptions, I would commend only the prospects for agricultural and raw material prices as an area for concerted study in the hemisphere, commodity by commodity. The two exceptions— where concerted action based on a hemispheric consensus would be useful—are with respect to oil and the physical environment.

For oil and oil substitutes, the lead times for investment are so long that an alternative to a fractured producers cartel should be explored (see Figure 6.1). It remains to be seen whether producers and consumers can be brought together to agree on long-term stable or slowly changing prices, sufficient to generate drilling for the replacement of oil reserves (or increased capacity in oil substitutes). These prices should not be so high as to produce the grotesque and costly oscillations that we have experienced since 1973, however.

With respect to the physical environment, it is time for a concerted effort throughout the hemisphere—North and South—to check and roll back gross environmental degradation. This is primarily, of course, a task for each nation. But the governments would each be strengthened in undertaking national programs of this kind, if their action was part of a hemispheric enterprise. Some of the tasks are inherently international, and investment support from the World Bank, the IADB, and U.S. aid programs would be appropriate.

## VI. THE INESCAPABLE RESPONSIBILITY OF THE UNITED STATES

In international affairs it is generally unprofitable to spend much time allocating blame for how one has gotten into a mess if the common objective is to get out of it as soon as possible. In any case, there is usually an ample supply of blame to be shared—as with the current debt problem in the hemisphere.

But it is a critically important fact that the United States has conducted an economic policy since 1979—primarily for domestic reasons—that has gravely complicated the development tasks of Latin America. Specifically, it has kept real interest rates higher than they should have been, slowed down the growth rate in the world economy, generated enormous fiscal and balance of payments deficits, the latter resulting from a grossly overvalued dollar; and it has stimulated, despite a continued flow of free trade rhetoric, important protectionist barriers. I would underline, however, the unpredicted impact of U.S. domestic economic policy on the dollar has constituted a significant countervailing subsidy to exports from certain Latin American countries—for example, Brazil—to the United States.

Right now the United States, with some cooperation within the OECD, is seeking to correct these costly distortions. Everyone would like what is called a "soft landing"—that is, gradual reductions in the U.S. fiscal deficit, the trade deficit, the overall balance of payment deficit, interest rates, and in the value of the dollar. All of this needs to be conducted in an environment of low inflation rates, an expanding U.S. economy, and liberalized trade, with Latin American debt burdens eased by lowered interest rates and expanded exports. Such a soft

130

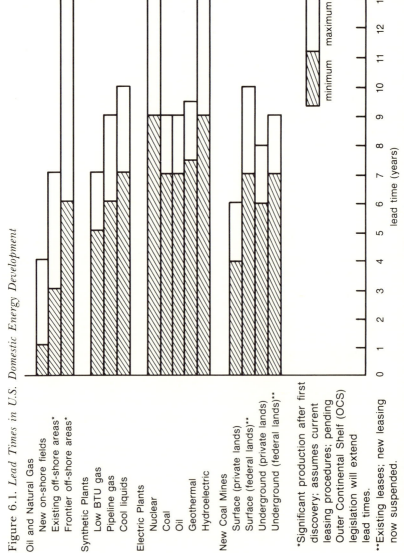

Figure 6.1. *Lead Times in U.S. Domestic Energy Development*

Oil and Natural Gas
New on-shore fields
Existing off-shore areas*
Frontier off-shore areas*

Synthetic Plants
Low BTU gas
Pipeline gas
Cool liquids

Electric Plants
Nuclear
Coal
Oil
Geothermal
Hydroelectric

New Coal Mines
Surface (private lands)
Surface (federal lands)**
Underground (private lands)
Underground (federal lands)**

*Significant production after first discovery; assumes current leasing procedures; pending Outer Continental Shelf (OCS) legislation will extend lead times.

**Existing leases; new leasing now suspended.

minimum  maximum

0 1 2 3 4 5 6 7 8 9 10 11 12 13
lead time (years)

*Source:* Modified from National Academy of Engineering (1973) and U.S. Geological Survey (1975) by Bureau of Economic Geology, University of Texas at Austin.

landing is not impossible to envisage. But, if it is to be sound, it must begin with a determination among the people of the United States to pay our way at home, to pay our way abroad, and to meet our responsibilities to the world community. We have done none of these things since 1979. And no future hemispheric partnership will be worth a damn unless the U.S. political system faces up to these homely tasks.

## VII. OUR COMMON RESPONSIBILITIES TO THE WEAKER ECONOMIES IN THE HEMISPHERE

I turn now to the fifth item on my proposed hemispheric agenda: concerted, patient, long-run assistance to the weaker economies in the hemisphere. It is one thing to create a partnership that will accelerate the movement of Latin American countries through the drive to technological maturity; it is quite a different kind of task to see what can be done to assist, say, Haiti in its frustrated efforts at modernization, or to design long-term policies that would permit the Caribbean islands or the small countries of Central America to establish viable roles in the hemispheric economy. These are difficult problems. If they were easy, they would have long since been solved. They are, moreover, problems to whose solution the more advanced countries of Latin America can greatly contribute, out of their own hard-won experience.

For reasons with which I shall not burden you, I have been engaged lately in a review of theories of economic growth generated over the past two-and-a-half centuries. As an economist, I have been proud to see that, from the very beginning, a revolt against the dehumanizing consequences of poverty has been the dominant theme and driving force in our profession. As more and more developing countries move through take-off and beyond, they should join in the effort to bring forward those who face special difficulties of one kind or another. In that reaching back, the more advanced Latin American countries have an opportunity to show the way.

## VIII. THE HEMISPHERIC TASK IN A LARGER PERSPECTIVE

Let me conclude by switching from the role of a former public servant, recommending an operational five-point policy for the future, to the perspective of the academic historian and economist I am pleased, in fact, to be.

If one pulls back the camera and tries to put in perspective the extraordinary story of our hemisphere since the Napoleonic Wars broke the back of colonialism in Latin America, what do we see? We see almost two centuries of effort, by the countries that emerged from colonialism, to modernize their societies in ways consistent with their complex cultural inheritances. Along the way we see an array of social and political problems that had to be solved—different in each country but usually difficult and slow to resolve. The existence of these overriding noneconomic problems postponed the coming of modern industrialization. For most of Latin America, in fact, the take-off began only fifty years ago, in the 1930s—about a century after the take-off of the United States. We are all aware of the urgency of the debt situation and other current problems that have damped the momentum of Latin American progress. But, looking back to the 1930s, Latin American economic and social progress has been extraordinary; and looking ahead, I, at least, do not doubt that in technological virtuosity as well as income per capita Latin America, taken as a whole, will continue to narrow the gap with the advanced industrial regions of the world economy.

I believe that within our hemisphere as well as in the Pacific Basin it will gradually become clear that the great common task in, say, the next half century will be to make the mutual adjustments required as late-comers to modern economic growth move toward economic and technological parity with the early-comers, e.g., the United States and Canada. The countries in this hemisphere should also work to preserve a system of open communication within the community of industrial, civilized nations. This spirit—which John Kennedy brought to the Alliance for Progress—should permeate the new phase of cooperation that our interdependence and common interests require.

## NOTES

1. *World Military Expenditures and Arms Transfers, 1971–1980* (Washington, D.C.: U.S. Arms Control and Disarmament Agency, March 1983), pp. 35–36.

2. The phrase is quoted in William P. Glade, "Economic Policy-making and the Structures of Corporation in Latin America," offprint ser. no. 208 (Austin: Institute of Latin American Studies, University of Texas at Austin, 1981).

3. For further discussion, see W. W. Rostow, *The Barbaric Counter-Revolution: Cause and Cure* (Austin: University of Texas Press, 1983), especially pp. 54–60 and 88–94.

4. I should like to take the occasion to call the reader's attention to a series of articles by Simón Teitel bearing on the extremely important but little studied question of technical change in what he called "semi-industrialized

countries" and I would call countries in the drive to technological maturity. Teitel's papers, originally published in various economic journals, are helpfully reprinted in the Inter-American Development Bank Reprint Series. They include "Towards an Understanding of Technical Change in Semi-Industrialized Countries," reprint ser. no. 118 (1981); "Creation of Technology Within Latin America," no. 120 (1981); "Tecnología, Industrialización y Dependencia," no. 125 (1981); "Indicadores Científico-Tecnológicos: la América Latina, paises industrializados y otros paises en vía desarrollo," no. 139 (1985); "Technology Creation in Semi-Industrial Economies," no. 150 (1984).

5. Our report was entitled "Hemispheric Cooperation and Integral Development," presented to the Secretary General of the Organization of American States, July 14, 1980.

# SEVEN

# India and the
# Fourth Industrial Revolution

*This chapter is based on the Vikram Sarabhai Memorial Lecture delivered on October 18, 1983, at the Indian Institute of Management in Ahmedabad. Sarabhai was a remarkable Indian scientist, engineer, and entrepreneur.*

*As I have already noted, the new technologies proved to be an almost obsessive subject of interest in 1983–1984 when my wife and I traveled to some thirty-four countries in twelve months. I was asked to give a good many talks like this, attempting to relate my notions about the Fourth Industrial Revolution to particular countries. I believe I learned a good deal from those exercises.*

*I might add that the courtyard of the Indian Institute of Management, where I delivered this lecture at dusk, with birds scudding about overhead and students on the balconies, was as graceful and benign a setting as I had ever encountered.*

### I

I was given this morning a packet of materials bearing on the remarkable and luminous man whose memory we honour this evening. It included pieces about him and his career as well as extracts from his own statements. I was transfixed when I came across the following observation:

The primary task of fundamental research is to discover, of Research and Development is to optimize, and of industry to produce; and one of the main problems faced in the organization of innovative institutions or establishments is to link these three cultures and to provide a basis by which transfer of knowledge of men and technology can proceed from one step to another interacting freely and benefiting one another.

Sarabhai's thesis about the need to link the "three cultures", articulated before his death more than a decade ago turns out to be my central theme tonight.

## II

I shall begin the elaboration of that theme with an observation about economic theory. From Adam Smith to contemporary mainstream economists, theorists have been schizophrenic in dealing with technology. On the one hand, in a part of their minds, they have understood that the flow of new technology is fundamental to economic progress. On the other hand, they could not figure out how to deal with that flow in a realistic and useful way. They have tended, therefore, to set it aside or deal with technical change in a highly abstract or over-aggregated way.

Adam Smith, for example, enunciated one of the abiding grand themes of dynamic economic analysis when he contrasted the prospects for diminishing returns to agriculture with the prospects for increasing returns to manufactures. The theme has recurred periodically down to the Limits to Growth debate of recent years. But *The Wealth of Nations* was completed in 1776 without the author being aware that in textiles and iron-making major inventions were being transformed into powerful innovations, and down in the basement of his own Glasgow University a tool-maker was making revolutionary improvements in the steam engine. Adam Smith missed the fact that the First Industrial Revolution was about to happen. His most important proposition bearing on manufactures related not to new technology but the potentialities of specialization with existing technology in the face of a widened market.

There are two abiding reasons for the discomfiture of mainstream economists with technological change. First, such change does not take place in GNP or a broad aggregate like Adam Smith's agriculture or manufactures. It occurs in particular narrow sectors. Such sectoral changes may—and often do—have a significant impact on a broader aggregates; but that is just the problem. Our conventional division between macro- and micro-economics provides no satisfactory and systematic method for linking the two domains. The second source of difficulty is that, for more than two centuries, economic theory has mainly regarded technological change as exogenous. Taking these two weaknesses together, we emerge with an aggregate capital-output ratio arbitrarily inserted in Harrod-Domar or neo-classical growth models; Solow's black-box "residual"; calculations for "additions to knowledge" in the productivity studies of Denison and John Kendrick.

I raise these large questions because, for our purposes, I take the generation and diffusion of innovations to be a complex sectoral process, endogenous to the workings of the economic system. But I would add a Marshallian *caveat*. Alfred Marshall, more than any of his predecessors or successors, was extremely sensitive to the meaning for formal economic theory of technological change. Quite particularly, he perceived that the case of increasing returns rendered impossible the definition of stable equilibrium in micro-economics and plunged the analyst into the dynamic but dishevelled world of "organic growth" in which all dimensions of a society were in play. This is one major reason Marshall, one of the best mathematicians among economists, took so limited a view of the usefulness of mathematics in economics. It is ironic that he should be best remembered for his formulations of the short period which he regarded as a limited and inadequate introduction to the subject.

## III

In any case, the implications I would draw for India (and other countries) of the group of innovations I define as the Fourth Industrial Revolution depend on three departures from conventional mainstream economics: innovation is viewed as an endogenous interacting process, engaging all of Sarabhai's three cultures in the spectrum from basic science to production; the spectrum embraces aspects of a society's performance beyond the economic system, narrowly defined; and, although the analysis takes its start in the particular sectors where innovation occurs, it attempts, in the end, to suggest the broad consequences for the economy as a whole of technological change.

So much by way of introduction. Now: is the concept of a Fourth Industrial Revolution justified? The answer is: more or less. The notion should be taken seriously, but not too seriously.

I include in the Fourth Industrial Revolution innovations in micro-electronics, communications, the offshoots of genetics, the laser, robots, and new synthetic materials. There are elements of both over-simplification and reality embedded in the notion that innovations come in groups which justify the designation of a sequence of definable industrial revolutions.

All innovations, clearly, do not come in such grand clusters. To start at the less glamorous end of the spectrum, a great deal of invention and innovation of great importance has gone on since the

1780s which consists of incremental improvements in existing technologies. Some of these incremental improvements find their way into patent records, many do not. The rates of productivity increase we observe in history are significantly determined by this kind of endemic, incremental invention and innovation. The path of refinement by small steps is subject to diminishing returns, as particular technologies age and potentialities for improvement decline.

Second, innovations of varying significance, creating new industries, large and small, are initiated, in modern time, over a wide front; and they are by no means all related to each other. One authority has identified, for example, 17 substantial innovations, rooted in technologies and processes known before 1914, which played an important part in the relatively depressed inter-war years, between say 1920 and 1939. They range from aircraft to ball bearings to more efficient office machinery and canning methods.

I would underline that I am talking here not about inventions but about innovations; that is, the actual introduction of an invention into the economic system on a cost-effective basis. I have little confidence that inventions can be satisfactorily dated or that such dates tell us a great deal. If one presses hard one is soon back in Leonardo's notebooks, the Sung Dynasty, mediaeval India, Greece or Rome.

A more recent study lists 62 innovations for the period 1920–1970. They range from the zip fastener, the ballpoint pen, and cinerama to electronic digital computers, DDT, and synthetic fibres.

But economic historians and some economists have recognized that, in addition, there have been, before out time, three giant innovational clusters: factory manufactured textiles, Cort's method for making iron from coke, and Watt's steam engine, all of which came on stage in a substantial way in Britain of the 1780s; then the railroads, making considerable commercial headway in the 1830s but generating substantial booms in Britain, the American Northeast, and Germany in the 1840s and leading on to the revolution in steel making in the 1870s; finally, electricity, a new batch of chemicals, and the internal combustion engine. These became significant round about the opening of the 20th century and, in its various elaborations, carried economic growth forward through the 1960s in the advanced industrial countries. This grouping of innovational giants has still a good deal to commend it, although it is, of course, highly over-simplified.

Since the dating of the initiation of these clusters is arbitrary, one could adjust them to say, a 60 or 70 year periodicity; but I do not believe there is a rational reason to assume a uniform rhythm for such grand innovational cycles.

There is, I suspect, more willingness to accept the notion that we are now passing through a powerful technological transformation in the world economy than there was, for example, in the mid-1970s. When I was writing a book on policy at that time, called *Getting from Here to There*, I found a considerable literature which argued that diminishing returns had, at long last, set in for man's creativity. Analysts of this bent concluded, much as some economists concluded in the 1930s, that the advanced industrial countries had come to a time of secular stagnation. I devoted two chapters in my book to investigating that proposition, concluding that it was not valid. But it even found its way into the Brandt Commission Report *North-South*. The case for mass transfers from North to South was, you will recall, argued, in part, on the grounds that the North lacked adequate investment opportunities to generate full employment and, therefore, massive transfers to the South which would stimulate the North's export industries were required to achieve full employment.

There is, of course, considerable debate and difference of view about long run employment prospects in the North; but I doubt that it would be widely argued, as we move into the mid-1980s, that mankind's scientific and technological creativity had waned. On the contrary, one major fear—which I do not share—is that the new technologies of the Fourth Industrial Revolution will cause high chronic unemployment.

I should note, however, that all analysts do not look at these matters as I do. Some would not accept my designation of the new technologies as the Fourth Industrial Revolution. For example, Christopher Freeman of Sussex would designate plastics, synthetic fibres, and the early rounds of computers as the Fourth Industrial Revolution and judge that phase of innovation to have decelerated since the late 1960s.

I am more inclined to treat plastics and synthetic fibres in continuity with the chemical revolution proceeding since the early years of the 20th century. We agree that deceleration occurred and when; but his writing does not yet recognize a new innovational wave under way. I cite these differences not to criticize Freeman, whose work I greatly respect, but to underline the element of arbitrariness at work in trying to make shape of the flow of innovations over long periods.

Another difference enters on the question of whether there has been a true cycle operating to produce waves or clusters of innovations. As I noted, it is not difficult to adjust the dates to produce a periodicity of 60–70 years. And one serious student of the subject, Gerhard Mensch, has advanced the hypothesis that periods of acute depression generate an environment of inventive creativity which results in a concentrated innovational surge in the next period of expansion. A

Figure 7.1. *The Four Industrial Revolutions*

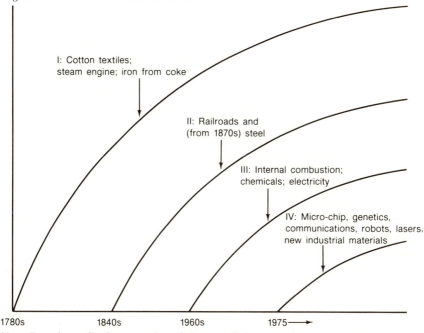

I: Cotton textiles;
steam engine; iron from coke

II: Railroads and
(from 1870s) steel

III: Internal combustion;
chemicals; electricity

IV: Micro-chip, genetics,
communications, robots, lasers,
new industrial materials

1780s     1840s     1960s     1975——▶

Note: For a less stylized presentation of these predictions see Figure 2.1 in Chapter 2.

number of economists and historians, including myself, do not believe this hypothesis is theoretically or historically well grounded. But, again, I cite it not to argue one position against another but to suggest that the analysis of historical and current patterns of innovation is a lively and contentious field—certainly livelier than it has been for a half century or so.

## IV

I turn now to three general characteristics of the Fourth Industrial Revolution, as I perceive it, all of which, if I am correct, are relevant to India.

First, rather more than most of the industrial revolutions of the past, this one is closely linked to areas of basic science which themselves are rapidly evolving. This is one reason that Sarabhai's dictum I quoted earlier is so germane. When Watt produced his steam engine with a separate condenser, Cort his method for making iron, and various characters made it possible, up to a point, to match the skill of Indian hands with machines in British factories, those devices could be progressively refined and rendered more efficient in small increments by skilled mechanics and engineers on the job. The users of these machines did not have to turn to basic scientists to solve their problems. And so it was with the railroad, most aspects of pre-1914 steel and metal-working, and, even, the internal combustion engine. It is clearly not the case with genetic engineering, the forthcoming rounds of computers, and other dimensions of the Fourth Industrial Revolution. The fate of particular sectors and even whole national economies is likely to depend substantially in the generation ahead on success or failure in bringing into firm and steady partnership the domains of basic science, R&D engineering, and entrepreneurship.

A second characteristic of the Fourth Industrial Revolution is that it seems fated to be ubiquitous. It is likely to transform—indeed, it is already beginning to transform—the older basic industries. I would guess that in the advanced industrial countries motor vehicles, machine tools, even steel itself will be high-tech industries in a quite thorough-going way in a decade or so. But the new technologies will equally suffuse agriculture, forestry, and animal husbandry; and, as is already observable, they will have revolutionary effects on a wide range of services: communications and medical care, education and banking. Some believe the effects of the new technologies on communications will be so powerful as to constitute, in effect, a transport revolution; that is, the transmittal of information may substantially substitute for the movement of people.

A third characteristic of the new technologies is that in different degree, they are and will increasingly be relevant to all the developing countries. As we all know, what we call developing countries cover an enormous spectrum not only in levels of real income per capita but also, and more significantly, in their capacities to absorb efficiently the pool of existing and emerging technologies. Nevertheless, the Fourth Industrial Revolution is relevant even at the lower end of the development spectrum; for example, a good many countries in Africa south of the Sahara. There, aspects of the new technologies that bear on agriculture, forestry, animal husbandry, and communications, as well, of course, as medical care will be immediately applicable. At the other end of the spectrum, a country like South Korea has pretty well absorbed the technologies of the Third Industrial Revolution. Talking in Seoul, just before coming here to India, I said that I would guess that by the end of the 1980s South Korea would have pretty well completed the absorption of steel, heavy as well as light engineering, chemicals and the early forms of electronics; and it would have to move rapidly to high-tech status to maintain its momentum. But most of the population of the developing world lives in societies which I would define as in the midst of the drive to technological maturity; and they are likely to be in an intermediate position with respect to the new technologies.

## V

The drive to technological maturity, you may recall, is, in my vocabulary, the post take-off stage during which a society generates the capacity to move out beyond the sectors which lead the way in take-off—usually incorporating fairly simple technologies, applied rather unevenly with respect to regions—and come to absorb efficiently the whole pool of existing technologies relevant to its particular mix of natural resources. It is, to put it simply, the time when modern technology, in all its complexity and diversity, is gradually absorbed throughout an economy. The drive to technological maturity reflects the widening pool of scientists, engineers, and entrepreneurs as well as the rising skill of an increasingly literate and well-trained working force. In the pre-1914 world the take-off usually took about 20 years; the drive to technological maturity, about 60. In the post-1945 era it has proved possible to transit those stages more swiftly in some societies. For example, in South Korea, I would guess, they went through both stages in about a third of the typical pre-1914 time.

For our purposes, however, the point is that a country in the midst of the drive to technological maturity—and that is clearly where India now stands—will be concerned simultaneously with bringing some sectors and regions forward in terms of technologies of the Third (or even earlier) Industrial Revolutions while also establishing which of the new technologies are relevant, in what sectors, and proceeding to absorb them. For some time, then, we can continue to expect India to present the spectacle of a society co-existing somehow—sometimes confortably, even gracefully, sometimes awkwardly—with a full spectrum of technologies from the most ancient to the most modern. That is precisely what one expects to see in a large country undergoing the drive to technological maturity.

But there is an important complexity here: Economies do not evolve by repeating in a simple, straightforward way the technological history of societies that entered take-off earlier. Technological leap-frogging is possible and going on every day. For example, many developing nations of the 20th century did not repeat the history of the railway age, including the electric tramway. They moved into the age of the motor truck and motor bus permitting much more flexible movement of goods and people. Looking to the future, should our genetic scientists and engineers learn how to fix nitrogen for many plants from the air, in a cost-effective way, the results would be promptly useful in agriculture everywhere.

There is another related complexity, that is, when will an older technology serve well as an "appropriate" technology, and when must a developing country move immediately to one of the new emerging technologies. The object, of course, is to save scarce capital, to employ a maximum of the work force, and to exploit in international competition the comparative advantage bestowed by cheap but competent labour. But what if the application of the new technologies permits the advanced industrial countries to revive the competitive position of industries that seemed destined to move quite naturally to the developing regions? That, I can tell you, is a fear that I found throughout developing Asia. We do not yet know the extent to which that fear is justified. We are talking about possible quantitative changes in relative costs without any knowledge or very good feel for the numbers. But the point I am raising has two implications. First, it is possible that a developing country will wish to introduce a sophisticated technology earlier than it might have earlier thought rational in order to counter its use elsewhere and to preserve its comparative advantage derived from lower labour costs. Second, the possible relevance of this point suggests that, if we can induce our economists to take technology seriously, and free themselves from the not very helpful formulations of Western mainstream economics, we need them in the partnerships that must also embrace scientists, engineers, and entrepreneurs.

## VI

Now, what more narrowly can one say about India's prospects with respect to the Fourth Industrial Revolution?

First, it must be said bluntly that India's relatively slow rate of growth will reduce its capacity to make the most of the new technologies. A society experiencing a high marginal capital-output ratio, low capacity utilization, an excessive brain drain, and the other familiar ills of the Indian economy is unlikely to be voracious or even very quick off the mark in absorbing new technologies. In the 13 days I have been in India, I have discovered that the analysis of these and other economic and political problems is a major national sport pursued with a knowledge and sophistication I certainly do not command. From my perspective—that of a development economist and friend, observing your vicissitudes and triumphs from a long distance for more than 30 years—I would say that Indian progress since the First Five-Year Plan has been palpable. It is to be observed not only—or even mainly—in the aggregate data of real GNP per capita. Progress of a kind never before known in Indian history is to be seen in the lengthening of human life; the expansion of educational opportunity; the drawing of first-rate talent to the private sector; a remarkable diversification of manufactures. Since the late 1960s India has also moved to render itself, for the time being at least, self-sustaining in food suplies even if at lower nutritional levels than we would all wish to see. Given the rate of population increase this has been a quite remarkable achievement. And in what I have often said was the greatest social science miracle of the third quarter of the 20th century, India has done these things while maintaining, aside from the Emergency, a working democracy.

We are all aware of the other side of the balance sheet: an agonizingly slow decline in birth rates; the excessively intrusive role of the state, inappropriate to the increasing diversity of the Indian economy and the rising level of entrepreneurship in the private sector; excessive protectionism and insufficient domestic competition. But all these familiar issues and others daily debated in every part of this highly articulate society are not my business today. My only point here is that the existence of these unresolved problems and the retardation they impose on the Indian economy will slow down the effective absorption of the Fourth Industrial Revolution in much the same way, I might add, as the slow average growth of the American economy in recent years is having the same consequence in the United States.

Nevertheless, the absorption of the Fourth Industrial Revolution has already begun in India; and I have not the slightest doubt that it will proceed. Aside from the rate of growth of the economy as a whole and the pace at which certain structural and institutional problems are solved or mitigated, the pace of absorption will depend on how wisely the public and private sectors deploy India's greatest asset; that is, its large pool of scientists, engineers, and increasingly skillful and adventurous entrepreneurs.

If I am correctly informed, the pool of scientists and engineers in India has increased from 190,000 in 1960 to 1.78 million in 1980. Some Indians have argued that this astounding almost ten-fold increase has not been sustained without a loss of quality. This is a matter I can not assess; but I am sure that India's technical capacity to absorb the new methods and devices is high. And it is backed by another rather extraordinary quantitative fact. About nine per cent of the relevant age group in India is enrolled in higher education, about three times the percentage for any other country in South Asia. The proportion of these students enrolled in natural sciences, engineering, and medical science is also much higher than the regional average.

Taken along with the large absolute size of India's population what this means is that India is quite capable of assembling the critical mass of scientists and R&D engineers required to solve the kinds of problems increasingly posed by the Fourth Industrial Revolution and its efficient absorption.

In short, I suspect India's central problem is not the size or quality of its pool of scientists and engineers. The central question is whether India can achieve, over a wide range of sectors, the bringing together in partnership of Sarabhai's three cultures which has already happened in a few sectors. It has happened in India in atomic energy, space, and, to a significant degree, in agriculture. The linkage has not been effectively made in a good many industrial sectors. The same, incidentally, can be said about the United States. The United States is suffering considerable competitive difficulty in some older industrial sectors where, for historically explicable reasons, the link between R&D and entrepreneurship was not sustained; e.g., motor vehicles, steel, machine tools. On the other hand the United States continues to do rather well in three sectors which arose out of laboratories and where the linkage between science, engineering, and management has remained close and interactive; i.e., chemicals, aerospace, and electronics. The same unevenness in sectoral performance, stemming from effective linkage of the three domains or failure of linkage, can be observed in the economies of Western Europe, the Soviet Union, and the People's Republic of China.

On this matter I conclude that India's fate in the Fourth Industrial Revolution is likely to depend heavily on how well it brings together Sarabhai's three cultures in the various sectors; that India has already demonstrated in a few sectors that it knows how to do this; and that it commands a sufficiently large pool of scientists, engineers, and entrepreneurs to be effective. Indeed, I would guess that if these linkages began to firm up in one sector after another, the Indian brain drain would begin to reverse.

As an economic historian I confess I derive a certain satisfaction from the emergence of this three-way linkage as critical to the world economy over the next several generations; for it was the formation of this linkage in the late 17th and 18th centuries that explains the coming of the First Industrial Revolution; and, in my view at least, it was certain aspects of British society of that era that made the linkage there particularly close, that helps explain why Britain (rather than, say, France) was the first country to experience an industrial revolution. I shall elaborate this point a little because, in the end, it leads to a challenge I shall lay before the Indian Institute of Management and its Director.

Briefly, what happened is that the scientific revolution, building momentum for two centuries after Copernicus, came to a kind of climax with the publication of Newton's *Principia*. Few read it, but the notion, articulated even earlier, that the physical world was knowable in terms of relatively few fixed laws and was capable of systematic manipulation to man's advantage, spread rapidly. Thus Charles II was induced to form the Royal Society and Colbert induced Louis XIV to form the French Academy. Both institutions were caught up with invention as well as science in some purer sense; but the Royal Society contained a particularly rich blend of scientists, gadgeteers, and businessmen. But even more important were the regional clubs such as Birmingham's Lunar Society. There the three cultures, not yet sharply delineated, interacted intensely; and these provincial groups, not matched in France, may have been Britain's secret weapon in the race to the take-off barrier.

Be that as it may, here is my challenge to this distinguished management institution. Surely we can agree that one of the critical tasks of management, in both the private and public sectors, for the foreseeable future is to handle in a reasonably orderly way the absorption of the technological revolution clearly under way. That task implies that managers work regularly, day-by-day, in confidence and mutual understanding, with scientists and inventive engineers. Would it not, then, be appropriate for the Indian Institute of Management to take the leadership in beginning to bring together, in this vital part of India, scientists, engineers, and entrepreneurs to explore together the directions the Fourth Industrial Revolution is taking; the technologies likely to be immediately or soon relevant to the needs of the Indian economy; and, when these are isolated, how best they might be efficiently introduced into the production process?

Once started, I would guess the issues dealt with would move from the general to the specific; and quite particular problems would be isolated for protracted examination. I would also guess that one of the most important positive products of the effect would be the emergence of the habit of easy communication among the parties concerned.

## VII

I turn now to certain international aspects of the Fourth Industrial Revolution. Thus far the bulk of the new technologies I include under this rubric have been generated in Western Europe, Japan, and the United States. Serious creative work is going forward in parts of the developing regions, and, with the passage of time, I would expect increasing contributions from Latin America, Africa, the Middle East, and Asia. But right now and for the foreseeable future the acquisition of the new technologies will involve a good deal of North-South transfer.

As we all know the transfer of technology—the means to accelerate it and render it less costly—is high on the agenda of the New International Economic Order. I do not wish on this occasion to be diverted into a discussion of the rather sterile state of North-South negotiations under United Nations auspices. I would only observe that a considerable air of unreality surrounds the discussion of the transfer of technology.

The international transfer of technology has been going on systematically since the 18th century, less systematically for a much longer period. There has always been, incidentally, an element of industrial espionage; in the 18th century the French sent well-paid spies to Britain when they sensed the British might be surging ahead in textile machinery; and the American industrial revolution can, with a little exaggeration, be said to have begun in a serious way when Francis Cabot Lowell stole not only British machinery designs but also an experienced foreman, Mr. Moody. They set up shop in a large mill in Lowell, Massachusetts, and proved large profits could be made by using capital-intensive methods to manufacture a simple product with a mass market.

There has been an enormous transfer of technologies after 1945, not only across the North Atlantic and North Pacific, but also North-South. Although it is only a rough index, the categories in the Indian Census of Manufactures have increased from 63 in 1950 to 350 in 1980, a diversification reflecting a good deal of international technology transfer.

More generally, many developing countries, acquiring the capacity to absorb an increasing proportion of the large global backlog of technologies, have moved beyond take-off into the technologies of the Third Industrial Revolution: steel and metal-working, chemicals, electricity, radio, and television. At every step the international transfer of technology has taken place.

Essentially, there are four necessary and sufficient conditions for the transfer of technology—in the longer past and at present:

- First, there must be an adequate supply of scientists and engineers within the recipient society to understand and, if necessary, modify for local conditions the technology being absorbed. India, for example, has benefitted, as have a great many other developing countries, from the new wheat and rice strains, generated by international cooperation in Mexico and the Philippines. But they had to be adapted to Indian conditions by Indian scientists and agronomists or the transfer could not have taken place successfully; and the work at the Indian end was of a very high order indeed.

• Second, there must be at the receiving end entrepreneurs, managers, and a working force sufficiently skilled to produce efficiently on the basis of the new technologies.

• Third, there must be a market setting which makes production and sale of the products using the new technology profitable— a function also of the entrepreneur.

• Fourth, the technology must be acquired. This is the easiest part of the whole business because the sale of technology is generally a highly competitive affair; and if the technology cannot, for any reason, be acquired from an American firm, it or a close substitute can be acquired from a Japanese or European firm and increasingly from a firm in Brazil, India, South Korea, or wherever. It is true, of course, that firms wish to be paid for transferring technologies in which they have patent rights. But new technologies are created by the investment of capital and highly skilled and creative manpower. They ought to be paid for, if created by private firms, like any other factor of production. And payment should recognize that, like the drilling of oil and gas wells, research and development is a form of investment with many dry-hole failures until success comes in like a gusher.

Difficulty may arise for developing countries when a firm decides to try to use its patent rights for monopolistic purposes and refuses to sell or lease the technology it has created. The laws permitting this to happen have for centuries recognized that monopoly rights related to patents could exist for only limited time periods. Even then, reasonable substitutes are likely to emerge in the modern world even before patents run out. The general lesson here is that we are dealing with a question of time and usually not long periods of time. At least that is the way it has been for two centuries. And this is true of even more serious efforts to shield military technology from one form or another of "transfer." The most one can hope for is a transient technological advantage.

If one looks about the developing world at countries where more advanced technologies have or have not been transferred it is palpable that the first three of the conditions cited here have been decisive in determining the outcome; and of them, I would rate the first as the most important. The local supply of scientists and engineers is fundamental; and the more modern forms of technology are distributed about the developing world in rough proportion to their pools of scientists and engineers. Put another way, the largest contribution the United States is now making to the transfer of technology is incorporated in this rather odd fact: American graduate schools of engineering are training more students from abroad than Americans.

To use a phrase from development economics of the 1950s where "absorptive capacity" exists, technology transfer is likely to occur.

## VIII

There is a narrower problem of technology transfer related to the Fourth Industrial Revolution which has not yet been recognized in discussions of international policy. Its reality has been forced upon us in every one of the dozen countries my wife and I have visited before we came to India. And it has certainly arisen vividly in a number of talks in different parts of this country. The problem can be described as pre-commercial. It is: How can a country not engaged on the frontiers of the Fourth Industrial Revolution understand where science and the R&D process are heading; in what directions are practical results likely to emerge in five or 10 years time; in what fields should talented young men and women be trained and other time-consuming preparations be made to understand and make the most of the technologies when they come on line. Only against the backround of that kind of knowledge and preparation are the four conditions for successful technology transfer I outlined earlier likely to be promptly met.

In any case I have come to a conclusion that I did not have when I left Austin, Texas, on July 6th. The conclusion is that there is great scope at many levels for scientists, engineers, and entrepreneurs from advanced industrial countries to meet systematically with similar groups from less developed countries to discuss in particular fields where the Fourth Industrial Revolution is heading and what forthcoming technologies are likely to be relevant to particular developing countries or groups of them at similar stages of growth. I would now argue that this kind of discussion has a significant place on a sensible North-South agenda.

I would suggest one rule for such discussions: they must be conducted solely by men and women who bear direct responsibility in each field considered, whether from the private or public sectors. A failure to follow this rule is, in my view, one major reason for the failure over the past decade of North-South negotiations.

## IX

Now, a brief, casual observation about the probable impact of the Fourth Industrial Revolution on our societies which I make simply because, if I am correct, it is an outcome that rather pleases me. I believe the Fourth Industrial Revolution will force within our societies and among them intensified partnerships. I have in mind not merely the linkages among the scientist, engineer, entrepreneur, and hopefully, the economist. The general application and diffusion of the new technologies will require areas of partnership between the public and private sectors, notably with respect to large R&D projects. It will require collaboration between management in the public and private sectors and the workers who must not only be persuaded that, on balance, the new technologies will work to their advantage, but they may also have to be re-trained. Internationally, the range and diversification of the new technologies will, I would guess, lead to at least as much international collaboration and interdependence, as between private sectors in different countries, as it will to competition; for no one country is going to establish a comparative advantage in all the multiple branches of the Fourth Industrial Revolution. And, as I have suggested, collaboration with respect to the new technologies could help move us toward the North-South partnership that our heightened interdependence requires but which our political leaders have thus far failed to establish.

## X

Now a final word in which I take my theme from a statement of the Prime Minister when she commented on Sarabhai at the time of his death in 1971: "Apart from his research, what lifted him above the ordinary was his intense concern with the relationship of science to the larger purposes of human life." I have thus far spoken on the assumption that high real growth rates and the progressive absorption of new technologies on which they depend are a good and legitimate objective. On the other hand, in all I have written over what is now getting close to being a half century, I have treated economic growth and the modernization of societies as a derived demand—an activity pursued for larger purposes. Nations have taken the painful steps to uproot traditional societies and to try to find paths to modernization consistent with their cultures for two reasons, both essentially non-economic. First, to sustain positions of national independence and dignified interdependence with other nations in a world in which they learned that these objectives required a grasp of modern technologies.

Put more bluntly, intrusion from abroad or feared intrusion by the more technologically advanced has, for more than two centuries, been the most powerful single force making for the modernization of societies. Alexander Hamilton's dictum of 1791 remains the dominant banner of most developing countries: "We need manufacturers not merely for the prosperity but for the independence of the country."

The second motive for modernization has been simply human. If it were possible, men and women wanted for themselves and the children longer lives, better food, better medical care, a chance to widen their opportunities and fulfill their innate talents through education; and, in what appears to be a virtually universal human trait, they wanted a chance to satisfy their curiosity as to what's down the road and over the horizon. I am of course aware that there are some who argue that economic growth is materialistic, destructive, not related to an improved quality of life and not a legitimate objective. Knowing what poverty was like in the 18th century British villages where men and women gladly moved to the mills of Manchester; what a Welsh mining village was like in the 1930s or, for that matter, an American mining village in Appalachia; and what life is like in the rural and urban slums of a good many developing countries, I remain, for this stage of history, pro-economic growth. If one surveys the real but incomplete progress of the past 35 years in the developing regions, it is clear that the aggregate statistics of real growth are not some kind of statistical artifact. The young live longer, are better educated, are provided with more medical care than their parents; and the area within which they can express their talents and make their choices is widening. There is, of course, more to the quality of life than progress of this kind. But I commend to you both the limitations and the glory of Keynes' 1945 toast before the Royal Economic Society, shortly before his death: "To economics and economists who are the trustees not of civilization but of the possibility of civilization."

# EIGHT

# The Pacific Basin
# and the World Economy

*This chapter is based on a paper delivered on the Asian Development Bank Special Day at Expo '85, Tsukuba, Japan, May 22, 1985. Expo '85 was organized around the technologies of the next century, although I was pleased to note the longest lines were for a ride on a rather conventional Ferris wheel. I was also delighted to observe that a complex Japanese robot, capable of reading music and playing the organ (badly), was completely upstaged by a stylized film of a lovely (nude) Japanese dancer projected on the wall of the room in the Japanese pavilion in which the robot was performing Protestant hymns.*

*It was evident that my Japanese (and other Asian) colleagues fully understood the relevance of David Hume's 1758 dictum to the future of the Pacific Basin.*

## I. INTRODUCTION

Thinking about the world economy last month in preparation for a conference at Ditchley in England, I was struck by the following thought. Every major country and region is now caught up in a rather painful historical transition. The transition can be defined bluntly as follows: the ideas on which we operated in the 1950s and 1960s no longer work. That was proved in the 1970s and first half of the 1980s. We are groping—all of us—towards new concepts and new policies. But we haven't found them, except perhaps in one country, on which I shall comment later.

Reprinted from the *Asian Development Bank Quarterly Review* (July 1985), pp. 4–9.

At the risk of some over-simplification, let me summarize briefly both the forces that carried us through the 1950s and 1960s and the nature of the transition through which we are passing. I shall deal, in order, with the major countries of the OECD, the developing regions, and the USSR.


## II. OECD: ATLANTIC WORLD

The unprecedented boom in the advanced industrial countries of the OECD during the 1950s and 1960s was based on the convergence of two powerful forces. First, the decline in basic commodity prices, yielding a favorable shift in the terms of trade from 1951 to the mid-1960s. Second, the backlog of unapplied technologies available to Western Europe and Japan, relating to automobiles and durable consumer goods, as well as the newer technologies—television, plastics, synthetic fibers and atomic energy—available for all. The favorable terms of trade lifted real incomes to a point where the mass ownership of automobiles and durable consumer goods became possible in Western Europe and, after the mid-1950s, in Japan as well. The absorption of the technological possibilities linked to these sectors drove forward the OECD economies at rates never before sustained. In addition, OECD social expenditures, in a revolutionary surge, rose from about 14 per cent of GDP to 24 per cent in the two decades after 1960. Between 1950 and 1975 GDP grew at 5 per cent, social expenditures at 8 per cent. Since trees do not grow to the sky, these rates could not continue. They slowed down in all major OECD countries after 1975 except France, although the deceleration was relatively minor in Japan. Overall the rate of increase in social expenditures was 4 per cent in 1975–1981, 3 per cent, excluding France and Japan.

Deceleration of the OECD economy itself began in the mid-1960s: the terms of trade levelled off; output in the leading sectors of the boom slowed down; and productivity as well. In a perfectly normal process, diminishing returns asserted itself in leading sectors which had carried forward the boom for almost a generation. Then came the price explosion of 1973 and 1974; a brief and incomplete recovery; the second oil shock; and, after a sharp recession, a second sluggish revival with unemployment in Western Europe hovering about 10 percent in 1985, 7 per cent in the United States. For reasons to which we shall return, Japan has been something of an exception.

Three related technical factors account for the sluggishness in the Atlantic world since 1973.

- The institutional rigidities which developed in the easy full-employment days of the 1950s and 1960s, especially in Western Europe, but to a degree also in the United States.
- Difficulties in reconciling rapid growth with control over inflation in the current international price environment. It was, for example, the American attempt to reconcile rapid growth with price stability through an extravagant Keynesian tax cut and an excessive monetarist reliance on high interest rates that brought about the large U.S. balance of payments and budget deficits, and the over-valued dollar.
- And Western Europe's slowness, relative to Japan and the United States, in generating and applying the new batch of technologies which began to assert themselves strongly in the mid-1970s—technologies which, as an economic historian, I identify as the Fourth Industrial Revolution.

These three technical problems define, after a fashion, the transition faced in the Atlantic world. But, in fact, the transition confronted in the Atlantic world is deeper and has a longer history.

For a century now—from, say, Bismarck's first major social legislation in 1883, the emergence of the Fabians and Labor Party in Britain, the Grangers and Populists in the United States—the central problem addressed in the Atlantic nations has been: How can we build industrial societies which reconcile efficiency with the humane values in which Western culture and its religions are rooted? In politics, the process often assumed the form of debate and struggle within a zero-sum game which allocated resources as between the less affluent and more affluent.

Clearly, the central issue of domestic political life in the Atlantic world can no longer be defined in terms of the allocation of a bit more or less to social welfare. Two issues, above others, appear fundamental if the erosion of the social and physical infrastructure of the West is to be avoided: the mounting of long-term policies capable of reconciling relatively high rates of growth with control over inflation; and the bringing together of scientists and engineers, entrepreneurs and the working force to generate and absorb efficiently—and across the board—the new technologies. In my view at least, the former objective requires effective long-term incomes policies, as well as a judicious blend of fiscal and monetary policies. Evidently, incomes policies are essentially political, social, and institutional rather than narrowly economic arrangements; and much the same can be said of the partnerships rendered imperative by the peculiar character of the new technologies.

Looked at in this way, the advanced industrial countries of the West are caught up in a transition between the struggle over the allocation of resources that marked the evolution of the welfare state over the past century, and the need for sustained communal cooperation if growth and control over influation are to be reconciled and the new technologies find an appropriate role in their societies.

## III. OECD: JAPAN

At first sight Japan appears to have escaped these transitional problems; and, therefore, it appears better geared to the tasks of the generation ahead than the major countries of the Atlantic world. From, say, the first ineffectual Factory Act of 1898 (which aimed to protect women and children) down to about 1936, Japanese social legislation followed, with a lag, a sequence not unlike that to be observed in the Atlantic nations at similar stages of growth. But a generation of war, physical destruction, and postwar recovery broke the pattern and forced Japan into a sequence of communal efforts climaxed by its extraordinary surge of growth since the mid-1950s. Its social expenditures rose from 8 to 17 per cent between 1960 and 1981; but that is the lowest figure for the major OECD countries. There are strong and understandable pressures in Japanese political life to raise the level of social outlays. Responding to those pressures, the rate of increase of social expenditures has been sustained at higher levels in Japan than in the Atlantic world; but there also appears to be a more solid consensus than in the Atlantic world that these zero-sum contests are less fundamental than the common effort to assure a steadily expanding pie to be appropriately divided. A lively sense of the communal stake in the continuity of high growth rates survives; Japan enjoys a quite well institutionalized incomes policy; and it has adjusted its institutions with alacrity to the imperatives of the Fourth Industrial Revolution.

These qualities render Japan an extraordinarily strong unit in the world economy; but, as Prime Minister Nakasone dramatized last month, Japan is also caught up in a difficult historical transition, but one quite different from that of the Atlantic world.

Japan's transition, as we all know, is to assume the degree of responsibility for the viability of the world's trade and financial system its economic power requires. Japan is now the third economic power in the world in terms of the production of goods and services, closing quite fast on the Soviet Union with only 44 per cent of the latter's population. This is an extraordinary achievement for a country whose take-off began just about 100 years ago, in the mid-1880s with the success of the Matsukata currency reform.

Confucius once observed—long before John Maynard Keynes—that a man's way of thinking was established by the age of thirty. When most Japanese now in authority arrived at their thirtieth birthday, Japan produced only three to four per cent of the world's gross product. The figure is now about 10 per cent and rising. I cite those familiar numbers not merely to express my respect for Japan's performance since 1885—and since 1945—but also to underline that the opening up of its markets to imports and the full internationalization of its capital markets is not a matter of reacting to U.S. pressure, nor, as some Japanese say, is it a necessary "sacrifice". It is a matter of direct and fundamental Japanese national interest. No country in the world has a greater stake than Japan in the viability of the world's trade and monetary system. For a good part of the past 40 years Japan could concentrate on its tasks at home and on the widening of its export markets, leaving the fate of the system to others. Those days are over, because the system is not viable if Japan continues to run a balance of payments surplus of the kind which now exists—a trade surplus estimated at $44 billion in 1984, of which 84 per cent is with the United States.

I know well that much work is going forward in Japan on these issues; and the dialogue between our two governments aimed at solving the problems between us, as the friends we must be, is intense.

But as one who for more than 20 years has treasured his ties to Japan, I would make this observation. There is something inappropriate about Americans trying to negotiate specific changes in Japanese practice that would increase U.S. exports to Japan. Japanese understand how their institutions work much better than Americans. It would be wiser and, in a sense, more dignified for both our peoples for Japan to set a target of eliminating its surplus with the United States at the rate of, say, $10 billion each year for the next four years and then to do whatever was necessary to meet that target. Obviously, the United States, as well as Japan, has major responsibilities in the process of eliminating its present trade and payments deficit. What is required is a plan—initially bilateral, but then widened out—to eliminate the U.S. deficit and the Japanese surplus without inducing a U.S. recession and without resort to further U.S. protectionism. As I have argued at length on many occasions, I do not believe this adjustment can be effectively accomplished without a rigorous American incomes policy.

Putting aside specific lines of action, if we fail to work together to this end, an extremely disruptive recession and phase of mercantilist protectionism is possible, with grave security implications.

One further observation as an historian. We Americans understand—or we should understand—the difficulty of the transition through which Japan is passing. It is much like the transition we confronted after the First World War. We had come to status as the world's largest and most powerful economy. The question was: Would we meet our responsibilities? We Americans failed to meet the test. At a critical moment we raised our tariffs; and we failed to meet our obligations to the system as a major source of international capital. Our failures on both counts helped make the depression after 1929 deeper and more prolonged than it need have been; and, in that sense, our economic action and inaction helped bring on the Second World War.

I cite that painful story now not because I believe a third world war is likely. On the contrary, I do so to underline how important it is that a new major economic power shake off the images and habits of its early days and assume the inescapable responsibilities of its role as a leader in the human family. A failure to assume those responsibilities can be extremely costly to all—without exception.

Now a more modest suggestion. It arises not from my work as an economist and historian but from experience at The University of Texas at Austin. Some years ago a creative member of our faculty, the late Mrs. Victorine Abboud, developed a unique, totally computerized system for teaching Arabic. It is approximately four times as efficient as conventional methods, in some fundamental aspects of language teaching; and it is being further developed by Mrs. Abboud's colleagues. The principles of this system are capable of being applied to the teaching of other languages. Japan is obviously at a stage where many people from abroad should be learning the Japanese language. I know that I would have been a better scholar and a better public servant if I had learned Japanese. And with Japan's ties to the outside world expanding so rapidly, many Japanese would also profit by learning foreign languages. I understand Japan is making great strides in computerized translation. I am suggesting, then, that it may be of interest for your talented experts, here in Tsukuba and elsewhere, to consider the possibility of allocating some of their virtuosity to the accelerated teaching of languages.

## IV. THE DEVELOPING REGIONS

I turn now from the problems, possibilities, and transitions of the advanced industrial world to those of the developing regions. As we all know, the developing regions have demonstrated in the past two generations both an astonishing vitality and a capacity to generate a great many difficult problems. Excepting the first few years of the 1980s, they sustained average per capita growth rates substantially higher than even the greatest optimists of the 1950s predicted—over 3 per cent per capita from 1960 to 1979. But their performance was also marked by agonizingly slow reductions in birth rates, insufficient domestic competition, government price and subsidy policies that damped agricultural production and otherwise distorted prices and the fiscal system. Perhaps the greatest transition confronted in the developing regions is the need to shift the balance of power significantly from "the state bourgeoisie" that have grown up since the 1950s to the competitive markets in the private sector.

The excessive powers of the state over the economy in the developing regions arose in the 1950s from a convergence of economic and political forces.

On the economic side, there was the inability to earn or borrow, at tolerable rates, sufficient foreign exchange to avoid highly protectionist import substitution policies. These led directly to insufficient competition in domestic markets. Foreign exchange rationing was also a policy that required large powerful bureaucracies to decide what should be imported. On the political side there was the fear of explosions in the volatile cities and a decision, in effect, to exploit the farmer on behalf of the urban population just as most of the OECD countries exploit the urban population on behalf of their farmers. In the developing countries this had, of course, the effect of reducing incentives in the agricultural sector and slowing the rate of increase of agricultural production, forcing increased grain imports at the expense of industrial development.

With respect to attitudes, the 1950s were times when capitalism was an unpopular word, socialism a popular word in the developing regions. Capitalism was often associated by political leaders with colonial or quasicolonial status. There was also considerable sentimental appeal in socialism during the 1950s: some of the European social democratic governments were doing quite well; Mao's Great Leap Forward and Chinese Communist policy in general generated a considerable appeal among those who did not investigate it too deeply; and even Khrushchev's boast that the USSR would soon outstrip the US in total output had a certain credibility in the late 1950s. To all this one can add that many of the emerging political leaders were intellectuals or soldiers, both types inherently suspicious of the market process and inclined, for different reasons, to have excessive faith in the powers of government administration.

Obviously, the answer now should not be a compulsive Friedman-esque reliance on the market process. As Adam Smith and most political economists since his time have recognized, there are major inescapable economic tasks for governments to perform. But the time has come to examine afresh and sceptically the accumulated economic functions of government, and to strike new balances between the public and private sectors—balances which would exploit the potentialities of private enterprise and competitive markets a good deal more than they are exploited at present.

There is a quite particular reason why such a shift of balance is appropriate. Most of the population in the developing regions now live in economies undergoing the drive to technological maturity, if I may use the vocabulary of my stages of economic growth. This is the stage beyond take-off when a society progressively demonstrates the capacity to absorb efficiently technologies of increased sophistication over a widening range of sectors. Production diversifies. The whole process is underpinned by an increase in absorptive capacity rooted in an enlarged corps of well-trained entrepreneurs and an increased proportion of the population with a secondary and higher education. To use the World Bank's vocabulary rather than mine, between 1960 and 1981 the proportion of the relevant age groups enrolled in secondary schools for "Lower middle-income" countries rose from 10 to 34 per cent; in higher education, from 3 to 9 per cent. For "Higher middle-income" countries the increases were, respectively, from 20 to 51 per cent and from 4 to 14 per cent. These apparently pedestrian figures reflect truly revolutionary change in the productive potential of the developing regions and in their absorptive capacity.

This transformation is relevant to the public-private sector balance because public authorities have proved everywhere peculiarly clumsy and inefficient in trying to manage the production of the highly diversified manufactures which characterize the drive to technological maturity; and, much more than was the case a generation ago, the private entrepreneurs now exist in the developing world capable of producing diversified industrial products competitively for world markets.

It is encouraging that leaders in a good many developing countries have publicly identified the need to rely more than at present on competitive private market sectors. The most remarkable such public acknowledgment has come from China. The Chinese government has already acted in a quite revolutionary way in agriculture; and it is seeking to introduce elements of a competitive market system elsewhere in the economy. We cannot now predict firmly the economic and political outcome of the reform process under way; but it is probably fair to say that China has, since the end of the Cultural Revolution, moved further along in its necessary historical transition than any other major country.

The shift in balance towards competitive private markets does not, of course, exhaust the list of transitional problems in the developing regions. For reasons considered later, developing as well as developed industrial countries confront the adjustments required to absorb efficiently the technologies of the Fourth Industrial Revolution. And this appears true even for some of the most dynamic developing countries of Asia that have managed to avoid gross imbalance between their public and private sectors. We shall return to the transition imposed by the Fourth Industrial Revolution a bit later in discussing the Pacific Basin.

## V. THE USSR

I turn now briefly to the character of the transition which challenges the Soviet Union. In a remarkable post-war effort the Soviet Union concentrated its resources on physical reconstruction and building the heavy industry foundations for military status as a truly global power. There was some movement from the mid-1950s forward towards durable consumer goods and private motor cars; but it was exceedingly weak as compared to the major OECD countries, and the Soviet Union fell behind in some of the important technologies related to the stage of high mass consumption. Nevertheless, Khrushchev's boast at the close of the 1950s that the Soviet Union would overtake the United States in production did not seem empty at the time.

It is now evident that the concepts and policies of the 1950s and 1960s become every day less relevant and helpful to life in the Soviet Union. The transition confronted in the Soviet Union is, perhaps, the most difficult of all, because it appears to require more profound political change than the transitions faced among the OECD and developing countries; and the Soviet Union has not experienced the kind of struggle which took place in China during the Cultural Revolution whose terrible human costs may have had some compensation in permitting more rapid movement through the Chinese transition than would otherwise have proved possible.

In any case, forces at work in Soviet demography, agriculture, raw materials supply, and industry have produced a striking deceleration in the productivity of investment (a rise in the capital-output ratio); and these forces have been compounded by the allocation to military production and space of an extraordinarily high proportion of resources, including scientists and engineers, competent foremen and skilled workers. Moreover, the institutions of Soviet society render the task of elaborating and applying across the board the technological possibilities of the Fourth Industrial Revolution exceedingly difficult. The modernization of the Soviet economy is, then, a formidable economic, social, political and cultural challenge.

Soviet society contains a great many talented, energetic and highly motivated men and women who understand better than any of us outside the Soviet Union the dilemmas they confront at the present time. I would not rule out the possibility that they will make some progress in resolving them. But for our purposes today it is enough to suggest that the USSR shares with the other nations and regions the challenge of moving through a major historical transition if its citizens are to enjoy the level of welfare and productivity Soviet resources and technological capacity could permit.


## VI. THE PACIFIC BASIN

Assume for a moment that my quick sketch of the world economy has some elements of truth; that is, the portrait of a global community in transition, made up of countries and regions struggling to find new concepts and policies to replace the eroded patterns of the 1950s and 1960s. Returning to the title of my talk, the question is: What, if anything, has that proposition got to do with the Pacific Basin?

The answer I suggest is this: The early emergence of the Pacific Basin as a regional intergovernmental economic organization could substantially assist and accelerate the transitional process for both the advanced and developing countries of the area.

It has taken some time, but I believe a consensus is now emerging that the key to a successful organization of the Pacific Basin is a recognition that if it is to succeed it will have to be an institution of direct and authentic interest to both its advanced industrial and developing members. That is why initial analogies of a Pacific Basin organization to the European Economic Community and the OECD failed to generate a credible and acceptable program.

Specifically, I would suggest four initial items for the Pacific Basin agenda; a method of organization; and a doctrine.

The first item of business is, clearly, the one that is already on the table; that is, Human Resource Development. This field for Pacific Basin cooperation was proposed by Indonesia on July 12, 1984, at the historic Six Plus Five Pacific Basin session in the wake of the ASEAN meeting in Djakarta. Although a great deal of international work goes forward every day in human resource development, two quite different challenges in this field have not been fully gripped in the region: human resource development in a good many of the Pacific islands whose modernization in productive ways poses extremely difficult problems which any Pacific Basin organization will have to consider; and human resource development to increase the capacity of the developing countries of the region to absorb the relevant technologies of the Fourth Industrial Revolution. In 1983–1984 my wife and I visited 34 countries, about 100 cities—from Auckland to Glasgow, from Cairo to Uppsala. We found a virtually universal awareness that profound changes in education are required in every country, without exception, that wishes to generate and absorb the new technologies. Such changes are already under way in the more advanced of the developing countries of the Pacific region; for example, in Taiwan and South Korea.

My simple point is, then, that there are major opportunities for international cooperation within the Pacific Basin to increase the capacity of all its countries to make the most of potentialities opened up by the Fourth Industrial Revolution by enlarged efforts in the field of human resource development. I would hope these opportunities will be exploited as the ASEAN initiative is explored and brought to life.

But human resource development does not exhaust the potentialities for increasing technological absorptive capacity. I suggest—as a second agenda item—that the Pacific Basin organize on a regular basis an exchange of information which would permit experts in every country to know the directions in which the R&D process is moving and the kinds of innovations likely to be possible just over the horizon; say in 3–5 years time. I am not talking about passing out patents but about circulating the kinds of information which would permit countries to begin to identify the innovations likely to be relevant to their particular mix of natural resources and stage of economic growth. I can attest from my tour through the area that a serious interest in this kind of cooperation is widespread.

A third area for Pacific cooperation is in the broad area of natural resources. I was much struck, in preparing this paper, that 65 per cent of the ADB's lending of almost $16 billion since 1967 was for agriculture, energy and water supply. For the year 1984 the figure was 73 per cent. This allocation correctly reflects the pressure of the high rates of growth in population and output in the region at a time when a good many of its countries have come to the stage when they can efficiently absorb sophisticated, energy-intensive and resource-intensive industries.

What I suggest here is that special Pacific Basin committees might look collectively further down the road than is now conventional in energy and agriculture and go to work operationally on a sector which, I suspect, needs more priority and resources than are now being allocated to it in the Pacific Basin. I refer to the enormous tasks of reforestation.

My fourth proposed agenda item is trade. There is, of course, no multilateral substitute for the measures Japan and the U.S. must undertake in parallel and, perhaps, in collaboration to end the dangerous current trade imbalance. But once each government sets in motion effective programs to this end, I believe the world economy—as well as the whole Pacific Basin region—would benefit from regular regional discussions on trade and payments.

This is not a pious platitude. Multilateral discussion of a problem of this kind has two virtues. First, it inevitably comes to rest on basic objective principles rather than competitive, bilateral bargaining. The latter is bound to be touched by an element of confrontation. Second, in a multilateral setting, opportunities are likely to open up for the balancing of accounts by changes in trade or payments patterns involving third parties.

My initial agenda for a Pacific Basin organization is, then:

- Human resource development, with special emphasis on the requirements generated by the Fourth Industrial Revolution.
- Multilateral examination of future innovations likely to be generated by the Fourth Industrial Revolution.
- Systematic examination of future basic resource requirements, with special initial emphasis on tasks of reforestation.
- Multilateral examination of the problems and possibilities of achieving dynamic trade and payments balance within the Pacific Basin.

Now, how should a Pacific Basin economic organization be institutionalized? Long before I was asked to speak on this occasion, I came to a conclusion on this point; expressed the conclusion in talks delivered in this region in 1983; and incorporated the conclusion in the draft of a book soon to be published entitled: *The United States and the Regional Organization of Asia and the Pacific: 1965–1985.* My conclusion was and is that a regional economic organization for the Pacific should be built on the foundation already provided by the Asian Development Bank.

I take this position for several reasons:

- In general, I believe it is wiser, to build on existing institutions, adjusting them as new problems and possibilities emerge, than to create new institutions. This is not merely a matter of economy; but institutions maintain their vitality over time by taking on the challenge of new problems as solutions to older problems become bureaucratized or diminish in relevance.
- A good deal of the staff work required for a Pacific Basin organization could be done by experts already working within the ADB, and if new expertise is required (e.g., in the new technologies), staff can be expanded with minimum additional overhead cost.
- The outcome of at least some of the work on the proposed agenda (e.g., reforestation and basic resource production) is likely to yield projects justifying investment; and some of this investment might well be undertaken by the ADB.

## VII. A DOCTRINE FOR THE PACIFIC BASIN AND BEYOND

Now a final word about a doctrine for the Pacific Basin—although it might well be extended to the world economy as a whole.

I have recently had occasion to go back and read again the works of the eighteenth century economists. As you know, modern economics emerged, in part, as a struggle against mercantilist doctrines. Those doctrines were generated in an era of chronic warfare between nation states. Mercantilism counseled not only that a favorable trade balance, and an influx of gold and silver, were essential for the security of the state, but also that the more advanced nations should try to prevent progress in manufactures in the less advanced.

This was a period before the great innovational breakthroughs of the First Industrial Revolution occurred in the 1780s. Nevertheless, levels of real income varied depending on the extent of trade, comparative advantage, and virtuosity in what were called the "mechanical arts". David Hume, Adam Smith's older friend—philosopher, psychologist, historian and economist—addressed this question: What would happen to the more advanced countries of his day as their example set in motion a "fermentation" (as he called it) in the less advanced; and they too acquired the advantages of trade and skills in the "mechanical arts".

In this wide Pacific Basin, where we have seen over the past century the rise of Japan to status as a great economic power, and behind Japan we have seen in the past 30 years a number of other countries stirred into "fermentation" by the example of Japan and the Atlantic world, we should I believe, firmly adopt the doctrine that splendid Scotsman David Hume enunciated in 1758.

> . . . where an open comunication is preserved among nations, it is impossible but the domestic industry of every one must receive an increase from the improvements of others. Compare the situation of Great Britain at present, with what it was two centuries ago. . . . Every improvement . . . has arisen from our imitation of foreigners. . . . Nor need any state entertain apprehensions, that their neighbours will improve to such a degree in every art and manufacture, as to have no demand from them. Nature, by giving a diversity of geniuses, climates, and soils, to different nations, has secured their mutual intercourse and commerce, as long as they all remain industrious and civilized.[1]

To a Pacific Basin, then, of "open communication," "industrious and civilized"!

## NOTES

1. "Of the Jealousy of Trade", in Eugene Rotwein, ed., *David Hume: Writings on Economics* (Madison, University of Wisconsin Press, 1955), pp. 78–79.

# NINE

# Is There Need
# for Economic Leadership?
# Japanese or U.S.?

*On our 1983–1984 year of travel, I received a request from Charles P. Kindleberger to write a paper for the annual 1984 end-of-year gathering of economists. Kindleberger had responsibility for the program, a burden imposed on the incoming president of the American Economic Association.*

*As a friend and, for four intervals, a colleague in war and peace, over a span of more than forty years, I have never been able to refuse one of Kindleberger's requests. The following essay resulted, published in the* American Economic Association Papers and Proceedings, *vol. 75, no. 2, May 1985.*

*The "Djakarta initiative" referred to in the last sentence proposed that the Pacific Basin governments begin to work together on human resource development. The move was something of a surprise because the conventional wisdom had it that the ASEAN was extremely reserved about a possible intergovernmental Pacific Basin organization. In 1986, after some staff work, the initiative is stalled because neither the U.S. nor the Japanese government (nor the Asian Development Bank) appears willing to allocate additional resources to the proposal.*

There are two reasonably unambiguous definitions of the inherently ambiguous concept of economic leadership. Definition One relates to innovation and leading sectors; that is, the relative primacy of a country in commercializing a new technology and establishing, for a

Reprinted with permission from the *American Economic Association Papers and Proceedings*, vol. 75, no. 2 (May 1985), pp. 285–291.

time, a dominant position in a major sector. In that sense, Britain led in the first phase of the cotton textile revolution (say, 1783–1832), and the United States led in the first phase of the mass automobile revolution (say, 1909–29).

Definition Two relates to policy; that is, the assumption of responsibility for the successful operation of the world economy as a whole by a single country. I shall consider later the necessary conditions for such leadership.

The leading sector and policy definitions are partially linked because only an economic power quick off the mark in converting new inventions into profitable innovations is likely to be able to sustain the balance of payments implications of policies of responsible leadership in the world economy.

I shall now respond to the subject of this paper in terms of each definition of leadership. First, the new technologies and their implications for leadership in the inovational, leading-sector sense. By new technologies I refer to the microchip, genetic engineering, the laser, robots, new communication methods, and new industrial materials. Although germinating for some time, the innovational stage of this technological revolution will be dated by historians, I believe, from, roughly, the second half of the 1970's.

Somewhat arbitrarily, I am inclined to regard this rather dramatic batch of innovations as the fourth such major grouping in the past two centuries. The fourth industrial revolution has some distinctive characteristics as compared to its predecessors. It is more intimately linked to areas of basic science which are themselves undergoing rapid revolutionary change. This means the scientist has become a critical actor in the drama; and the successful linkage of the scientist, engineer, and the entrepreneur has become crucial to the generation and diffusion of the new technologies. The new technologies are also proving ubiquitous, progressively suffusing the older basic industries, agriculture, animal husbandry, and forestry, as well as all manner of services from education and medicine to banking and communications; and they are, in different degree, immediately relevant to the economies of the developing regions, depending on their stage of growth, absorptive capacity, and resource endowments.

For our purposes, the extraordinary range and diversity of the new technologies bear directly on the prospects for leadership by Japan, the United States, or anyone else. I find it most improbable that any one nation will achieve and sustain across-the-board technological leadership in the fourth industrial revolution, or, indeed, leadership in a major area such as micro electronics or genetic engineering or new industrial materials. Each such area represents, in fact, a group of highly specialized and differentiated activities. Given the reasonably even distribution of scientific, engineering, and entrepreneurial talent among the advanced industrial countries—and the similar educational level and skills of their working forces—with the passage of time, specialized comparative advantage is likely to be distributed among a considerable range of countries; and one is likely to see a great deal of cooperation and trade in the new technologies, as well as competition. Indeed, if one examines the pattern of joint ventures across international boundaries and the expanding trade in high-technology sectors, the process can already be seen to be under way, despite the somewhat slower start of Western Europe than Japan and the United States in exploiting the new possibilities.

The diffusion of virtuosity in the new technologies will be accelerated by their indirect impact on the developing regions. Over the next decade we are likely to see the new technologies vigorously applied in the motor vehicle, machine tool, steel, textile, and other industries rooted in the longer past. One result of this conversion to high tech along a broad front is that the more advanced developing countries will no longer be able to count on generating increased manufactured exports simply by exploiting their lower money-wage rates. There is a lively awareness of this change in prospects in the Pacific Basin because of palpable Japanese progress in applying the new technologies to the older industries. In consequence, there is intense interest among the newly industrialized countries in acquiring the emerging technologies. The Republic of Korea, for example, is gearing its current Five-Year Plan to the rapid absorption of the new technologies, including quite radical changes in education policy. (For an extended discussion, see my 1983b book.)

Each developing country differs, of course, in both the extent to which the new technologies are relevant and in its capacity productively to absorb them. But, in general, potential absorptive capacity is higher than relative per capita levels of real income would suggest.

Consider the case of India, a country with an exceedingly low average real income per capita, conventionally measured. The pool of scientists and engineers in India has increased from about 190,000 in 1960 to 2.4 million in 1984 (see Government of India, 1984); and it is sustained by the fact that something like 9 percent of the Indian population aged 20–24 is now enrolled in higher education, three times the proportion twenty years earlier. Taken along with the large absolute size of India's population, this means that India is quite capable of assembling the critical mass of scientists and R&D engineers required to solve the kinds of problems increasingly posed by the fourth industrial revolution and its efficient absorption.

The central question is whether Indian society can achieve, over a wide spectrum of sectors, the bringing together in partnership of scientists, engineers, and entrepreneurs which has happened in atomic energy, space, and, to a significant degree, in agriculture. The linkage has not been effectively made in a good many industrial sectors. I would guess that if these linkages began to firm up in one sector after another, the Indian brain drain would begin to reverse.

While the Indian case is rather dramatic, given the country's size and relatively low real income level, the revolutionary expansion of higher education over the past generation is quite typical of the developing world. For middle-income economies as a whole, the higher education proportion of the relevant age group rose from 3 percent in 1960 to 11 percent in 1979. (See World Bank, 1983.) It will certainly take time for these more advanced developing countries to bring about the partnership of scientists, engineers, and entrepreneurs the absorption of the Fourth Industrial Revolution requires. (It is, indeed, taking quite a lot of time in Western Europe and the United States.) But I do believe it will happen; and the process will strengthen the diffusion of technological virtuosity within the world economy.

Now, what about the second definition of leadership, in terms of policies reflecting responsibility for the viability of the world economy? The capacity to lead, in this sense, depends in part, of course, on a nation's proportionate role in the world economy; its relative contribution to global GNP and international trade; and the strength of its capital markets and the scale of its international lending. Britain's contribution to global industrial production may have fallen from 32 to 14 percent between 1870 and 1913, its foreign trade from 25 to 16 percent (see my 1978 book); but its large and active capital market, combined with the maintenance of a free-trade policy, permitted Britain to remain an acknowledged leader in the world economy down to World War I.

There was, however, more to it than that. British leadership was only possible because the United States, the major states of Europe, and the component regions of the British Empire by and large conducted their business in ways compatible with London's rules of the game. They did not generally share London's passion for free trade; but that fact did not prevent the relatively easy flow of goods and capital and people and the acceptance of transmission mechanisms which kept the world economy roughly in step with respect to prices and cyclical fluctuations.

At the base of the system was a fundamental, shared agreement in domestic politics; namely, that tariffs apart, there was no realistic alternative to accepting the domestic consequences of the vagaries inherent in a competitive, largely private enterprise global system of trade and capital movements.

The tragic experiences of the world economy from 1920 to 1939 radically altered both the international and domestic aspects of the pre-1914 consensus. At the close of World War II, the United States, conscious of its interwar derelictions and of its extraordinary relative economic strength in a war-damaged world, explicitly accepted responsibilities for economic leadership, including initially high levels of official grants and loans to foreign governments.

The U.S. role was sustained by a widespread consensus on appropriate international and domestic rules of the game, the latter including the acceptance by governments of responsibility for both the domestic level of employment and the expansion of social services.

Over the past forty years, the relative role of the United States in the world economy has declined with the revival of Western and Eastern Europe; with the extraordinary surge of Japanese growth; and with the expansion of the developing economies at overall rates averaging higher than those in the advanced industrial economies. As of 1980, the United States contributed perhaps 23 percent to global GNP, the figure having declined from about 33 percent in 1950. (The U.S. and Japanese GNP data in relation to global GNP are from Herbert Block, 1981, pp. 30–32, Appendix Table 1.) The Japanese GNP proportion rose between 1950 and 1980 from about 3 to 8.5 percent.

Despite the sharp relative rise of Japan, the capacity of the United states to lead, in terms of my second definition, is evidently still greater than that of Japan; and that capacity is enhanced, as was that of pre-1914 Britain, by the continuing large role of the United States as a capital market. But the fact is that, no more than Edwardian Britain, does the United States command the power to impose its leadership on the world economy. The distribution of effective economic and political power is, in fact, greater now than then.

My interim conclusions, then, are these. First, whether one uses leading sector Definition One, or rules of the game Definition Two, forces are at work tending to diffuse, rather than concentrate, the power to lead. Second, an overwhelming concentration of power in a single country does not appear to be a necessary condition for effective leadership in the world economy, if there is an effective working consensus on economic rules of the game, domestic as well as international. It is here, I believe, in domestic policy that the critical problem lies which led us to focus this session on the question of leadership in the world economy.

The circumstances that emerged in the world economy in the early 1970's broke up the consensus on domestic economic policy that had emerged after World War II and acquired legitimacy with the historically unique growth rates of the 1950's and 1960's. No viable successor consensus on domestic economic policy has yet emerged. And it is the lack of an effective consensus on domestic policy in Western Europe and the United States which mainly accounts for the rise of protectionism, distorted real interest rates, precarious debt structures, a grossly overvalued dollar, and other pathological aspects of a disheveled world economy. Specifically, international economic policy is likely to remain ineffectual until the West learns how to reconcile relatively full employment (and reasonably high and steady growth rates) with control over inflation, and how to generate and absorb rapidly the technological possibilities inherent in the fourth industrial revolution.

This judgment stems from a particular view of where the Atlantic world stands in the sweep of modern history. For a century now— from, say, Bismarck's first major social legislation in 1883—the central problem addressed in the advanced industrial nations of Western Europe and North America has been, how can we build industrial societies which reconcile efficiency in a world of rapidly evolving technologies with the humane values in which Western culture is rooted? In politics the process often assumed the form of debate and struggle within a zero-sum game which allocated resources as between welfare and private consumption and investment, as between the less affluent and more affluent. It is one of the major achievements of the Western democratic process that this muted form of class struggle proceeded in relative peace, reaching in the decades after World War II a remarkable apogee. The proportion of social outlays rose in seven major OECD countries from 14 to 24 percent of GDP between 1960 and 1980 (see *OECD Observer*, 1984)—a truly revolutionary shift.

Since trees do not grow to the sky, the expansion of social outlays at rates higher even than the extraordinary real growth rates of the 1950's and 1960's was bound, in time, to cease. Pressures to contain these outlays increased sharply with the explosion of oil prices, exacerbated inflation, and high unemployment rates of 1974–80. After three years of remission, a similar traumatic sequence occurred in 1979–80. This time, the recession continued for a further two years, in part due to U.S. domestic economic policy. The GDP per capita, which has grown at 3.8 percent per annum from 1950 to 1973 for the advanced industrial countries, decelerated to 2.0 percent for the period 1973–79, and averaged slightly negative over the next three years. Meanwhile, amidst these setbacks the fourth industrial revolution asserted itself on the world scene with its potentialities, challenges, and dangers for those who lagged in its exploitation.

Clearly, the central issue of domestic political life in the West could no longer be defined in terms of the allocation of a bit more or less to social welfare. Two issues, above others, appeared fundamental if the erosion of the social and physical infrastructure of the advanced industrial countries was to be avoided: the mounting of long-term policies capable of reconciling relatively high rates of growth with control over inflation; and the bringing together of scientists, engineers, entrepreneurs, and the working force to generate and absorb efficiently—and across the board—the technologies of the fourth industrial revolution. In my view at least, the former objective requires effective long-term incomes policies, as well as a judicious blend of fiscal and monetary policies. Evidently incomes policies are essentially political, social, and institutional, rather than narrowly economic arrangements; and much the same can be said of the partnerships rendered imperative by the peculiar character of the fourth industrial revolution.

Looked at in this way, the advanced industrial countries of the Atlantic world are caught up in a transition between the struggle over the allocation of resources that marked the evolution of the welfare state, and the need for sustained communal cooperation if growth and control over inflation are to be reconciled and the new technologies find an appropriate role in their societies. If one pierces the veil of political rhetoric—which is exceedingly slow to change— one can observe the transition as a halting de facto process in Western Europe and in the United States.

Assuming this view has a reasonable degree of validity, it throws some light on our instinctive feeling that, somehow, Japan is, at the moment, better geared to the tasks of the generation ahead than the major countries of the Atlantic world. From, say, the first ineffectual Factory Act of 1898 (which aimed to protect women and children) down to about 1936, Japanese social legislation followed, with a lag, a sequence not unlike that to be observed in the Atlantic nations at similar stages of growth. (For a brief summary of this sequence, see my 1971 study, pp. 149–52.) But a generation of war, physical destruction, and postwar recovery broke the pattern and forced Japan into a sequence of communal efforts climaxed by its extraordinary surge of growth since the mid-1950's. A lively sense of the communal stake in the continuity of high growth rates helps account for the fact that Japan has, in a sense, already made the transition towards which much of the Atlantic world is moving rather slowly and with some pain; that is, Japan enjoys a quite well-institutionalized incomes policy and has adjusted its institutions with alacrity to the imperatives of the fourth industrial revolution. There are within Japan debates and struggles about the appropriate proportionate level of social outlays and about income distribution, and these could become more acute; but there is also a more solid consensus than in the Atlantic world that these zero-sum contests are less fundamental than the common effort to assure a steadily expanding pie to be appropriately divided.

These qualities render Japan an extraordinarily strong unit in the world economy; but its capacity to lead is restricted by its incomplete acceptance of the trade responsibilities that leadership demands, the still limited, if expanding, capacity of its international capital markets, and, above all, by the lack of consensus on domestic economic policy in the rest of the OECD world.

I conclude, then, that forces at work in the world economy are likely to diffuse, rather than concentrate, leadership over the time ahead under either of the two definitions with which I began; that such dilute multilateral leadership is quite feasible if a reasonably wide consensus exists on the economic rules of the game, both domestic and international; that the United States is in a position to provide, potentially, a higher degree of leadership than Japan; but it is gravely inhibited because it is still caught up in a transition to a new post-welfare-state consensus on domestic economic policy the Japanese have substantially made.

To answer directly the question posed in the title of this paper—the world economy needs the leadership of both Japan and the United States, but, for different reasons, neither is in a position to supply it at the moment and neither can do the job alone.

The extent to which the United States can provide its share of leadership, over the next several generations, will depend substantially on how fast we diffuse the new technologies across the old basic industry sectors as well as agriculture and the services. I emphasize diffusion rather than generation because, by historical accident—including the land grant colleges and the commitment to serve the economy in which they are rooted—we are almost certainly the best positioned of all the advanced industrial countries to build the close, flexible working partnership of scientists, engineers, and entrepreneurs necessary to create and innovate the new technologies. Indeed, we are in tolerably good shape in three major sectors which arose from laboratories and have managed to maintain the interactive osmotic partnership between scientists and the production process necessary for competitive viability; that is, electronics, chemicals, and aerospace. But our entrepreneurs in steel, motor vehicles, machine tools, and some other basic industries have not worked well with the R&D process in the post-1945 years.

I might add that our problem has been compounded by business schools that teach their students how to maximize the bottom line with fixed production functions, but not how to operate in a world of rapidly changing technological possibilities and accelerated obsolescence. And we economists haven't helped much. For more than two centuries we have failed to build the process of generating and diffusing technologies into the mainstream propositions of macro and micro theory.

Nevertheless, I would guess that with costly time lags, the United States will solve the critical problem of diffusion and meet rather well the challenge of the fourth industrial revolution.

But there is a lion in our path—that is, the four interlocked pathological problems that now have us in their grip: excessively high interest rates, a grossly overvalued dollar, a scandalous balance of payments deficit, and a federal budget deficit running at 5 percent of GNP. Sooner or later we shall have to deal with these problems that we are now pushing down the road by borrowing on a profligate scale. The question is whether we can move to a more viable balance without triggering a grave national and international economic crisis.

This is clearly not an occasion to offer detailed policy prescriptions. I would only observe that it seems most unlikely that those now deeply rooted problems will be resolved merely by a somewhat easier monetary policy, a somewhat tighter fiscal policy. I believe at some stage a rigorous incomes policy will be required, not merely to contain the inflationary effects of the necessary dollar exchange rate adjustment, but also to render credible the decline in interest rates and to assist in narrowing the federal deficit.

We have been living grossly beyond our means and we won't get our books into balance merely by a bit of jiggery-pokery with macroeconomic policy.

But I doubt that American political life has the capacity to face these problems until we are in much worse trouble than we are right now. We are more likely to operate on the principle Jean Monnet set out in his *Memoirs*: ". . . people only accept change when they are faced with necessity, and only recognize necessity when a crisis is upon them" (1978, p. 109).

As an economic historian, I have long rejected the convenient but illusory theoretical distinction between the long run and the short run. The Marshallian long run is moving every day of our lives. Put another way, the long run is simply the accumulation of what happens over short periods of time. Therefore, there is a clash between my temperate optimism about the United States and the challenge of the new technologies, and my temperate pessimism about our capacity to correct the distortions in our economy without major crisis. A crisis is likely to slow up, for a time, the pace at which we carry forward the fourth industrial revolution.

But looking ahead over the 1980's and 1990's, my net judgment, for what it may be worth, is that Mancur Olson hasn't gotten us yet, that we remain a resilient continental society, with many changing centers of energy and initiative, and that we will sustain a vital role in the economic life of the world economy, as the inevitable and wholesome diffusion of economic power continues as it has since the late 1940's.

But is the diffusion of economic power consistent with leadership and a reasonable degree of order? Or, are we on the road to perpetual chaos in the world economy? On this matter I would supplement my earlier observation on the importance of consensus concerning domestic rules of the game with an institutional recommendation. We are most likely to master chaos in a world of diffuse power by going to work, in the first instance, regionally rather than globally; that the Pacific Basin is a promising arena for demonstration; and the place to start is with the Djakarta initiative of ASEAN of July 12, 1984.

## REFERENCES

Block, Herbert, *The Planetary Product in 1980: A Creative Pause?*, Bureau of Public Affairs, Department of State, Washington: USGPO, 1981.

Monnet, Jean, *Memoirs*, Garden City: Doubleday, 1978.

Rostow, W. W., *Politics and the Stages of Growth*, Cambridge: University of Cambridge Press, 1971.

——— , *The World Economy: History and Prospect*, Austin: University of Texas Press, 1978.

——— , (1983a) *The Barbaric Counter-Revolution: Cause and Cure*, Austin: University of Texas Press, 1983.

——— , (1983b) *Korea and the Fourth Industrial Revolution*, Seoul: Korean Economic Research Institute, 1983.

——— , *India and the Fourth Industrial Revolution*, (Dr. Vikram Sarabhai Memorial Lecture), Ahmedabad: Institute of Management, 1984 [reprinted here in Chapter 7].

Government of India, *A High Tech India Needs You to Take the Right STEP* (The Science and Technology Entrepreneur's Park), New Delhi: Department of Science and Technology, 1984.

OECD, "Social Expenditures: Erosion or Evolution?" *OECD Observer*, No. 126, January 1984, 3–6.

World Bank, *World Development Report 1983*, New York: Oxford University Press, 1983, Table 25, pp. 196–97.

# TEN

# How the Cold War Might End

*I was drawn back from work on economic problems to take stock of the cold war by a request to participate in an imaginative symposium organized by John Gaddis at Ohio University in Athens, Ohio, April 17–18, 1986, as part of the Baker Peace Studies program.*

*The resultant essay reflects three distinct strands. The first is my long-held view that economic, political, and effective military power have been diffusing away from both Washington and Moscow since, say, 1948, when the U.S. Congress voted the Marshall Plan legislation and Tito successfully defected from Stalin's Eastern European empire. The second grew out of a conversation in Moscow in May 1984, initiated when I was asked by two Soviet officials: "How have U.S.-Soviet relations gotten into such a mess? What lessons would you draw? How do we get out of it?" My response at the time and later reflections have strengthened my judgment that cyclical oscillations in U.S. policy and the nation's performance on the world scene have contributed substantially to the persistence of the cold war. The third is a growing conviction, arising out of my current work in economic theory and history, that the new technologies (i.e., microelectronics, genetic engineering, etc.) will diffuse to the developing regions over the next several generations (notably, to Asia and Latin America) posing challenges and opportunities that may well render the cold war irrelevant as well as palpably anachronistic. Without excessive optimism, I would argue here that it would be helpful to the human race if Moscow and Washington would act together—and with others—on that perception.*

## I. INTRODUCTION

One cannot answer the grand question posed by this symposium without some notion of what the cold war is all about and without

175

some concept of its dynamics; that is, what has determined the pattern of its movement through time. Those judgments will determine how we think it might end. Because there is no agreement on these matters, I am quite conscious that what I have to say tonight is simply one man's view.

My talk is advertised in our program as "A Policy-Maker's Perspective." That is partly true. I've been involved in U.S.-Soviet relations, in one way or another, since the day the Potsdam communiqué was published, August 2, 1945. That was also the day I went to work in the State Department on German-Austrian economic problems. But some forty-one years of seniority does not, unfortunately, guarantee wisdom; and my talk tonight is based at least as much on my views as a historian and economist as on my experiences as a public servant.

Against that background I shall try to do three things: state my view of the origins and dynamic character of the Cold War; define where it now stands; and then outline how it might peacefully end.

## II. THE COLD WAR: ORIGINS

One is tempted to begin by evoking once again Alexis de Tocqueville's remarkable, almost mystical, prediction a century and a half ago.

> The Anglo-American relies upon personal interest to accomplish his ends and gives free scope to the unguided strength and common sense of the people; the Russian centers all the authority of society in a single arm. The principal instrument of the former is freedom; of the latter, servitude. Their starting-point is different and their courses are not the same; yet each of them seems marked out by the will of Heaven to sway the destinies of half the globe.[1]

One can see how a thoughtful and imaginative Frenchman, looking east to a great continental, essentially feudal monarchy, just beginning to acquire some of the technologies of the First Industrial Revolution, looking west to a young agrarian but technologically competent democracy, evidently destined to dominate another continent—one can see how he might predict the outcome he did. And he was correct in his view that each in its period of maximum relative power would stand before the world as champion of a quite different ideology, although Karl Marx was only seventeen years old when the first volume of Tocqueville's *Democracy in America* was published.

I would not underestimate the element of ideological commitment and evangelism that suffuses the foreign policies of both the Soviet Union and the United States;[2] and surely the geographical location, size, and resources of both powers are relevant. But, in my view, the origins of the cold war are best understood, in first approximation, as the fourth major effort in the twentieth century by a late-comer on the world scene against those nations whose industrialization came earlier and had already reached the limit of and consolidated their international positions.[3]

Think for a moment of how things stood in 1870 when Bismarck consolidated the German Empire. Great Britain accounted for 32 percent of the world's industrial production; Germany, 13 percent; France, 10 percent; Russia, 4 percent; across the Atlantic, the United States, 23 percent; the Japanese, only two years beyond the Meiji Restoration, did not make the cut.[4]

The German take-off began in the 1840s; the Japanese, in the 1880s; the Russian, in the 1890s. By 1914 Germany had acquired all the then existing major technologies, as had Japan and the Soviet Union by 1941. They had come, in my vocabulary, to technological maturity. Here are the figures comparable to 1870 for 1936 to 1938: Great Britain 9 percent; Germany 11 percent; France 5 percent; the Soviet Union 19 percent; the United States 32 percent; Japan 4 percent.

Stripped of details, what we have seen in the past century are two attempts by Germany, one by Japan, and since 1945 one by the Soviet Union to achieve strategic hegemony in their respective regions, although Soviet ambitions in the cold war evidently reach beyond Eurasia—as did Germany's at the peak of its ambitions. In all four cases the United States has thus far played an important part in frustrating these late-comers' drives for hegemony.

What about the United States? Did some special dispensation of grace exempt us from the late-comers' imperial impulse? By no means. Our take-off (putting New England's precocious industrialization aside) comes at about the same time as Germany's, in the 1840s and 1850s. Our instinct to deploy our new consciousness of power was expressed, in the first instance, in completing the consolidation of the U.S. continent; and then in asserting ourselves in the Pacific, the Caribbean, Central America, and Mexico. But, however strong the imperialist impulse may have been among some Americans in the pre-1914 generation, it was reined in by three forces: an ideological sense among a good many other U.S. citizens that imperialism was incompatible with the values on which domestic society in the United States was built; disconcerting confrontations with nationalism (in, for example, the Philippines and Mexico), which resisted U.S. intrusion; and then, starting in 1917, the recurrent problem of dealing defensively with the efforts of the sequence of late-comers to achieve hegemony at one end or the other—or both—of the great Eurasian continent.

If one plays over the last seven decades of history without a soundtrack—putting aside the rhetoric, debates, and oscillations of U.S. foreign policy—the United States has behaved at times of crisis in a quite consistent way. We have acted systematically as if we were mortally endangered should a single power or coalition achieve hegemony in Western Europe, in Asia, or both. (We have also, of course, reacted systematically when a major extracontinental power threatened to install substantial military force in this hemisphere and, in the nuclear age, when we judged ourselves potentially threatened by a first strike that might radically reduce our second-strike capability.)

### III. THE POST-1945 SETTING

Let us assume that my characterizations of the Soviet Union and the United States are roughly correct: the Soviet Union a still ambitious late-comer to the arena of world power; the United States a nation whose take-off came a half century earlier, whose phase of conventional imperialism was foreshortened by the need to cope defensively after 1917 with the efforts of other technologically mature powers to achieve hegemony on the Eurasian continent. What does this stylized perspective on the two major actors tell us about the character of the cold war?

My first proposition is that it was not unreasonable for Soviet planners, as Allied victory became increasingly certain after the great turnaround in the autumn of 1942—at Stalingrad and at both ends of North Africa—to set their sights high for the postwar extension of Soviet power. And immediate postwar events and circumstances appeared to justify that assessment.

In Europe, the Soviet armies were on the Elbe; Germany was devastated and impotent; Great Britain and France gravely weakened at home and confronting serious problems in the Mediterranean, the Middle East, and Asia; the United States was unilaterally disarming and behaving as if it were about to repeat its convulsive withdrawal from responsibility of 1919 and 1920. It appeared every day to be confirming President Franklin Roosevelt's opening statement at Yalta, when he made what Churchill described as the "momentous" prediction that the United States would not keep a large army in Europe and that its occupation of Germany could be envisaged for only two years.

In Asia, the United States was firmly anchored in Japan; but elsewhere the evidently forthcoming end of colonialism and the civil war in China offered opportunities that a Marxist-Leninist view of the world tended to heighten.

This is certainly no place for an account of what has unfolded over four decades from the extraordinary circumstances of the immediate postwar years—circumstances in which a victorious but badly wounded Soviet Union could look out from its central position and not rule out the possibility of becoming the dominant power from one end of continental Eurasia to the other. But a word is required about the dynamics of the cold war, which assumed the form of three cycles.

## IV. THE THREE COLD WAR CYCLES: 1945–1955, 1955–1973, 1974–1986

The first cycle might be called the Truman-Stalin duel. It begins with U.S. weakness and confusion in 1945–1946 and progressive movement toward the division of Europe in the latter year. Then, in 1947 came the first of the three belated U.S. cold war reactions— the Truman Doctrine, followed by the Marshall Plan, and later the creation of the North Atlantic Treaty Organization (NATO).

As Europe moved toward stalemate in 1948 and 1949, the scene shifted to Asia. There Mao moved toward victory while the French continued the struggle against the Vietminh to maintain their hold in Indochina. Guerrilla war erupted in Burma, Malaya, Indonesia, and the Philippines; and the Korean War was planned (according to Khrushchev) in Moscow early in 1950 by Stalin and Mao. By 1953, when Stalin died, Asia, like Europe, was close to stalemate except in Indochina, and that also appeared to have been sealed off by the Geneva Accords of 1954. The Austrian State Treaty and the Geneva Summit of 1955 appeared to signal, perhaps, an end to the cold war after a decade of thrust and counterthrust amidst the dishevelment of post–World War II Eurasia.

But in 1955 the second round was, in fact, already under way, symbolized by Khrushchev's public nuclear threat in Birmingham and the Egyptian arms deal. The Soviet thrust consisted of a counterpoint of thermonuclear-tipped missiles—used to apply political pressure on Western Europe—and the extension of cold war initiatives into the Middle East, Africa, South Asia, and, before long, Latin America. Soviet momentum accelerated after the first Sputnik and the decisions that followed at the Communist summit meeting in Moscow of November 1957. There were Soviet initiatives in the Congo, the Caribbean—where Castro came to power—and Indochina where war was revived in 1958 by Hanoi; and nuclear blackmail assumed a quite lucid, operational form with Khrushchev's rolling ultimatum on Berlin with its explicit threat to Western transport routes. The U.S. response to nuclear blackmail built up to related climactic crises in Berlin in 1961 and early 1962, and then the Cuba missile crisis of October 1962. The Congo gradually calmed down under UN auspices, and the Laos Accords of 1962 appeared briefly to have again yielded calm in Indochina. But, as in the first cycle, there was a second round, which focused on a conventional war in Indochina in 1964 and 1965, the Malaysian confrontation, and the attempted Communist coup in Indonesia. These hostilities were exacerbated by the multiple conflicts of the Middle East. The latter reached a temporary climax in the 1947 Arab-Israeli war, the former in the peace agreement of early 1973.

With the beginnings of the normalization of U.S. relations with China and the Nixon-Brezhnev summit meetings, including the first Strategic Arms Limitation Talks (SALT I), again there was, in the early 1970s, as in 1953 to 1955, an illusory interval in which it appeared the cold war might be subsiding.

Then came the third cycle, triggered, in my view, by the convergence of the self-destruction of a U.S. president via Watergate, throwing the whole political system out of balance for the better part of the 1970s, and the underlying schisms, traumas, and uncertainties generated by the protracted U.S. engagement in Southeast Asia. The result was not only a remarkable period of unilateral reduction in U.S. military expenditures relative to GNP but a general across-the-board weakening of U.S. will to deal with strategic reality. In any case, perhaps a bit to their surprise, Soviet planners, conducting their correlation of force analyses in 1973 to 1975, perceived the most attractive array of opportunities since the first Sputnik in October 1957—or, perhaps, even since Franklin Roosevelt's opening statement at Yalta. Again, there was an exercise in nuclear blackmail against Europe with the buildup of the SS-20s. There were thrusts, exploiting the Cubans and Vietnamese, into the Caribbean and Central America, Angola, Ethiopia, Aden, and Indochina. The Soviet base in Cuba was strengthened and important naval and air bases acquired in Indochina. Finally, there was the Soviet invasion of Afghanistan in 1979. This triggered the third belated reactive turnaround in U.S. policy, parallel to those early 1947 and 1961.

Seven years after the turnaround of 1979, we are here in the days of the Strategic Defense Initiative (SDI); contras in Central America, Africa, Afghanistan, and Kampuchea; Pershings and cruise missiles in Europe; and, hopefully, another meeting of Mr. Gorbachev and Mr. Reagan.

## V. CYCLES AND UNDERLYING TRENDS

I have, with purpose, evoked this dreary forty-year saga as if the most powerful force at work in the world arena was, in fact, the U.S.-Soviet cold war duel, and as if each of the three cyclical rounds of the duel was of equal significance to the relative power of the two major contestants. In my view, neither proposition is true.

If my underlying analysis is correct, it was historically understandable, if not quite inevitable, that the Soviet Union try for hegemony in Eurasia and that the United States react, even if belatedly. But a lot more was going on in the world than this deadly struggle damped just short of all-out war.

First, I would argue that the stakes for each side in each of the three rounds of the cold war progressively diminished. The first round, after all, concerned regions and nations that determine the strategic balance in Eurasia. It settled the initial postwar orientation of Western Europe, Germany, Eastern Europe, Japan, and China. The second round concerned extremely important but perhaps not quite such basic issues: Berlin and the diplomatic threat to Western Europe via nuclear missiles; the acceptance or rejection of Soviet missiles in the Western Hemisphere; the future of Southeast Asia.

The intensity of nuclear blackmail via the SS-20s in the third round, with its denouement in the votes of Western European parliaments accepting the Pershings and cruise missiles, did not match the intensity of the Berlin and Cuba missile crises twenty years earlier. Similarly, the ample supply of trouble generated in recent years in Southeast Asia, South Asia, the Middle East, Africa, and the Caribbean did not appear to have quite the strategic importance of the earlier crises in the Third World.

Why should this be so? One reason is that the orientation of the major strategic regions had been settled in the first cold war cycle and was not subsequently upset. But it is also the case that quietly, erratically, the capacity of the developing regions to shape their own destiny had been increasing. In part, nationalism, always fundamental, gathered strength. In part, economic, social, and technical progress reduced the possibility of external manipulation. In Southeast Asia, for example, the members of ASEAN used the time bought in Vietnam between 1965 and 1975 to good effect and rallied together rather than collapsed when Saigon fell. In the Middle East, for example, the Iranian Revolution and the Iran-Iraq War symbolized that the countries of the region were not wholly the playthings of cold war manipulation or ideology and would increasingly go their own, not always attractive, ways. Historians may well assess this powerful trend as more significant, over the past quarter century, than most of the cold war clashes that dominated the headlines and that I have tried tersely to evoke.

There was still another trend quietly at work reshaping the world arena of power over this interval: the relative decline in the economic power of the Soviet Union and the United States as Western and Southern Europe, Japan, the developing countries of the Pacific Basin, and some of the more advanced developing countries in other regions came forward more rapidly. Both historically and in the contemporary world, nations in what I call the drive to technological maturity tend to grow faster than the most advanced nations. This is the case because they have generated the capacity to absorb the backlog of unapplied technologies available to them. More advanced nations have already absorbed the backlog and only have available what is being generated on the technological frontier.

To sum up the dynamics of our story: the three rounds of the cold war have been conducted by the Soviet Union and the United States in a pattern of Soviet initiative and belated U.S. response, as befits the historical and strategic character of the struggle. The issues at stake in each round have been increasingly less fundamental to the strategic position of the two central players: in part, because the struggle shifted from the core of Eurasia to the periphery; in part, because the capacity of the Soviet Union and the United States to influence the behavior of the developing nations progressively declined with the rise in the power and assertiveness of nationalism. The Soviet Union and the United States maintained throughout the two greatest concentrations of nuclear power. These proved to be of some limited military and diplomatic significance; but usable military power as well as economic capacity tended to diffuse away from both superpowers.

In short, barring an irrational stumbling into nuclear war, the underlying natural forces at work would appear to decree that the Soviet late-comer's drive for hegemony will fail like the earlier efforts of Germany and Japan. If the United States were engaged in such a hegemonic effort, it also would fail. The second half of the twentieth century has proved a bad time for empires. The twenty-first century promises to be worse. The question is: Can we bring the cold war to an end without the kind of major conflict that ended the German and Japanese efforts, which, in a nuclear age, would constitute a disaster for all humanity?

## VI. IS A SOFT LANDING POSSIBLE?

I believe a soft landing is possible but not certain. It is possible because both positive and negative forces are at work that in time may make an end to the cold war both safe and logical—if not inevitable—for the Soviet leaders and wholly acceptable to the United States.

It would be safe because a radical change in policy could be made without fear that the Soviet Union could be subjected to successful external military attack by the United States or anyone else. Whatever changes there may be in military technology, none is in sight that would render a first strike on the Soviet Union rational—if, indeed, any circumstances can be conceived when a first strike by either party might be rational.

On the other hand, there are four solidly based reasons that could—and may—lead the Soviet Union to end the cold war or, more likely, leave it gradually to wither away. Three of these reasons are familiar in Sovietology and can be briskly stated. The fourth will require a bit more exposition.

First, the arms race. Barring radical political change on either side of the Atlantic, it is not likely that either with respect to the central front in Europe or the United States that circumstances will arise in which it would be profitable for the Soviet Union to use military force. Moreover, having twice attempted nuclear blackmail in Europe without success, it is also not likely that a third effort would prove successful. And as French and British nuclear stockpiles become less trivial, such Soviet pressure loses further credibility.

Second, given the now familiar corrosive problems at work in the Soviet economy and the challenge posed by the lead of Japan, the United States, and Western Europe in the generation and diffusion of the new technologies, it will make less and less sense to tie up such a high proportion of the best scientists, engineers, managers, foremen, and workers in the Soviet military-industrial complex. Only in that complex has the Soviet Union managed to put together the osmotically interacting teams required by the new technological revolution. Either that complex will have to teach the rest of the Soviet economy how to operate in the new technological setting or it will have to take over significant aspects of civilian production.

Third, the thrust for national independence and increased human freedom is certain to rise with the passage of time and the succession of generations in Stalin's Eastern European empire. The pressure to find some alternative way to satisfy legitimate Soviet security interests in Europe is bound to increase.

Fourth, and least familiar, the shape of the world arena is likely to change as radically in the next half century as it did between, say, 1890 and 1939.

The basis for that change lies in the revolution in higher education taking place in the developing regions and the consequences of that revolution for their capacity to absorb and apply efficiently the new technologies. Not only has the percentage of the population enrolled in higher education greatly increased since the 1960s, but the educational emphasis has shifted radically. In my view, these changes foreshadow a dramatic adjustment over the decades ahead in world politics and power as well as in the world economy. Moreover, although 24 percent of the world's population lives in advanced industrial countries (including the USSR and those of Eastern Europe), at least 56 percent live in countries that I expect will reach technological maturity during the next fifty years. And in the near future the population will increase more rapidly in the less developed countries. Thus a transformation in the balance of power is destined to occur— one at least equivalent to the rise in power over the past century of the United States, Germany, the Soviet Union, and Japan relative to, say, Great Britain and France.

What follows from this proposition? As some of you may know, I have been arguing since the late 1950s that the most powerful underlying force at work in the world arena is the diffusion of effective power away from both Washington and Moscow. The data I have just cited and the trend they foreshadow strengthen this long-held conviction. For example, I observed at a Pugwash conference in Moscow in December 1960 that the Soviet Union and the United States have three possible courses: a catastrophic war; a continuation of the cold war leading to a progressive decline in the power of either Moscow or Washington to control events; or cooperation in seeking to ensure a reasonably orderly diffusion of power. This is the limit of their historical powers. I hope that they will choose the third course. If rationality were to prevail, the deadend character of the arms race, the deeply rooted economic problems of the Soviet Union, the rise of nationalism and the desire for freedom in the Soviet empire, and the prospect of a relative rise in economic power and technological prowess, as well as national assertiveness in the developing regions, should lead the Soviet Union to abandon its drive for hegemony and seek safety not only in its own great defensive capability but also by working with others for the peaceful diffusion of power.

## VII. WHAT WOULD THE END OF
## THE COLD WAR LOOK LIKE?

If my initial characterization of the basic U.S. posture in the cold war is more or less correct, a Soviet decision to end the conflict on these terms would be wholly acceptable to the American people and government. But ending the cold war would not be quite as simple as that. The Soviet Union and the United States both have abiding interests to protect as nation states; they would have to look after those interests; and a new flow of difficult but hopefully more benign problems would arise. Diplomatic and military history would not end.

What then, in very rough outline, would the end of the cold war look like? Essentially, initial understandings would have to be reached in three areas; and in all cases, while U.S.-Soviet understandings would be basic to a successful outcome, the interests of many other states would be involved, negotiations would be complex, and the outcomes would only be stable if new common law rules of the game were established over a long period of time.

The first critical area would, of course, be the nuclear arms race. Here three conditions would have to be satisfied: a securely inspected U.S.-USSR nuclear balance sufficient to guarantee, at lower overall force levels, secure second-strike capabilities but no capacity for nuclear blackmail; agreements on nuclear force ceilings with other nuclear weapons powers; and against this background—and efforts to settle regional conflicts—a drive to implement more firmly the nuclear nonproliferation treaty.

The second area would be a reorganization of NATO and the Warsaw Pact in ways that satisfied three interests: increased scope for national political freedom in Eastern Europe; partial U.S. and Soviet force withdrawals from Western and Eastern Europe; agreed force levels, securely inspected, for residual NATO and Warsaw Pact forces. The most complex issue certain to arise is the degree and character of German unity.

Finally, the third area would be the settlement, to the extent possible, of regional conflicts with a cold war dimension and the development— probably the gradual development—of new, longer run rules of the game. In the short run, intimate Soviet ties to Hanoi, Havana, and Kabul might provide the basis for settlements in which existing governments would remain but were effectively confined within their own borders without the presence of external military forces. In the long run, the United States and the USSR would have to agree to live with outcomes determined by strictly local historical forces. The Middle East would, of course, be extremely difficult to sort out given the limited powers of the United States and the USSR in the region. But, as elsewhere, those powers would still be formidable if rooted in a joint conviction that the cold war was no longer a sensible framework for the conduct of U.S.-USSR relations.

## VIII. TWO GREAT OBSTACLES

So far as long-run historical forces are concerned, I'm reasonably confident that there is a good deal of realism in this scenario of how the cold war might end. As I said earlier, I believe a soft landing is possible but not certain. My uncertainty, however, is serious and comes to rest on two critical questions: one concerns the USSR; the other, the United States.

The set of changes in Soviet relations with the United States, Western and Eastern Europe, and the developing regions implied by this scenario are quite significant. So are the changes required in Soviet society and its institutions to render the economy efficient and capable of absorbing in all sectors the remarkable flow of new technologies. These kinds of changes evidently require changes in politics and the language of politics.

It is not difficult to take the view that the Soviet political leadership is and will remain so deeply committed to indefinite expansion by Russian history, Communist doctrine, and institutional vested interest that only defeat in bloody war could bring about a Soviet Union that, like other late-comers, came deeply to accept that hegemony was beyond its grasp and that its task was to look after Soviet interests in an increasingly complex multipolar world. Soviet leadership may even fear that such a change in perspective would undermine fatally the legitimacy of Communist party rule over the Soviet Union. I am inclined to believe that, with the passage of time, the latter problem, however real it may earlier have been, has diminished. Perhaps the turning point was the defeat of Germany in the Second World War. At the moment, one cannot help feeling that the viability of Soviet domestic rule hinges rather more on the progress of the economy than on the continued expansion of Soviet power. But what matters are not the views of external observers but those who operate the Soviet system.

In any case, I would judge that it is on the willingness of the Soviet leadership to make the requisite domestic changes that a soft landing depends; but I would note that the posture of the United States might affect that willingness to the extent that it generates a sense of insecurity, security, or revived hopes for hegemony in Moscow.

This brings me to my second uncertainty: Is the United States, as a society, capable of a reasonably steady performance in military and foreign policy? We have oscillated since 1945 between slack complacency and feverish, belated efforts to halt or roll back Soviet expansionist initiatives launched to exploit those intervals of U.S. slack complacency. We have survived on the basis of Dr. Samuel Johnson's dictum: "Depend upon it, Sir, when a man knows he is to be hanged in a fortnight, it concentrates his mind wonderfully." We can never re-run history; but I'm inclined at least to contemplate the possibility that the third cycle was unnecessary. It may well have never happened without Watergate and all that followed in the Congress. Put another way, a soft landing from the cold war is a U.S. as well as a Soviet responsibility; for a steady United States, strong but not aggressive, can help make the transition easier and more secure for the Soviet leadership; a United States that once again slid into slack complacency could set in motion once again a dangerous cold war cycle.

But, be that as it may, I am sure Soviet behavior cannot be predicted unless one answers the question: What is the Soviet view of the strength, unity, and will of the United States?

## NOTES

1. Alexis de Tocqueville, *Democracy in America* (New York: Alfred A. Knopf, Vintage Books, 1954), vol. I, p. 452.

2. For my view of the complex interrelations of ideological and conventional power motives in Soviet policy, see *The Dynamics of Soviet Society* (New York: W. W. Norton, 1953), pp. 3–14; in U.S. policy, *The United States in the World Arena* (New York: Harper & Row, 1960), pp. 12–38 and 543–550; and *The Diffusion of Power* (New York: Macmillan, 1972), pp. 605–611.

3. For an extended analysis of aggression in relation to stages of economic growth, see W. W. Rostow, *The Stages of Economic Growth* (Cambridge: at the University Press, 1960, 1971), pp. 106–122.

4. W. W. Rostow, *The World Economy: History and Prospect* (Austin: University of Texas Press, 1978), pp. 52–53, where original sources are indicated.

# Index

Abboud, Victorine, 156
ADB. *See* Asian Development Bank
Aden, 180
AFDB. *See* African Development Bank
Afghanistan, 180
African Development Bank (AFDB),
  117–118
Agriculture, 42, 124
  in developing countries, 157
  policy, 95
  postwar, 30
  productivity, 86, 95, 96(table)
  railroads and, 89
Alliance for Progress, 120, 123, 132
Angola, 180
Arab-Israeli War, 180
Argentina, 59(fig.), 71(table), 122
Arms race, 183, 185
ASEAN. *See* Association of Southeast
  Asian Nations
Asian Development Bank (ADB), 118,
  161, 162, 163
Association of Southeast Asian Nations
  (ASEAN), 94, 161, 181
*Attack and Other Essays, The* (Tawney), 20
Australia, 59(fig.)
Austrian State Treaty, 179
Automobiles, 23(fig.), 31(table), 32, 34,
  82, 152

Belgium, 58, 61, 70(table)
Berlin Crisis, 180, 181
Beveridge, William Henry, 47(n10)
Bismarck, 68
Bissell, Richard M., 5
Block, Herbert, 78(n39)
Boulton, Matthew, 88
Brandt Commission Report, 138
Brazil, 59(fig.), 67, 71(table), 122, 129
Brezhnev, Leonid, 180
Burma, 179

*Business Cycles* (Schumpeter), 80

Canada, 33, 59(fig.), 71(table), 73(table),
  132
Capitalism, 107, 124, 157
Carter, Jimmy, 38
Castro, Fidel, 179
Chile, 122
China, 50, 55, 59(fig.), 61. *See also*
  People's Republic of China
Churchill, Winston, 3, 178
Cisneros, Henry, 69
Clark, Colin, 80
Clayton, Will, 77(n11)
Colbert, Jean Baptiste, 145
Cold war, 73, 75–76, 175–187
  cycles, 179–180, 181, 182
  end of, 184–185, 186, 187
Colombia, 122
Colombo Plan, 32
Commercial revolution, 50
Commodity prices, 97, 128
  cycles of, 21, 25–28, 84–87, 90
  decline in, 33, 34
  import, 36
  post-1972 explosion, 37–38, 152
  relative, 27(fig.), 28, 34, 35–38,
    84–85, 90, 103(n11)
  trade expansion and, 80
*Commonplace Book* (Tawney), 20
Communal cooperation. *See*
  Cooperation, intersectoral
Comparative advantage, 10, 13, 14, 16,
  51, 52–53, 54, 57, 167
Confucius, 155
Congo, 179, 180
Consumer durables, 82, 152
Cooperation
  international, 42, 43, 75, 115, 126,
    128, 154, 167, 171
  intersectoral, 69, 98–99, 115, 134–135,
    136, 139–140, 144, 154, 171

189

## DATE DUE